UNDER-STUDIED RELATIONSHIPS

UNDERSTANDING RELATIONSHIP PROCESSES

Series Editor
Steve Duck, *University of Iowa*

This series of books on the theme **Understanding Relationship Processes** provides a coherent and progressive review of current thinking in the field. Uniquely organized around the notion of relational competence, the six volumes constitute a contemporary, multidisciplinary handbook of relationship research for advanced students and professionals in psychology, sociology, communication, family studies, and education.

Volumes in the Series

1. INDIVIDUALS IN RELATIONSHIPS

2. LEARNING ABOUT RELATIONSHIPS

3. SOCIAL CONTEXT AND RELATIONSHIPS

4. DYNAMICS OF RELATIONSHIPS

5. CONFRONTING RELATIONSHIP CHALLENGES

6. UNDER-STUDIED RELATIONSHIPS

EDITED BY

JULIA T. WOOD
STEVE DUCK

UNDER-STUDIED RELATIONSHIPS
Off the Beaten Track

UNDERSTANDING RELATIONSHIP PROCESSES SERIES
VOLUME 6

SAGE Publications
International Educational and Professional Publisher
Thousand Oaks   London   New Delhi

Copyright © 1995 by Sage Publications, Inc.

For information address:

SAGE Publications, Inc.
2455 Teller Road
Thousand Oaks, California 91320

SAGE Publications Ltd.
6 Bonhill Street
London EC2A 4PU
United Kingdom

SAGE Publications India Pvt. Ltd.
M-32 Market
Greater Kailash I
New Delhi 110 048 India

Printed in the United States of America

Library of Congress Cataloging-in-Publication Data

Main entry under title:

Under-studied relationships: off the beaten track / edited by Julia
   T. Wood, Steve Duck
      p. cm. —(Understanding relationship processes series ; v.
   6)
   Includes bibliographical references and index.
   ISBN 0-8039-5650-9.   — ISBN 0-8039-5651-7 (pbk.)
      1. Interpersonal relations. 2. Social interaction. I. Wood,
Julia T. II. Duck, Steve. III. Series.
HM132.U54 1995
[v. 6]
302—dc20   95-5097

This book is printed on acid-free paper.

95 96 97 98 99 10 9 8 7 6 5 4 3 2 1

Production Editor: Diane S. Foster   Typesetter: Christina Hill

Contents

Series Preface

This short series of books on the theme "Understanding Relationship Processes" responds to recent calls for attention to *processes* in relationships. A close look at the nature of processes in relationships will reveal that, over and above the importance of change, temporality, and an orientation to the future, there also lies beneath most process thinking on relationships the implicit notion of competent use of knowledge across time. For example, this assumption is true of many elements of the work on relationships, such as the (competent) transition to marriage, (skilled) conflict management, (appropriate) self-disclosure, and (orderly) organization or (satisfactory) maintenance of relationships diachronically. The assumption also is contained in any discussion of intimacy assessment or creation of "a couple" (by which authors evaluate, usually implicitly, the degrees of intimacy or progress that are adequate, allowable, suitable, or competent) and is latent in discussion of relationship breakdown, in which researchers treat breakdown as failure or incompetence, contrasted with skill or competence.

Such competence is evident in, and constrained by, a variety of influences on behavior. In focusing on some of these topics, this series moves conceptually outwards: That is, the series began with the contributions of individuals—and their developmental experiences—to relationships and moved toward the social context and interpersonal interaction. Individuals bring into relationships their individual characteristics and factors that reflect their point in the life cycle and their developmental achievements. Individuals are influenced by the social setting (situational, cultural, linguistic, and societal) in which relationships take place; they are constrained and influenced by the structural, transactional, behavioral, and communicative contexts for their relationships; and they sometimes conduct the relationships in dysfunctional environments or disrupted emotional contexts. The series takes these contextual themes in sequence and deals with the latest research and thinking that address these topics.

Accordingly, each volume focuses on a particular context or arena for relationship activity. The volumes of the series are as follows.

Individuals and Relationships (Vol. 1) deals particularly with the ways in which internal or intrapersonal context is provided by structures of the mind or of knowledge that are prerequisite for success in relationships; however, rather than focusing on such knowledge styles and structures as if they were the end of the story, the chapters place them in context by referring frequently to *behavioral* effects of such structures.

Learning About Relationships (Vol. 2) covers especially the skills and experiences in childhood that lay the groundwork for competence as a properly functioning relater in adult life; the volume emphasizes the wide range of social sources from which development of competence is derived and the richness of the social sources from which developing minds acquire their sense of relationship competence.

Social Contexts of Relationships (Vol. 3) focuses especially on the social structural constraints within which relationships are located and the ways in which the two partners must negotiate and deal with the dialectical and interior pressures that are created by such contexts.

Dynamics of Relationships (Vol. 4) deals with the dyadic management of relational conduct in the context provided by the earlier volumes, and explores the issues of competent relational management that are created by the transactions of relating—not the factors that influence or prepare the ground for relationships, but the actual *doing* of them.

Confronting Relationship Challenges (Vol. 5) turned the series toward the difficult side of relationships and away from any implication that relationships are only good and delightful. Relationship processes encompass "binds" as well as "bonds" (in the elegant pun in Wiseman, 1986), and both must be included in an understanding of relationship processes.

Under-Studied Relationships: Off the Beaten Track (Vol. 6) recognizes and begins to rectify existing scholarship's tendency to focus only on particular types of relationships and particular issues in relationships and thus to ignore or underacknowledge the range of real-world relationships and the myriad processes they entail. A full understanding of relationship processes must include consideration of theoretically inconvenient and/or socially disfavored instances as well as instances (or phenomena) whose value and importance traditionally have been acknowledged in research.

STEVE DUCK

Volume Preface

The first four volumes in this series considered the roles of individual cognition, developmental learning, social contexts, and relationship dynamics in understanding relationship processes. Extending beyond those concerns, Volume 5 concentrated on relationships that are particularly challenging or that pose special difficulties for participants. The present volume, which completes the series, simultaneously initiates new lines of inquiry and new ways of thinking about existing lines.

This volume's specific aim is to inaugurate inquiry into relationship types and processes that have been largely overlooked. Research in general and this series so far have neglected many kinds of relationships and many facets of relational life that are socially and personally important and also theoretically significant. To date, scholars have concentrated primarily on romance, friendship, and marriage among young, white, middle-class, heterosexual Westerners whose relationships are conducted in the open and are often studied in truncated environments that are unconstrained by many of the contextual forces that influence real-life conduct. Significantly less effort has been devoted to studying non-Anglos or couples in which one or both partners are disabled or elderly, affairs in which one or both partners are married to others, intergenerational connections, extremely long-lasting marriages, or relationships that involve substantial risk to the health of participants. We also have limited insight into bases of commitment and satisfaction for lesbians and gays, dynamics of interaction between enemies, and the processes that operate between cohabiting partners. Although these types of relationships have existed for some time, they have not been widely studied. In addition, new forms of relationships are constantly emerging, and existing research has not yet mapped their processes and patterns. Among the dawning kinds of relationships in this era are commuter marriages, electronically mediated friendships, and "microwave relationships" that heat up more quickly than has been previously assumed to be normative.

Thus, when we move off the beaten track of research, we find both established relationships that have been overlooked and emergent ones that previous researchers could not have studied. The premise of the present volume is that investigation of such types of relationship will advance knowledge about social and personal relationships in two ways. First, inquiry into understudied relationships enlarges understanding of the range of ways in which people form and conduct relationships, as well as the meanings and motives associated with sundry kinds of connections. Because knowledge about a broader range of relationship phenomena increases awareness of variations in form, meaning, and substance, it cultivates appreciation of the pluralism characteristic of relationship life.

Second, an expanded scope of study allows fuller and therefore better development and testing of theories. For example, accounts of marital satisfaction that are derived from studies of young, white, middle-class heterosexuals are not rigorously tested when applied only to that same group of people. Instead, to determine the scope and limits of a theory, one must evaluate it in contexts and with people who potentially *challenge* its adequacy and accuracy. By moving off the beaten track, then, researchers are able to refine, revise, and fortify existing theories and, when appropriate, to develop new ones.

The eight chapters composing this volume begin the work of redressing some of the oversights in existing research. Launching this effort is the opening essay, in which Wood and Duck consider what has been neglected by relationship researchers and explore reasons for these oversights. Arguing that science is a social enterprise, we suggest that topics of inquiry and methods of conducting it result as much from the preoccupations of the times as from any intrinsic merit of the ideas themselves. At any given moment in a culture's life, certain relationships are legitimized, whereas others are unseen, denied, devalued, or marginalized. Although cultural ideologies and values equally infuse the thinking and activities of both dominant and marginalized groups, the mainstream perspective is normalized in a manner that obscures its biases and blind spots and also impedes awareness of the viewpoints of more peripheral groups. In other words, heterosexuals are no less culturally saturated than are gays and lesbians, Caucasians are no less embedded in their cultures than African Americans are in theirs, and researchers who rely on widely accepted theories and methods are no less ideological than those whose work lies outside of what academe currently designates as good scholarship. Thus the prevailing views of a culture in general, and research as a specific agency of that culture, reflect and operate according to particular values and viewpoints, even though these often go unnoticed.

By extension, in any era certain kinds of knowledge and means of acquiring it are authorized, whereas others are regarded as frivolous, "unscientific," "bourgeois," or otherwise undesired. In the introductory chapter we trace how the modern era authorized particular forms and foci of inquiry, and we then suggest changes in these inclinations that are occasioned by postmodern understandings of social life and academic research. No more immune than others to the influence of temporal-cultural horizons, our interest in under-studied relationship forms and processes is fueled, at least in part, by increasingly widespread awareness of social diversity and the blinders that accompany any perspective, especially dominant ones because their inclinations are typically taken for granted and hence are not interrogated critically.

The specific consideration of under-studied relationships in this volume begins with a discussion of relationships in later life. In her chapter on mature relationships, Fran Dickson explores processes in long-lasting marriages, which are increasingly common as life spans extend. Reviewing research from multiple disciplines as well as her own studies, Dickson sketches prototypical processes in both happy and unhappy marriages that endure over many years. Her conclusions indicate that although long-lasting marriages entail distinctive processes, they also parallel some of the patterns and dynamics that have been documented in younger marriages. The theoretical significance of Dickson's analysis is that it broadens the scope of existing theories beyond those used to develop and previously test relationship theories by noting the diversity of relationship forms that exist beyond the early parts of life.

Extending the analysis to other relationships beyond those traditionally taken as paradigmatic, Stanley Gaines' chapter on relationships between members of cultural minorities focuses on Hispanic and black families. Gaines illustrates how cultural ideologies shape values, meanings, and interactions that form and are enacted in personal relationships. Reporting that collectivism and familism are strongly salient values in black and Hispanic families, respectively, Gaines shows how they contour personal relationships of minority persons in ways distinct from those of the majority culture. Extending this theoretical argument, he demonstrates that cultural ideologies are equally influential in the marriages of Western Caucasians, who typically privilege individualism, which is prominent in the mainstream culture and, not coincidentally, is emphasized in much relationship research. Thus, Gaines argues that individualism, familism, and collectivism are all and equally culturally bound values, rather than the latter being a universal standard against which all others should be compared. His chapter, like others that follow it, demonstrates the potential of knowledge from under-studied relationships to reform general theories.

Stepping outside conventional frameworks in other ways, Michelle Huston and Pepper Schwartz offer a chapter on gay and lesbian relationships. Relying on interdisciplinary work, Huston and Schwartz report processes that lesbians and gays use to negotiate interaction in a largely heterosexual world. Going beyond existing research, they make original extensions that add to understandings of how gay men and lesbians meet, court, and enact relationships. In so doing, they point out ways in which gay and lesbian relations are similar to and distinct from heterosexual partnerships, yet they resist regarding heterosexual patterns as presumptive standards. Their analysis reminds us of the normalizing force of dominant ideology and its consequent tendency to obscure the cultural saturation of relationship forms and processes that are centrally positioned. Hence this chapter underlines the need for researchers to recognize and account for the dominant (and therefore taken for granted) culture and the relationships, values, and conduct it naturalizes.

Theodore Zorn discusses another kind of relationship, which is common but little studied, in his chapter on relationships that are simultaneously hierarchical (i.e., supervisor and subordinate) and personal (i.e., friendship). Concentrating on friendships between people of unequal professional status, Zorn probes dialectical tensions and sense-making patterns that guide interaction. His analysis clarifies unique processes and issues that mark relationships between bosses and buddies and, at the same time, suggests ways in which such relationships are similar to more routinely studied relationships. In so doing, he extends the volume's overall focus on how different cultures shape interaction.

Responding to the times, the final three chapters examine types of relationships that have emerged in recent years and that to different extents are made possible as a direct result of changes in both social values and technologies. John Cunningham and John Antill review research on cohabiting arrangements that are increasingly adopted by both romantic partners and friends. Their analysis sheds light on ways in which cohabitation differs from and resembles more traditional relationships. In addition, they invite us to develop theories that account for relationship motives, goals, and rhythms beyond those conventionally legitimized.

In her chapter, Mary Rohlfing highlights the unique psychological and practical difficulties that lace long-distance friendships and sheds light on some of the patterns and means of connection they embody. Arguing that long-distance relationships, whether romantic or friendship, entail distinctive motives, sensemaking patterns, and modes of communication, Rohlfing urges researchers to develop theories, concepts, and methods that fit the particular constraints and processes inherent in them.

Martin Lea and Russell Spears conclude the volume by focusing on the increasing number of people who develop and maintain relationships via electronic mail. As the much-touted information highway becomes an increasing fact of daily life for many people, electronically launched and conducted relationships promise to proliferate. In addition to drawing attention to this new relationship type, Lea and Spears point out challenges that it poses to existing theories and methods.

Although this volume does not map the universe of understudied relationships (for example, we would have liked to include a chapter on affairs), it is a first effort to enlarge understanding of the breadth of connections that enrapture, entrap, and entangle humans. In concert, the eight chapters composing the volume constitute a persuasive argument for the value of moving off the beaten track and into new frontiers of relationship research, which promise to inform us about previously neglected relationships and to enlarge and to revise our knowledge of ones more routinely studied. Expansion of the scope of relationship life enables fuller and more adequate testing of theories so that their values and limits may be recognized and their form revised to incorporate more clearly the relational processes and contexts that are emphasized in this series as a whole.

We hope these chapters are a catalyst for sustained efforts to expand the kinds of relationships studied and the frameworks in which we study them. If so, then we may look forward to greater scholarly attention to relationships that lie off the beaten track of academic research. We also hope to spark bolder thinking about the ways in which relating occurs in the often messy contexts of real lives and varied circumstances whose complexities preclude laboratory study and resist the unifying and simplifying tendencies of previous theories.

The limited relationships that have preoccupied researchers are actually small parts of the rich universe of relationship types, processes, and meanings whose character and consequences scholars and practitioners have not fully fathomed. We believe that the description and mapping of this universe are prerequisites to claims that we have knowledge about human relationships in general and any single instance of them in particular. So we now invite you to join us in venturing off the beaten path of relationship research.

JULIA T. WOOD
STEVE DUCK

1

Off the Beaten Track: New Shores for Relationship Research

Julia T. Wood

Steve Duck

Joyous we too launch out on trackless seas,
Fearless for unknown shores.
                    —Walt Whitman, *Leaves of Grass*

An acquaintance recently mentioned an "intimate" he met for the first time on a flight, spent a weekend with, and does not plan to see again. A colleague gauges himself by the enemies he makes and his ability to outmaneuver them in sophisticated verbal duels. An undergraduate complains that a course in families does not reflect her experiences as a Latina, and a graduate student transforms an assignment to define personal relationships into a critique of scholars' heterosexist bias and neglect of lesbian and gay attachments.

Happenings such as these expose lacunae in scholarship on relationships, which has generated much information about heterosexual romance in college, friendships among members of the middle class, and development and dissolution of love between white Westerners living in relative affluence. Enemies, non-Anglo relationships, instant intimacy, and gay and lesbian commitments are some of the threads missing in the fabric of social and personal relationships that academics have woven. The existence of affiliations other than those routinely studied is obvious; what they are, how they develop and operate, and what they mean to participants are far less clear. It is equally unclear how knowledge of under-studied relationships might usefully test, extend, revise, or disprove existing theories derived from study of a limited, and thus unrepresentative, sample of relationships.

Expansion of the boundaries of scholarship on human connections requires not only inaugurating inquiry into areas heretofore neglected but also asking how knowledge of under-studied phenomena might affect theories about relationships in general. We believe that no theory about relationships can be regarded as adequately tested until it has been applied to a broad range of situations, including relationships that have been routinely overlooked by researchers. In other words, it is insufficient to measure theories against null hypotheses and to carry out investigations that do not have the potential to *challenge* theories. Theories must also be tested in unfamiliar contexts and with participants other than those used to build those same theories. Pursuing these lines of thought, this chapter ventures off the beaten track to identify gaps in scholarship, explore reasons for them, and consider what might be gained by studying relationship phenomena that have fallen through the cracks of inquiry.

Why Move Off the Beaten Track?

It is axiomatic that a thorough descriptive base is a foundation for theories. Because creation of a representative base of knowledge about relationships requires investigation of a wide range of personal and social associations, we believe that an expanded scope of inquiry will enrich insight into relationships traditionally studied as well as ones generally overlooked. Our interest in moving off the beaten track of research is propelled by growing awareness of acute absences in existing scholarship and the questions that those absences raise about theories in general. We are also intrigued by cultural and intellectual shifts that promote new forms of relationships and new perspectives on established ones. Whether existing theories can explain emergent relationship forms remains to be seen.

Science as a Social Enterprise

Like all researchers, those who study relationships have been selective. They have limited the field's scope to a small sample of relationships and have adopted particular conceptual and methodological lenses, which have simultaneously sharpened and occluded vision. As Burke (1935) noted in an early work, "A way of seeing is also a way of not seeing—a focus upon object A involves a neglect of object B" (p. 70). Why do some and not other relationships captivate scholars' attention? Why do some perspectives, topics, and modes of inquiry prevail over alternatives? Is it, as Bateson (1975) once proposed, that there is a "natural selection of ideas" so that the fittest survive? Or is it, as Duck (1980) claimed in an early essay, that what scholars study at any time reflects not only the richness or power of ideas themselves, but also social forces and disciplinary predilections that encourage certain foci and ways of understanding while discouraging others?

The selectivity of research on relationships reflects science's social character. What ever else it may be—a search for "truth," a specialized method of inquiry—science is also always social, because it is conducted by humans who are embedded in social contexts that shape choices of issues, methods, and interpretations (Epstein, 1988). Because science is social, it is responsive to the particular mind-sets, problems, and mysteries ascendant at a given moment in a culture's life. Scientists in 1950 did not study HIV because either it did not exist or it had not been named, but they did study obedience, conformity, group behavior, and prejudice, all topics made salient by experiences in the military in World War II. Scientists in 1994 do study HIV, more in fact than other lethal medical problems such as breast cancer, and interest in obedience has waned even though the phenomenon is not yet fully understood. The attention scientists give to HIV or any topic depends less on the topic's intrinsic worth than on prevailing social views of its importance, prestige, and urgency. Nor is the appeal of particular topics unrelated to the willingness of funding agencies to support some, and not other, foci of inquiry.

As a social enterprise, science can be neither objective nor neutral. Indeed, Keller (1992), a mathematical biophysicist turned philosopher of science, explained that "science is the name we give to a set of practices and a body of knowledge delineated by a community" (p. 25). In this chapter, we mean to take Keller's claim seriously and ask what the community of relationship researchers has defined as its practices and knowledge. Equally important, we want to contemplate what has been left out of the delineation made by this community and how omissions may restrict tests of theory and awareness of its values and limits.

Defining a Field of Inquiry

In seeking to understand why some topics and viewpoints have enjoyed currency whereas others have not, we begin by noting that the methodological and substantive character of research is drafted by those who constitute a field. Judgments of which relationships are important and which conceptual and methodological lenses are superior reflect scholars' social situatedness (Burke, 1935; Keller, 1985) and the influence of powerful members of the field. Because historically most academics have been white, heterosexual, middle class, and surrounded by young students, courtship and marriage have emerged as the twin pillars of relationship research. Because historically most academics have been male, instrumental perspectives and foci have predominated in much relationship research. Thus exchange perspectives and study of outcomes and individuals have eclipsed attention to more usually feminine affiliative perspectives and study of communal orientations, processes, needs, and mutuality (Wood, 1993a, 1993b, 1994b, in press). In short, the theoretical and methodological demeanor of research reflects the values, experiences, and priorities of the group who traditionally made up the professoriate.

Yet academics are no longer a socially homogeneous lot. Increasingly, faculty represent both sexes and diverse ethnicities, races, religions, sexual preferences, and classes. Diversification of the ivory tower re-forms knowledge in two interrelated ways. First, and more obviously, members of historically subordinated groups fuel awareness of what lies outside the experience of those with majority status (Collins, 1986; Harding, 1991). Second, because new topics and knowledge are more than additive, they reverberate against prior understandings, revising them as well. Because new lines of study can alter understandings of relationships in general, they are social forces that shape the field just as previous foci of inquiry delineated the field's existing character.

The Value of New Perspectives on a Field

Academics with nonmajority standpoints call attention to absences and distortions in research and teaching about relationships (Wood, 1994b, in press). Pointing out that their experiences have been misrepresented or erased, nontraditional scholars insist that the prevailing picture of relationships is partial, reflecting primarily the experiences of white, middle-class, male, heterosexual, Western young people (Epstein, 1988; Wood, 1993b). Thus blacks may note, as Gaines does in Chapter 3 of this volume, that conventional definitions of family exclude nonlegal ties common in African American familial arrangements. Similarly, women may be more aware than men of sexual harassment (Wood, 1992b, 1994c) and caregiving activities (Okin, 1989; Wood, 1994d). Working-class individuals may realize more than members of the middle class the impact of financial strain and dead-end jobs on married life (Eckenrode & Gore, 1989).

Enlarging the traditional domain of scholarship yields knowledge not only about relationships routinely overlooked but also about ones assiduously studied. As Harding (1991) noted, any group learns about its own unquestioned, often unnoticed, patterns by encountering ones that differ. Echoing Hegel's (1807/1910) insight that slaves in particular and powerless groups in general have greater understanding of the lives of masters in particular and powerful groups in general than vice versa, Collins (1986) argued that black women sociologists have experiences not known to Anglo males and distinct perspectives on the lives of the upper class. Hence, she claimed, black women's perspectives are theoretically as well as personally significant. Noting that those whom research misrepresents have the keenest insight into scholarly bias, Goffman (1977) realized that "we have to rely on the discontented to remind us of our subject matter" (p. 301). Thus absences detected by nontraditional academics enlarge both the boundaries of study and the accuracy of theories.

The Postmodern Zeitgeist

As we have argued, the times themselves influence the preoccupations of scholarly minds precisely because the zeitgeist grows out of those minds. In other words, we *are* the zeitgeist; it is not some disembodied, abstract, external entity. Consequently the times and intellectual interests change as new voices call for the rethinking of theories about social and individual life. Every era has its upholders of tradition and its challengers who question the authority of prevailing wisdom and the comforting, albeit socially constructed, coherence of social life. By causing some expansion or redirection of existing views, pluralistic perspectives continually recreate the kaleidoscope of scholarly outlooks. Calls to rethink research in the present time reflect, in part, a larger cultural and intellectual shift into postmodernity.

Because scholarship on personal relationships arose during the modernist period, it is infused by the predilections of that epoch. Among the characteristics of modernity as an intellectual mind-set are belief in capital-T Truth (e.g., laws, generalizations, and grand models); emphasis on the autonomous, sovereign individual; a quest for control; and a view of stability and coherence as natural and, more important, as inherent in Nature. These features are evident in conventionally preferred topics and modes of inquiry in research on relationships (Duck, 1990; Wood 1993b, in press). For instance, relationship research historically favored control through lab study over investigation in real-life contexts, reliability of measurement over richness of data, and simple 2 × 2 explanatory matrices over more complex path analyses and interwoven complexities of interpretation. In contrast, a postmodern mind-set, which began emerging some time ago, is skeptical of the coherence of social life and of views of individuals who are relatively unencumbered by contexts (Wood & Cox, 1993). Here we sketch five implications of postmodern thinking for study of social and personal relationships.

Profound Contextuality

Postmodern perspectives are deeply contextual in their attention to individuals' embeddedness in multiple environments. With respect to research practices, contextuality summons researchers to realize that a perspective is an integral and unavoidable part of any observation. The perfectly neutral observation is a fictional concept because all observations are based on assumptions that must be understood and examined self-reflexively so that their capacities for shaping interpretation may be better recognized. Hence objective observations are not possible, and researchers are not independent of what and whom they study (Harding, 1991; Keller, 1985). It is possible and, we think, desirable to probe how the assumptions and sense-making systems that inhere in scholars' thinking affect the ways in which they conceive and conduct research. For instance, as Duck (1994b) observed, if researchers think of courtship growth as progress along a pathway, then it is unsurprising when they find "turning points" (Surra, 1987), and if researchers assume that relationships are transformations, it is unremarkable that they discern transitions (Conville, 1988). Because the subject matter is itself defined for each researcher on the basis of a set of starting perspectives and also is studied through perspectives and their consequences, data and interpretations are necessarily partial in two senses. They are incomplete, and they are inclined to favor seeing certain phenomena, and not others, and interpreting them in particular ways.

With respect to relationships, postmodernism extends system theory's dictum that phenomena can be understood only within their environments. Thus, in relationships, individuals and their activities reflect social locations that differ among various groups (Harding, 1991; Wood, in press). Material, social, and symbolic conditions affect what people experience as well as the ways they make sense of their experiences. Consequently, how individuals perceive closeness, conflict, or family depends on experiences available to them and interpretive frameworks authorized by groups in which they participate. For instance, what lesbians consider salient in relationships may be obscured by research questions, designs, and instruments derived from and appropriate for heterosexuals (Kirpatrick, 1989). To understand lesbian commitments, researchers must discern the meanings and significations authorized and embodied in lesbian communities. Only then may it be possible to assess whether present theories of closeness adequately gauge closeness in lesbian relationships.

Decentered Selves

The self, proclaimed McCarthy (1987), "has been definitively decentered" (p. 4) so that identity is no longer anchored in a stable core, as was assumed in the modern era. Instead, selves are recognized as contingent, forming and re-forming within diverse relationships and circumstances. In other words, an individual does not have a monolithic, lifelong identity, but instead assumes identity in response to others and activities in particular contexts. This relational self (Gergen, 1991) is not a fixed essence but a teeming mass of potentialities, any of which may be realized in particular moments and none of which is invariant across time and context.

The decentering of self makes it untenable to believe in an autonomous agent who stands apart from his or her surroundings. If there is no such thing as a sovereign subject, then the research tradition of focusing on individuals unencumbered by relational and contextual influences ceases to be viable (Lannamann, 1991). We cannot have confidence that a distinct self has cognitions, feelings, perspectives, and so forth independently of phenomena with which it is intimately entwined. Immersed in social processes, "individuals" are within, part of, and informed and formed by the ever-fluctuating situations in which they live their lives and conduct their relationships. Although this view does regard selves as complexly contextualized, it does not dispose of the concept of accountability. Instead, it suggests that individuals make choices not only about their actions but also about the contexts and circumstances within which they locate themselves and which, in turn, sculpt their interpretations and choices. Like all people, researchers are immersed in social and professional contexts that shape their interests, assumptions, methods, and explanatory inclinations.

Postmodernism thus assumes that identity is diverse, not singular, and changing, not stable. Inquiry based on the assumption that identity is continually in flux is less enamored of outcomes than of processes, changes, and the interesting variabilities (what modernists disparage as inconsistencies) in actors and situations. Further, postmodernity regards differences and changes as normal, not deviations from a static standard that has been designated normative. Inconsistencies, as Duck (1990) noted earlier, are not problems or inconveniences, but important data about what is happening in people's relationships and in their experience and understanding of those relationships. Postmodern views of selves as decentered and contextually encumbered, therefore, suggest that we should focus on, rather than try to eliminate or explain away, variability and the ways in which people cope with it as a continuous part of their experiences.

New Forms of Relationships

Developments in the postmodern era also make new types of relationships possible and, in privileging pluralistic perspectives, heighten the potential to notice them. In his analysis of postmodernism's implications for individuals and relationships, Gergen (1991) argues that an individual's consciousness is saturated by others as technologies make it possible to watch goings on in faraway countries, meet new people and form relationships via electronic mail, maintain ready contact with distant friends and colleagues, jet across the globe, and, in general, tune into more others than ever before. The sheer number of people a person encounters and the variety of relationships she or he knows about and/or engages in have exploded, transforming what it means to know another, be intimate, or be in a relationship. Emerging forms of human connection and enlarged awareness of neglected topics challenge scholars to develop concepts consonant with new relational forms and to explore whether existing theories need to be re-formed or augmented to account for previously under-studied relationships.

Language as Presentational

Perhaps postmodernism's most important contribution is highlighting the generative capacity of language to constitute social and personal life—that is, how our use of language shapes our experience. Some years ago Duck and Pond (1989) called attention to the presentational force of language. They noted that language not only composes and structures thought, serves as an instrumental vehicle for conducting relationships, and indicates what is happening in relationships, but also it is the experience of relating for most people most of the time. Arguing that researchers have overlooked the essential function of language, Duck and Pond proposed that communication embodies or creates relationships, and later research (Duck, Rutt, Hurst, & Strejc, 1991) shows that "just talking" is a large and important part of being in a relationship. Similarly, scholars in Europe and North America (Baxter, 1987, 1993; Billig, 1987; Billig et al., 1988; Shotter, 1993) have elaborated how linguistic processes actually compose human experience. Just as postmodern selves have no fixed character, language and one of its products, knowledge, are unfettered from stable referents. Sheer talking must be recognized as a social and epistemologically significant process through which meanings are formed, enacted, and shared between people.

Language is thus a social process in which selves and relationships arise and are altered, their meanings continually affirmed, challenged, negotiated, transformed, and celebrated in the ongoing conversation that constitutes and sustains human identity and connections (Berger & Kellner, 1975). In short, we and our relationships become, or arise, in discourse. Because it is presentational, our use of language not only shapes the meaning of our social experiences but also very much shapes our social identity by influencing how we think, the distinctions we note, the contrasts we recognize and articulate, and the meanings we construct for others, ourselves, and social activities. Echoing Gadamer (1989), Stewart (1991) noted that we are as much subject to linguistic resources as those resources are subject to us (p. 365). This implies that subjects and subjectivity do not precede but actually arise in language, which is an always operating process (Gadamer, 1989) that creates social and personal relationships. Thought and meaning cannot be distinguished from language because the former are constituted linguistically (Gadamer, 1989; Lannamann, 1991).

In an extended treatment of the role of talk in creating and sharing meaning in relationships, Duck (1994b) elaborated the consequences for research when such a position is taken seriously. As already noted, the language used by researchers must be understood as an influence on research (as in research on turning points and transitions). It is also the case that research often reflects the distinctive linguistic inclinations of particular disciplines. So, for instance, psychologists concentrate on individuals and on activities such as motivations, predispositions, and attitudes, whereas sociologists more typically direct inquiry toward structural matters such as social contexts and scenes. Each discipline, then, conducts its scholarly debates in terms that are framed by its terminology. This has the effect of making it difficult to conduct interdisciplinary discussions because the linguistic and assumptive frameworks of various disciplines differ.

Situated Accounts, Not Laws; Perspectives, Not Truth

Postmodern thinking also reconfigures the goals and meaning of research. With erosion of faith in Truth, autonomous individuals, objectivity, and language as representational of concrete reality, researchers can no longer be regarded as disinterested and findings can no longer be assumed self-evident. According to Stewart (1991), "Most postmodern authors do not purport to be providing objective accounts of 'reality' which are more 'accurate.' . . . Their appeals are argumentative rather than demonstrative, 'rhetorical' rather than 'scientific'" (p. 358). As a result, interpretations of data are recognized not as disembodied logic but as rhetorical arguments that are infused with the perspectives of researchers and that derive their credibility from sources germane to other forms of rhetoric. In place of formal criteria to justify the validity of claims, intersubjective and discursive bases of judgment assume salience. The value of findings hinges on their capacity to give an account of data that participants, audiences, and other researchers find credible, rather than on their ability to unclothe Nature. Scholars are thus not engaged in demonstrative proofs but involved in a persuasive activity in which they attempt to convince others of the merit of their claims. As a consequence, they become more responsible to those who read and participate in research than was the case when it was believed that "objective science" simply revealed the unvarnished Truth.

The goals of inquiry, too, are transformed by postmodern views of social life. Explanation and control as objectives of inquiry give way to understanding, which is presumed to be context bound, not universal. The traditional quest to build grand theories by accumulating incremental findings about a limited topic is augmented by efforts to gain insight into processes in specific circumstances that involve particularly located individuals. Although situated study may inform understandings of broad social activities, expansive generalization is not a primary goal of postmodern inquiry. Instead, such inquiry aims to increase insight into patterns and processes that arise in particular settings that are complex, varying, and nonuniform.

Postmodern conceptions of social life and inquiry refine received truths of academic life. No longer may researchers assume that universal theories can be developed for all subjects of inquiry; no longer may we see ourselves as distinct from those whom and that which we study; no longer may we act as if the language we use to conceive, conduct, and present research is neutral; no longer may we assume that coherence and order are natural. As much as it ushers in what modernists decry as chaos, postmodernity also energizes social and personal life and research about it.

The Beaten Track: An Abridged History of the Abridged Study of Relationships

A field labeled *social and personal relationships* would seem to comprise the range of close associations that people form. Yet this assumption is not borne out by the history of relationship scholarship. Instead, the research community has reduced relationships and aspects of relational life to a narrow and unrepresentative sample. To illustrate the limited scope of existing research, we consider several relationship types and topics that have dominated research agenda and ones that have been neglected.

Types of Relationships
Routinely Studied and Neglected

Research has primarily concentrated on friendship, courtship, and marriage among educated, white, heterosexual, middle-class persons. Because *Sophomorus academicus Americanus* is the favored research species, most studies are of college students' friendships and romances. As a result we have insight into dating behaviors of campus women and men (Pryor & Merluzzi, 1985; Rose & Frieze, 1989), symbols of relational identity in undergraduate friendships and romances (Baxter, 1987), and ways that heterosexual students experience love (Frazier & Cook, 1993; Hendrick & Hendrick, 1988). We know much less about symbols of relational identity among working-class and older couples, roles of mature women and men in dating situations, or how lesbians and gays experience and express love. The restricted scope of research impedes appreciation of varied forms, meanings, and pathways of diverse romantic relationships and simultaneously renders precarious theories about the relationships that have been routinely studied.

As with dating, studies of marriage have focused primarily on white, middle-class, heterosexual marriages in the West. Research has yielded considerable knowledge about how this group organizes married life (Fitzpatrick, 1988; Fitzpatrick & Best, 1979) and what enhances and erodes satisfaction and commitment (Riessman, 1990). We know comparatively less about relational structures of non-Anglos or couples in which one or both partners are disabled or elderly. We also have limited insight into bases of commitment and satisfaction for lesbians and gays.

Studies of courtship and marriage also reflect a bias that relationships are normatively positive. Duck's (1994d) insistence that less than pleasant, less than loving thoughts, feelings, and interactions lace most normal enduring relationships runs counter to general tendencies to view conflict, for instance, as a deviation from intimacy, and problems as impediments to closeness. Because challenges, problems, and tensions are ever-present in relationships, defining and responding to them is a continuous activity in normal relationships. Thus, existing tendencies to obscure or pathologize less pleasant types of interaction yield a false model that invites scholars, students, and laypersons to assume unrealistic standards for relationships and normality. Disregarding the dark side of interaction or separating it from normal, ongoing relationship life also narrows theoretical understanding of relationships to either-or, positive-negative dichotomies and simplistic generalizations that fail to capture the complex and multifaceted possibilities of social and personal connections. Relationships, we suspect, are not so cut and dried nor so normatively positive as prevailing theories imply. Instead, they are ongoing processes in which people confront and respond to the rough and the smooth, sickness and health, richer and poorer, and better and worse. Partners continually experience tensions between gratifying and frustrating experiences, hope and fear, anger and affection, excitement and boredom, connectedness and distance, and disappointment and anticipation. The process of relationships is how partners work out and/or live within these tensions and how they frame and attribute meaning to them (Duck, 1994b; Wood, 1995).

Studied and Neglected Relationship Phenomena and Processes

Not only have certain relationship forms been emphasized by researchers, but also selective aspects of relationship life have been granted preferential status. To illustrate, we note three favored foci that are far more salient and significant in research than in actual relationship life.

Self-Disclosure

Since the 1970s (Jourard, 1971), self-disclosure has been a hot research topic. Because it has been extensively studied, we know a good deal about why people do and do not disclose and what disclosures tend to produce—for example, trust (Berger & Bell, 1988). So spotlighted is self-disclosure that every textbook on interpersonal communication and relationships discusses it, usually in considerable detail. We do not doubt that self-disclosure influences relationships and therefore merits study; we do, however, question the way self-disclosure has been conceived and the importance conferred on it.

Widely defined as communicating private information about oneself to another person or persons, self-disclosure involves verbal expressiveness, although Jourard's (1971) original thinking included nonverbal behaviors as well. Exiled from the prevailing definition are a host of nonverbal ways individuals reveal personal information. For example, in traveling together, playing sports, or undertaking challenges, people disclose courage and fear, loyalty and betrayal, egocentrism and altruism. Similarly, caring and commitment are shown by doing things for others without verbal accompaniment. The broad spectrum of ways that humans self-disclose has been narrowed to verbal and explicitly affective displays, thereby reflecting a feminine bias for closeness in dialogue and obscuring more typically masculine closeness in doing things with and for others (Cancian, 1987; Swain, 1989; Wood & Inman, 1993). Given prevailing equations of self-disclosure and verbal expression, it is unsurprising that in a classic study, researchers did not classify a husband's washing his wife's car as an act of affection (Wills, Weiss, & Patterson, 1974). Among other things, moving off the beaten track involves enlarging views of activities such as self-disclosure to include, for instance, its role in education of adolescents through advice giving (Spencer, 1994), its strategic use as a power ploy (Spencer, 1994), and its role in self-definition and self-development (Dindia, 1994).

We also doubt that self-disclosure's prominence in research mirrors its actual presence and importance in relationships. Studies (Dindia, Fitzpatrick, & Kenny, 1989; Duck et al., 1991; Duck & Miell, 1984) show that self-disclosure makes up only a small portion of talk between intimates, a finding that hardly justifies the topic's popularity in published research. The vast majority of communication in social and personal relationships is mundane, unremarkable, and very, very important (Duck et al., 1991; Wood, 1993b). Through continuous thought about relationships (Acitelli, 1988) and mundane exchanges about the comings and goings of life, partners stay tuned into one another and constantly recreate familiar rhythms and patterns that simultaneously reflect and realize their connectedness (Wood, 1995). We hope that future research will be more attentive to everyday, ordinary processes that weave the ongoing fabric of intimacy.

Conflict

Another perennial research topic is conflict. Investigations inform us about common sources of conflict (Hochschild, 1989), responses to relationship distress (Rusbult, 1987), constructive and destructive patterns of managing conflict (Gottman, Markman, & Notarius, 1977), and violent forms of conflict (Goldner, Penn, Scheinberg, & Walker, 1990; Thompson & Walker, 1989). Although conflict deserves study, we urge reconsideration of its importance and particularly of the way in which it is viewed. Conflict is too often regarded as an aberration that must be "managed." Yet it is not necessarily symptomatic of relational pathology and may in fact be highly constructive in many instances.

If we suspend the prevailing view that conflict is negative, we may discover that it has constructive capacities to vitalize connections, negotiate relational dialectics (Baxter, 1993), fit lives together, and even rejuvenate relationships (Wilmot, 1994). Indeed, conflict should perhaps be reconceived as a natural and appropriate process in all relationships, rather than as a discrete occurrence that operates outside of ordinary relationship business. Such a conceptual and linguistic redirection encourages researchers to consider how conflict may constructively operate to invigorate relationships and coordinate lines of thinking and conduct between intimates. That conflict may enhance intimacy was evident in a recent study (Wood, Dendy, Dordak,

Germany, & Varallo, 1994) in which respondents described conflict as energizing relationships, heightening individuality, inspiring trust, and enriching intimacy. Conflict, then, appears to have broader and perhaps different functions than those widely assumed by relationship researchers. We hope that future scholars will venture off the beaten track to probe multiple meanings, manifestations, and consequences of conflict.

Social Exchange Frameworks

A third pronounced focus of relationship research is exchange perspectives. Although there are numerous versions of exchange theory, all share the basic assumption that social and personal relationships are essentially commercial arrangements in which participants calculate rewards, costs, and outcomes to determine whether to remain involved (Rusbult & Buunk, 1993). Despite repeated indictments of exchange models as ill adapted to the processes and meanings that make up real, everyday personal relationships (Bochner, 1984; Duck, 1994a, 1994b; Wood, 1993b, 1995, in press), the perspective continues to enjoy prominence and remarkably inventive efforts to camouflage or transcend its conceptual limitations.

Here we confine our criticism to arguing that exchange perspectives represent a standpoint not embraced by all members of Western society. Although the culture esteems individuality, profit, and competitiveness (Ting-Toomey, 1991; VanYperen & Buunk, 1991), these values do not uniformly permeate all pockets of society, but most strongly influence public and business spheres. In the "private sphere" of home and family, different ethics have held sway. Communality replaces individuality, particularly in Hispanic and black families, as Gaines, in Chapter 3 of this volume, points out; and cooperation eclipses competition as a modus vivendi. Several studies suggest that exchange principles are suspended in personal relationships (Clark, Quellette, Powell, & Milberg, 1987; Lund, 1985; McDonald, 1981; O'Connell, 1984). A communal orientation (O'Connell, 1984) more accurately captures how many, perhaps most, people seem to think about personal relationships (VanYperen & Buunk, 1991). Thus, as a perspective, exchange describes one set of principles that some people use in some relationships; as a model it falsely generalizes those principles to all people and all relationships.

We are troubled as much by what exchange theory overlooks as by the assumptions to which it cleaves. Without grave distortion, an exchange framework cannot account for parental sacrifices, caring for family members who may be senile and/or physically unpleasant, or soldiers who die to protect buddies. Such acts of devotion cannot be reduced to or explained by cost-benefit analysis. Yet few researchers have seriously looked for alternative frameworks that might operate in relationships between people outside of North America's social mainstream and the individualism, competition, and profit motivations it champions.

Relationship research is selective in many ways beyond the three we have discussed. For instance, the cultural regard for individualism suffuses study of personal relationships. Witness the attention to individuality in Fitzpatrick's (1988) work on marital types and individualistic explanations of relational phenomena such as violence and codependence. When violence between intimates is accounted for in terms of individual predispositions, for instance, critical social and relational dynamics that allow or inhibit realization of predispositions are ignored, a claim well supported by West (1995). When attachment styles are analyzed as individual qualities or tendencies, researchers obscure the ways in which activities such as talk realize relational proclivities in the process of interaction.

Scholars also make present thought and interaction the temporal axis of inquiry. In spotlighting the here and now, researchers neglect the powerful role of memory in constituting and sustaining human connections. Because its operation has been so little studied, we know little about the ways memory creates and affects social and personal relationships. Thus, we can only wonder about questions such as these: How do memories of past interactions configure current relationships? What various functions does memory serve for diverse people, during differ-ent stages of life, at sundry points in relational evolution? How do individuals and partners edit memories in ways that sustain views on which relationships' continuity depends?

Research has also focused intensively on satisfaction, which is assumed to influence relational health and stability. Yet sat-isfaction is most likely to be salient when (or if) more basic requirements for shelter, sustenance, and security are met, thereby allowing contemplation of less rudimentary needs. Those who are not economically privileged may not think a great deal about satisfaction as it is conceived by researchers and/or may define it in ways that prevailing conceptual frame-works would regard as undemanding. Satisfaction may in fact have less to do with whether some people stay in relationships than duty, religion, income, security, and so forth have. This may be particularly likely in cultures in which familial duty, for instance, is highly esteemed. To take another example, the widely held and asserted belief that marital satisfaction de-creases when children are present has not been tested in cul-tures less modern, individualistic, and wealthy than those of the West. In South Africa, for instance, a man's wealth and worth are judged by the size of his family, which suggests that many children would increase satisfaction—at least for South African males. To understand how satisfaction, memory, individuality, and other factors affect the range of human associations, re-searchers will need to investigate the rhythms, hopes, fears, ex-pectations, and meanings of relationships that are off the beaten track of relationship research.

Off the Beaten Track

Inquiry that probes relationships other than those historically studied may well require the development of new methods, theories, language, and interpretive lenses. This is to say, we cannot assume it is sufficient—or even appropriate—to use conventional frameworks to investigate under-studied types of relationships. It is likely that we will need to revise or generate concepts, terms, and approaches in order to tap into processes and phenomena beyond those that existing methods and concepts are designed to map. For instance, when an adult child is the primary caregiver for a parent, dialectical tensions and role strain are likely to arise. Yet how such tensions and strains are defined and managed may not be accurately captured by conventional terms and measures, and may also differ from patterns typical of college romances and marriage, which are the primary contexts in which theories of roles and dialectics have been developed and tested. If this turns out to be the case, then existing theories, terms, and measures will require revision.

In addition, there may be processes and phenomena unique to under-studied relationships that will beckon scholars to develop wholly new conceptual and methodological strategies as well as to frame novel questions to guide inquiry. For example, what existing term defines the relationship between a child and the female partner of the child's mother? Studying new types of relationships requires us to discern their distinctive character rather than to impose existing language, assumptions, and frameworks that may distort or neglect their particular integrity.

We believe that by venturing off the beaten track of scholarship and exploring new territory, research will enlarge awareness of the range of relational life and will advance theories by providing broader, more challenging measures of relationships' scope and character. If we test familiar theory in new terrain and discover new relational phenomena in previously neglected contexts, then we can enhance understandings of the multitude of ways in which humans create relationships and are, in turn, created within their relationships. A full understanding of relationship processes will be possible only when we include such multitudinous embodiments in our research. We believe that such rich knowledge requires us not only to maintain the well-worn paths of existing research but also to step off the beaten track and explore new territory.

The Best Is Yet to Be: Research on Long-Lasting Marriages

Fran C. Dickson

W: I think we have had a good life. I am very happy, but there have been very—not many times—several times when it's hard. You can't always see eye to eye on everything.

I: What was the hardest time together?

H: I don't know.

W: Nothing tremendous . . . little things.

H: I was out a job a couple of times, in fact back when I was 40, early 40s.

W: Yeah.

H: But it didn't put that much of a strain on our life, we weren't spending much in those days.

W: It wasn't much of a hardship.

H: No. We got along well.

I: What was the best time?

H: Now (laugh), now really, we enjoy life.

W: Yeah, really. There are very few pressures, very little strain, freedom, we do anything we like, often we do things on

AUTHOR'S NOTE: Parts of this chapter were presented at the annual conference of the International Network on Personal Relationships, May 1993, Milwaukee. This research, in part, has been funded by the University of Denver Faculty Research Council.

the spur of the moment. In Rochester, one time I remember, we were going to go out for dinner one night.

H: Oh, yeah.

W: And where do you want to go, what do you want to eat and we decided we wanted lobster. Well, in Rochester, where do you go for lobster? So I said if you really want lobster, you should really go to Maine, right? So, the next morning we packed up.

H: We packed up, we drove to Maine.

W: Yeah, the next morning we packed up and drove up to Maine, ate lobster three nights in a row, and then came home. (They both laugh)

This conversation between a couple married more than 50 years is a typical example of how many happily married, long-lasting couples view their lives together. The partners portray their life together as involving little pressure, much spontaneity, and enjoyment of each other. There are other long-lasting couples who are not as lucky—they view their marriages as riddled with conflict, emotional distance, and sadness. This chapter explores both happily and unhappily married long-lasting couples. First, I will discuss what we know about the later-life marriage. Second, I will present a typology describing long-lasting relationships, accompanied by new information that has the potential to increase our understanding about the later-life, long-lasting marriage.

Consistent with this series' focus on processes, my examination of long-lasting marriages concentrates on the types of processes that knit couples together as well as those that allow endurance even when closeness and satisfaction are not achieved. Both the topic of long-lasting marriages and attention to processes in them advance this volume's goal of moving off the beaten track of relationship study and into underexplored areas. In making this move, this chapter and the volume as a whole provide insight not only into relationships relatively neglected in research, but also into those relationships that have been more intensively studied. For instance, as the discussion that follows will demonstrate, some processes that seem characteristic of long-lasting relationships parallel ones documented in relationships of shorter duration and also enlarge the significance that perhaps should be attached to patterns that develop early in intimacy.

Framing this chapter is the fact that our society is aging rapidly. By the year 2030 more than 35% of people in the United States will be older than 65 (Cavanaugh & Parks, 1993; Nussbaum, Thompson, & Robinson, 1989). As longevity increases, so does the length of time people remain married. Of those who stay married, one out of five celebrate their 50th wedding anniversary (Ade-Ridder & Brubaker, 1983). Unfortunately, although the average longevity is increasing, there is not a concomitant increase in knowledge about the long-lasting marriage. Much of the research on aging focuses on retirement, health issues, and perceptions of life satisfaction among older adults. Relatively little attention has been devoted to exploring how later-life couples perceive the quality of their overall life together and what it means to be lifelong partners. Thus, this review summarizes general findings of research on marriage as well as the limited studies of long-lasting marriages.

Marital Quality Over the Life Stages

Research has consistently demonstrated an association between marital happiness and life events. For example, during the honeymoon stage the couple is typically happiest (Troll, 1982), and satisfaction with the marriage decreases somewhat during the child-rearing years (Belsky & Volling, 1987; Burr, 1970). After children leave home, levels of marital satisfaction increase, and most older marriages are relatively happy (Rollins & Feldman, 1970; Steere, 1981). This suggests a curvilinear trend of marital quality over time for couples with children, in which marital satisfaction is high in the early and later stages of the marriage and low during the middle, child-rearing years (Anderson,

Russell, & Schumm, 1983; Olson, McCubbin, Barnes, Larsen, Muxen, & Wilson, 1983; Rollins & Cannon, 1974; Tamir & Antonucci, 1981).

Although much of the life stages literature focuses on the traditional family structure with children, little attention has been directed toward long-term marriages that are child-free. Research has consistently demonstrated that marital satisfaction tends to be higher for child-free couples (Feldman, 1974). Yet we know little about whether these patterns continue into the later stages of life within long-term marriages.

Typically, two explanations emerge from the literature on the pattern of marital quality across life stages. First, cognitive consistency theory (Schumm, 1979; Spanier, Lewis, & Cole, 1975; Streib & Beck, 1980) states that the longer couples are married, the greater their investment in the relationship. Therefore, as consistently reported in the literature (e.g., Lee, 1988; Mathis & Tanner, 1991), later-life couples have a greater tendency to report having a happy marriage.

A second common explanation for marital quality among later-life couples is that of life continuity theory (Cole, 1984), which suggests that patterns of interaction and happiness of the couple during the earlier stages of marriage are the best predictors of marital satisfaction in the later stages. For example, couples who had low marital satisfaction in the initial phase of their relationship generally experience low levels of marital satisfaction throughout their lives together and tend not to recover from the stresses of the child-rearing years. If unsatisfying marriages endure, they are typically utilitarian and sustained more by instrumental functions than by social or emotional connections. Because spouses who are not highly satisfied often are child centered, their marital satisfaction level remains low or they divorce when the children are launched. This seems consistent with (though different from) the investment theory that spouses who are not satisfied with marriage invest less in the couple relationship and thus are more likely to end it when its functional value ends. For couples who report high marital satisfaction, retirement is far more enjoyable, and the couples reinvigorate the relationship that was established before child rearing.

Therefore, although most later-life couples report having a happy marriage, they may not all be experiencing the same degree of what they call "happiness." In general, those with happy early marriages tend to have more satisfying later-life marriages.

Role Differentiation in the Later-Life Couple

With one out of five marriages reaching its 50th anniversary, we wonder about the processes and perceptions in marriages that last so long. Small amounts of relevant research on this topic exist, but Nussbaum et al. (1989) believes that most statements about the later-life marriage are based on speculation. Research directly focused on older marriages has assessed variables such as health status, contact with family, income, and living arrangements. Particular attention has concentrated on role differentiation, or task specificity, which decreases in the later years of many marriages (Nussbaum et al., 1989). It is possible that the longer people live, the less sex-specific their behavior becomes, and that as couples grow older together there is less differentiation between the masculine and feminine and more similarity. A typical pattern is that older husbands are expected to share feminine-associated activities, such as food shopping, but are not responsible for those activities (Brubaker, 1985). Therefore, it is believed that in some later-life marriages, partners tend to be more psychologically androgynous (Gutmann, 1977) and less role differentiated than their younger counterparts.

Differences Between
Older and Younger Married Couples

Typically, research has indicated that patterns of interaction and quality of communication for couples remain constant. That is, as previously stated, the quality of the relationship before child-rearing responsibilities is most predictive of the quality of the relationship later in life (Cole, 1984). However, a more detailed examination of the literature reveals a number of subtle differences between older couples and their younger counterparts.

These differences may arise from the reality of retirement, absence of children in the household, and role readjustment. More specifically, retired couples have the potential to spend more time together than in the earlier, child-rearing years. The absence of children in the household may also increase the amount of couple time together. Therefore, one major difference between later-life couples and other couples is the amount of interaction and time together.

Tamir and Antonucci (1981) discussed how, after retirement, couples experience a number of other changes. For example, in the earlier stages of marriages, husbands are typically more concerned with career achievement, financial security, and prestige. During the middle and later years, husbands become more focused on affiliative concerns and maintenance of the family relationships. But at the same time that husbands are becoming more affiliative, wives are becoming more independent and shifting attention away from the spouse and children and toward their individual needs and concerns. Therefore, in the later years, husbands and wives may be moving in different directions, and this may create difficulty and tension in coordinating their relationships. Because research on these patterns is yet limited, well-founded conclusions are not possible. Although some studies have found that older wives become more assertive and instrumental, and husbands more affiliative and expressive, in later years (Grunebaum, 1979; Gutmann, 1977; Levinson, 1978), other researchers report that both the males and females become more expressive as they grow older (Lowenthal & Robinson, 1976; Troll, 1971).

The retirement process may also affect family roles. In younger and middle-aged couples with child-rearing responsibilities, role definition tends to adhere to traditional gender-specific prescriptions (Pearson, 1992). When the children have been launched and the couple has retired, the functionality of such role definitions attenuates. Husbands are more willing to participate in home maintenance tasks that they previously avoided (Cole, 1984). Husbands report becoming more involved in cooking, cleaning, and grocery shopping (Dickson, 1994). Specifically, older wives report that participation of their husbands in the home activities affects their feelings of competence. Wives with high self-esteem have an easier time adjusting to husbands' participation in home activities than do wives with low self-esteem (Keith, Powers, & Goudy, 1981). In addition, because husbands are often older than wives, husbands may retire before their partners. When the wife is the sole income earner, this can affect role responsibility within the home. For example, is the wife still responsible for the meals and food shopping, and who makes decisions about how to spend money?

In previous years when it was typical for the husband to be the provider, roles may have been more clearly defined; now that the wife may be the sole provider, do the roles remain constant or is she more of an equal participant in decision making and is he more of a participant in home maintenance tasks?

Communication and Interaction in the Later-Life Couple

Although the retirement process seems to proceed most smoothly for couples who have positive and productive communication skills, research findings regarding communication are mixed, and typically rely on cross-sectional samples. More multimethod research is needed to answer questions around patterns of relationships among later-life couples. For example, studies that rely on traditionally accepted measures of marital satisfaction may have misleading results because most of the measures rely on "agreement" as an indication of satisfaction. Couples who have been together for over 50 years are most likely to have high levels of agreement on many lifestyle issues;

however, that agreement maybe an indication of happiness, or it may just be an artifact of the length of time the couple has been together. Keating and Cole (1980) found that after retirement there is not an increase in the amount of communication, as one might expect because couples are spending more time together. However, an early study found that after retirement, couples enjoy the opportunity of sharing feelings and developing their relationship through participation in mutual interests (Stinnett, Carter, & Montgomery, 1972).

The retirement process forces many later-life couples to readjust and redefine their relationships. Although this period of adjustment for couples can be very difficult, it can lead to positive changes and new insights into the marital relationship. Typically, retirement is a time when older couples can renegotiate patterns of separateness and connectedness (Orthner, 1975). Research (Keith et al., 1981) has indicated that many wives have a more difficult time adjusting to their husbands' participation in the home than husbands have adjusting to being home. The husband's presence in the home creates some tension for the wife, who typically views the home as her territory. Wives report having mixed feelings about having their retired husband around the house more often (Cole, 1984).

The few studies focused on communication patterns among older married couples indicate that older and younger couples focus conversations differently. For example, Treas (1975) reported that older couples talk about their children much less than their younger counterparts do and that older couples' topics of conversation are very conventional, such as church, home, and health. However, more recently, Dickson (1994) found that older couples, who completed interaction diaries over a 2-week period, talk about a number of different topics such as leisure activities, plans for the future, social and political events, and their families, with little discussion of the past and health.

A recent study explored relational themes that emerged for married couples (Sillars, Burggraf, Yost, & Zietlow, 1992). This study found that life stage was positively associated with communal themes such as togetherness and communication. In other words, the longer the couple was together, the more communal themes emerged in their communication. They also found that older couples were more interdependent and conventional than younger couples and that they made less reference to personality and separateness themes than did younger couples. Finally, they concluded that middle-aged and older couples had more uniformity and stability in their relationships than did younger couples (Sillars et al., 1992).

Pearson's (1992) book is rich with descriptions of older marriages, analyzing couples married for 45 or more years. Consistent trends tend to characterize these later-life couples. First, older couples are less concerned with autonomy than younger couples, and Pearson (1992) believed this is because their autonomy needs may have been met earlier in their lives. Second, older couples spend most of their leisure time together. Third, it appears that time and life together have given later-life couples the ability to mind-read. In shorter term and younger marriages, this is considered a negative behavior (Markman, 1988); however, in older marriages, it is an indicator of closeness and time together. Perhaps what is happening here is that older couples tend to mind-read better (that is, more accurately), whereas younger couples are still learning how to do it and so get it wrong more often.

Although older marriages benefit both parties, older husbands, in general, benefit more from marriage than their wives, a finding consistent with disparity in younger marriages (Brehm, 1992). Men typically receive more help from their spouses and are more satisfied with the marital relationship (Keith & Schafer, 1985). Marriage appears to be a mediating variable that facilitates a smooth, positive retirement process for men (Cole, 1984). Huych and Hoyer (1982) summarize this position quite well by stating that older marriages are a good source of social support and a good way to avoid loneliness.

Older married people tend to be healthier overall than their younger counterparts, and older marriages are more conventional, having less passion (Huych & Hoyer, 1982). It is apparent that the later-life couple has unique circumstances that create particular challenges for relationship maintenance and satisfaction. Because the later-life marriage is such an under-studied phenomenon, we know relatively little about the unique circumstances and relationship dynamics of this fascinating type of relationship. The next section of this chapter presents details of an ongoing project that is one of the few studies to examine later-life couples' communication by analyzing joint storytelling of the couple.

Understanding Long-Lasting, Later-Life Couples

I have been involved in exploring couples who have been married for more than 50 years. Through an analysis of couples' narratives of their life stories, I have developed a classification of couple types and have gained a greater understanding of long-lasting, later-life couples. This research has been heavily influenced by the works of Baxter (1988) and Fitzpatrick (1988). Baxter (1988, 1990) conducted a number of studies of relational dialectics, one of which is the autonomy-connection dialectic. The theme of connectedness and separateness is very similar to that of autonomy-connection in Baxter's research, but Baxter's research was not conducted on long-lasting relationships. We will see that consistent patterns did emerge for long-lasting relationships as they did for relationships in their earlier stages.

Fitzpatrick's (1988) work on couple types also influenced this research. Fitzpatrick identified three couple types: traditionals, independents, and separates. Here too, I have identified couple types and patterns that to an extent parallel Fitzpatrick's typology. However, forthcoming research will indicate that Fitzpatrick's methodology and typology do not discriminate among long-lasting marriages.

The data and findings reported in this chapter grow out of a 2-year, ongoing project that investigates narratives and storytelling among later-life, long-lasting couples. Couples participated in three 1-hour interviews in which they were asked to report at least one story that defined them as a couple for each life stage. This strategy was used in order to anchor the storytelling for the couples, and of course couples told many more than just one story for each life stage.

After the interviews were completed, my research team and I began to analyze the interview tapes. Before the data could be analyzed, each interview was transcribed, resulting in thousands of pages of data. In terms of the analysis, first we identified consistent themes for each couple across the stories told for each life stage. In analyzing the couples' storytelling, we are focusing on the couples' *own* experience of their life together. Second, we analyzed the styles and processes each couple used to tell their stories. Finally, we analyzed traditional measures of marital satisfaction (Locke & Wallace, 1959) and relationship typology (Fitzpatrick, 1988).

Cohort Effects on Later-Life Couples

Couples married for more than 50 years are clearly influenced by larger historical events occurring during their lifetime. Virtually all were affected by the Depression and World War II. The Depression had a large impact on their perceptions of their financial status. For example, the dialogue presented at the beginning of the chapter discusses a time when there were financial hardships for the partners. However, they report that the lack of money did not create a large problem for them, because they really needed little and were used to spending less. We also believe that the Depression affects how couples view the quality of their marital relationships. Spouses who survived the Depression learned to be satisfied with less, both personally and financially. Therefore, their expectations about intimate relationships could be different from those of younger couples today.

The following dialogue reveals how one couple experienced the Depression. This couple adopted traditional roles: He would make a decision and she would follow along without questioning. Yet although he clearly dominated the decision-making process, she dominated the storytelling.

H: The Great Depression came . . . and I lost my job at Westinghouse. . . . Things were terrible. . . .

W: Well, I worked too. . . . I made a nice little sum of money. My parents were in no position to help me, and it worked out nicely, and we were in no position to say we were going to get married because things were terrible at that time. And I worked there on Wall Street, and people were absolutely committing suicide because they didn't have any money. . . . Joseph and I decided several times that we would try and see our way through to get married, but it was almost impossible. So we were dating each other for at least 4 years (pause) and then we decided to get married. It wasn't easy . . . but we saw it all through, and in 1933, Joseph was a little more settled and I was a little more settled, ah, we decided to get married in January 7 of 1933, and we did exactly that.

H: It was a time of hardships, my father had suffered some hardships in business. He lost his business and lost quite a bit of money, and fortunately they had a home out in New Jersey. And I was an only child of parents in later age, and he was getting to a point where he wanted to retire anyway but he didn't have the way with all [sic] to live in the manner he was accustomed to before, so I did everything I could to help him. . . . So with that responsibility and other things not going so good, Ann always hesitated, and I brought it to a head one time when we met when I said, "We have been together 4 years now, you better make up your mind, either we decide on a marriage date right now or else let's break up." She chickened out fast, and that's when we set a date for marriage.

W: The first place we lived in was a brand new house that the people who owned couldn't afford it. We rented from them, which helped them out a bit. . . . Then they wanted the house back when they got on their feet. . . . We moved to Atlanta, lived there for 5 years, it worked out beautifully. Then we moved to Michigan and that worked out well too. . . . Now you can continue with yours.

H: It is of interest to know that when we moved to different locations it was my wishes completely, and Ann would always go along with them, she never objected. When I decided to move up to my parents' house to save the expense of the rent and to be a little closer to them, . . . it was a difficult decision to live with my parents. . . . She never once objected to it, and she had some trying times. I made the decision to move from there because I knew she was not happy there and I wanted to move on in business.

World War II also had a strong impact on later-life couples. As a result of the war, many couples spent their courtship and early stages of marriage communicating through letters. Couples were married when the men were on furlough, and then lived apart for great lengths of time. In some cases, couples courted through letter writing, decided to marry through letter writing, and then after marriage were apart, experiencing the early stages of marriage through letter writing. The lack of proximal interaction during the early stages of the relationship and marriage seems to have shaped long-term expectations for the relationship. Again, as with the Depression, couples had to be happy with less.

The following dialogue is an example of how one couple experienced World War II. This couple is discussing the early years of their marriage, how the father of the wife was not happy with his new son-in-law and how that attitude changed.

H: He took an interest in me since I was shot down and a prisoner of war.

I: Un huh.

H: He kept charts of where I was and all.

I: So he adjusted to you?

H: Oh, yeah, and when I came home, he's all right, he wasn't bitter.

I: What was it like when you were a prisoner of war?

H: Best I don't talk about that.

I: Okay.

W: Harry, I think that's interesting.

H: Well, it is.

W: It's just like with one of your kids, Jim or Scott, asks you that question . . .

H: Oh, yeah.

W: I think you should answer honestly, okay?

H: I'll answer honestly. (laugh) (pause) It wasn't good at all. I went from 205 pounds to 128. . . . I was in four different camps altogether. . . . Two, 3 years ago I had a six-artery bypass, and that was the cause of that. I don't know if it was.

W: That's what your POW book says. The book says that so many of you are having problems now.

H: Malnutrition was a big problem, it was cold, we didn't have heat.

W: You seen those pictures of Dachau where the beds are a few boards or so, they called bunks—that's the kind of thing he had for bunks.

I: What was it like for you (referring to W)?

H: It must have been awful (both laugh).

W: (laugh) I had a bed to sleep in.

H: It was warm.

W: I had a stove.

H: It was awfully hard on her.

W: I was told you were missing in action, MIA. We lost track of him, he was up in an area in Poland. (pause) I always said that if he's gone, I'd know he's gone, I'd know. (pause) That's why I wonder about these women whose husbands are still missing. (pause) Do they really think that their husbands are alive, can they let go or not?

This couple tells this story as if it is *their* story, with joint ownership of the POW experience. It appears that even with the great distance and lack of contact during that time, they still maintained a sense of connectedness, even with each other's pain. He appears more concerned with her well-being than his own during his time as a prisoner of war.

Types of Later-Life, Long-Lasting Couples

Themes of connectedness and separateness represent common tensions for families and couples (Baxter, 1988, 1990; Hess & Handel, 1959; Stamp, 1991; Stamp & Banski, 1992; Yerby, Buerkel-Rothfuss, & Bochner, 1990). For couples in this study, consistent themes tended to emerge in stories across life stages. In other words, if a theme of connectedness existed in the stories of the early stages of marriage, the same theme existed throughout stories about later stages.

Through an analysis of the themes that emerged for couples in their storytelling, we have identified three different types of long-lasting couples.

1. *Connected Couples* are characterized by high levels of closeness, intimacy, and dependency. They tell their stories as if they are jointly owned by both partners. Connected couples engage in frequent overlapping dialogue and validation of each other's statements. They tend to repeat the last few words of their partner's statements many times during their storytelling. Connected couples even report having the ability to read each other's minds. These couples are very happy and satisfied with their marital relationship. Their communication involves a great deal of respect, humor, politeness, and validation. These couples tend to enjoy sharing activities and spend a great deal of time together.

The following dialogue is an example of a connected couple in the later stages of life. This couple is discussing friends and the present state of their relationship. The connectedness between the partners is apparently intense, as they typify all of the characteristics of connected couples. This couple builds its conversation on each other's comments. They appear to let their stories spiral between each other.

H: We know a lot of people, no, not a lot, we have a few friends that go separate ways. Ah, can't think of them, Al and Barbara . . .

W: Yeah, they do nothing . . .

H: Nothing together.

W: They are both retired and they don't do much together at all.

H: Nothing at all, she loves shopping, he hates it.

W: Well, but, he goes . . .

H: He goes, yeah . . .

W: Yeah.

H: Like Tom and Joan . . .

W: Yeah, they just do different things.

H: He will go out Thursday night with the fellows and she goes out on the days with the girls or something and goes her own way. And we don't, we never have.

W: I think we are unusual, though, we spend 48 hours, no 24 hours a day.

H: Feels like 48. (laugh)

W: Yeah, it does, 6 days a week, and we spend all that time together. So that's a lot of time to spend together. But we enjoy each other's company.

H: We know what the other one's thinking. It's crazy.

W: That's the weirdest part of all for us is that we can be doing something, anything, and I'll think of something completely different from what we are doing. . . . We can just be sitting and reading or walking in the mall and I will think of something that has nothing to do with what we had been talking about, and 2 seconds later he will say, you know what I was just thinking of such and such a thing, and I will say, that was just running through my mind. (laugh) And it happens quite often. We can be sitting here reading and I'll say, you know what I just thought of, and he'll say, I was just thinking about that. It's weird.

H: It is weird, we are on the same wavelength or something.

I: Did this happen when you were first together, at all?

W: Oh, no.

W: No, that's only within the . . .

H: Oh, no, it comes with age.

W: No, no, the last few years that we think of the same things at the same time.

2. *Functional Separate Couples* consist of spouses who emphasize separate activities and are highly independent of one another. Storytelling for this type of couple is very much like that of connected couples, with a great deal of support, validation, positivity, and respect. What differentiates this couple from others is that there is a great deal of individual storytelling about the couple, family, and personal experiences. It is common for members of this type of couple to be involved in separate activities. Many have acknowledged the lack of common interests and have accepted it as part of their relationship. Noting that he enjoys doing things in the garage whereas his wife has interests in playing cards and her clubs, one husband concluded by saying, "That's just how it is and it's okay." It would also be common for one partner to tell a story and then say to the other, "It's your turn now." This conversational pattern appears typical for this type of couple, who nonetheless appear to be happy and satisfied with their marriages. They have established a level of intimacy that appears to be comfortable for them. Although on the surface partners may appear distant and disconnected, deeper analysis indicates that there is a great deal of caring that may be promoted by comfortable levels of distance.

The next dialogue is from a functional separate couple. This couple discusses feelings about the death of a partner. As you can see, they have very different perspectives on death and being alone. However, both are involved in the dialogue, listen to each other, add or comment on each other's position, and see humor in their partner's comments. Although this couple may appear to be very separate and distant, they are highly committed to each other and show positive affect when the other partner is speaking.

W: It's *inevitable,* and uh, how do we know? (pause) Um, (pause) if I could make it through the Depression, do I have to worry what's going to happen next year? I'm 76 this year, I don't.

H: In fact, I'd probably be unusually well prepared for losing you because of now, I go places by myself, I go on trips by myself, I fly my airplane by myself, I belong to clubs she doesn't belong to and environmental groups and everything.

W: And he can't be reached, you see. Something happens to me, um, he can't, he cannot be reached.

I: Right.

W: But the kids understand, I hope, we have to remind 'em again that they're not going to attempt to reach him, because . . .

H: And we're not going to have funerals and all that monkey motion.

W: Because he's on an ice cutter and he's up in the icebergs and why should he come home. (pause) I've thought I was dead a couple of times when he's flying to Vietnam, or going to die . . .

I: Uh-huh.

W: . . . and you just, you can't reach, so why do you have to, he's not gonna save my live or reincarnate me or whatever.

I: I see.

W: And I do want cremation. Instant.

I: No ceremony?

W: A memorial, 1 month later, just my family.

H: I'd like to have a good wake and all my friends come and . . .

W: Drink.

H: Have a glass of wine and sing bawdy songs and live it up.

W: You wouldn't be there to enjoy it. Although you might be.

H: I could pay for the wine, and food.

In the next example of a functional separate couple's dialogue, the couple members tell the same story but focus on their individual experiences. Their stories concern a house that he built and the death of their baby daughter.

H: Another thing that I look back on and I really enjoyed, I don't think Ida did quite so much. I built our house that we lived in. And, ah, I can look back during that construction of that house and I was in my 30s, wasn't I?

W: Yeah, late 20s.

H: Late 20s and early 30s, and, ah, when we go back to this town in Nebraska where this house is I would still like to go through the house again and some time but, uh, I look back and I think that's an accomplishment that I never half thought, uh . . .

I: So you actually built it yourself?

H: Yes, I hired a, or we hired, somebody to rough the house up and I did all the finishing the outside, the inside and Ida was busy with the twins and . . .

W: I was going to say that's why I didn't . . .

H: Yes.

W: I was too busy with them to even (laugh) to you know.

I: So it was Hank's project?

W: Mmm-hmm. We lived in the basement while he worked on the upstairs and that was it. It would rain and water would drip in and I had put the twins in, I had a buggy I'd move them all around with that top up on the buggy so they wouldn't get rain on them and stuff like that. Although that's why I don't look back on it with joy because it was a big job, it took a long time. But we did enjoy the house and I liked the house and we lived there a long time after it was finished.

H: Yeah, we designed the house and everything all by ourselves.

I: So you both had a kind of different perspective about the house as far as what it means to you that really is . . .

W: I think probably, yeah. Because it was an accomplishment for him, and I don't, I just look back and think about and see we had lost our daughter and then we had the twins and then we just, I don't know we, I, it wasn't a happy time for me, really.

H: I think it was a time for me that, ah, maybe an outlet for my feelings, you know.

W: And I think you kind of like to get a hammer and pound around.

H: Yes, I do. And do something with my hands, I think that's one reason I enjoyed the woodworking work and that, ah, but, of course, it was just working with your hands and, ah, if I could turn out some type of work that people would appreciate, then I thought that was an accomplishment.

3. *Dysfunctional Separate Couples* are characterized by distance and dissatisfaction with the marriage. In most cases, at least one or both couple members report and appear to be dissatisfied with the marriage. Partners in this type of couple have stated that they have different interests and tend not to support the other's interests. Their storytelling is punctuated by a great deal of contradiction, disagreement, and lack of listening and response to the other's stories. They tend not to build, support, or provide additions to the other's stories, and there is a great deal of individual storytelling. Much of the communication is characteristic of an unhappy couple, with complaining, criticism, and contradictions in information.

For example, one couple could not agree on who was present at their wedding, how long they dated before they married, or when they moved into different houses. For this couple, there appeared to be very different experiences of the same event or story. In another example, the husband admitted that he had nothing in common with his wife and she said nothing about it. He said there was a great deal of disagreement early in their marriage, whereas she said everything worked out fine. This couple, like many others in the study, reported that they had stayed together only because divorce was not an option when they were younger. Finally, some of the stories told by this couple type appear to have a strong fantasy element to them. For many dysfunctional separate couples, fantasy may have been instrumental in sustaining the marriage.

The following dialogue shows how couples expressed distance and separateness in their stories. This couple is discussing an event that occurred while their children were adolescents. This particular couple's courtship involved extensive letter writing during the war. They rarely saw each other and made the decision to marry through letters. Their relationship started with a high level of separateness that continued through later stages. This dialogue also demonstrates a level of relationship apathy for the wife. An upsetting event occurred when the husband acted unilaterally, and she did not even care enough to engage in conflict, even though she was clearly upset.

W: He wanted to put in a patio, pour cement, and I never wanted it. He waited till I went back to see my mother and he built the patio while I'm gone.

H: No, you went to the Gulf, remember? You took the kids down to Florida or somewhere down there, went on a trip.

W: I don't know, well, anyway, he waited.

H: I waited till they was gone and I had the stuff all ready to order and just ordered it and went to work before they got back, and they came back earlier, too, and that didn't help. (She laughs.)

I: Why didn't you want a patio?

W: A patio is always dirty, and it's always up to me to put up with it. He did the same thing out here, and there hasn't been anyone who cleans the patio off but me, and it blows the leaves and . . . and dirt in and covers the furniture. . . . We just found out the other day that he built it on top of the sewer line. . . . We will have to put in a new sewer line, we will have to break up the whole patio, I guess. (laugh)

I: What did you do when you saw the patio?

W: Nothing, what could you do?

I: Did you get mad?

H: No.

W: No. (pause) It was there, I dealt with it . . .

A second incident for this couple occurred in the later stages of their relationship:

W: I do a lot of things, he does his thing, works in the garage now, I work at the local library.

H: Remember I wasn't feeling right, thought my pacemaker was going?

W: Yeah, he woke up that morning said it wasn't working. I had to go to the library, had to work, (pause) so I went.

H: Got myself to the hospital. Walked into the emergency room, said my pacemaker was broken. They all got to me, real fast. Guess I had a loose wire.

W: I had to go down to the library.

In these two examples, the wife indicates their separateness first by stating that they have different interests and then by not offering assistance when her husband is having medical difficulty. He does not seem to react and behaves as if this is typical behavior in their relationship.

In the next sequence of dialogue, the couple discuss how they deal with conflict. When they tell their stories, they do a great deal of formal turn taking, actually saying, "It's your turn now." When one finishes discussing an event, the other tells another story. Many times the stories are not connected in any way. These spouses rarely validate each other, never finish each other's statements or laugh at the stories. This becomes most evident if you compare their dialogue to the connected couple's dialogue, which demonstrates high levels of connectedness. The dialogue presented below is a good example of separateness and distance that couples experience throughout their entire marriage. It is also interesting to note that the amount of time each couple member talks is significantly more than that of other couples in the study. Although this couple verbally report that they are very happy with their marriage, their dialogue offers little evidence of happiness.

H: You know, it's interesting that she gets along with me so well. I'm very strong willed, and when I want to do something, I don't yield very much. Until sometimes she can reason with me and I will, but if it's important things—things that I feel important to—I won't yield, and she yields, so we . . . we never had clashes because of that. We would have had clashes otherwise.

W: Well, I'm not as stubborn as he is, that's number one. Number two, at the beginning there was a strong love between the two of us, and it seemed like we'd fall back on that thought, you know, we really care. Whatever we are doing, we are doing because we care. We're not taking chances because we're doing it because it's laid out that way, so we didn't have problems like some couples have.

H: But, see, we don't have any, have any strong interests in common at all, (pause) which is interesting.

I: Uh-huh, it is.

H: And whatever we wanted to do, if we wanted to go on vacation or took a trip at all I was the one to always suggest let's do it, let's do that, and she went along and enjoyed it.

W: I didn't think that was such a terrible, a terrible thing to do. I thought it was beautiful, because he had the initiative, he had the willingness to do things and I never stopped him. I always said, I'll go along with you, and it worked very nicely. What do you gain if you're strong willed, and what do you gain if he's strong willed? You gain nothing. At least this way we matched everything. I thought that was a good way of living.

I: So you never resented that?

W: No, no. And what is the use of being stubborn? What is the use of making up your mind, letting someone else set out on the branch? Do it together. I used to take care of the children while he fished. I'm not a fisherman, what's so wrong with that? I did other things that were beautiful. He can't do anything that I do. When it came to the kitchen, it came to a party, it came to something very advantageous, I was the one that did all that. I have the skill for it, I have the knowledge for it and I went ahead and did it, and when it was done, it was beautiful. He couldn't do those things. (pause) But on the other hand, he does certain beautiful things that I can't do. He's an engineer, I'm not an engineer. Right?

I: Right.

W: He knows the beginning, how to put in a screw. With me watching him, I learned a lot. I take a screwdriver if I have to, I take a needle and thread if I have to, I wasn't taught.

I: Sounds to me like you are very satisfied with who you are.

W: Yeah, yeah, I do what I want to do. He does what he wants to do. But he does share it with me, too. Like if it's done, he'll say look at this. Fine, beautiful.

H: And with all our financial stress that we have had or even later on when money was easier, uh, we never had financial problems, never had any financially. I used to be worried, I'd always say, "We're going to go in the red now. I don't know what we're going to do."

W: Oh, I heard that so much, but I said, don't worry about it. We'll have a way of seeing that through, and we did.

H: Yeah, her wants were never such that we had to stretch anything to satisfy her wants.

W: I'll tell you what I did do. (pause) If he came home very uptight, very worried and he shared it with me, I didn't scream. I didn't say you deserve it or anything like that. I says, you don't worry, it's all going to correct itself, and it did. He went back to work and it was a different scenery already.
(pause)

H: Most of the dissention was around the children.

W: It worked out beautifully. I knew the kids better then he did. (pause) And I think the trouble today with our young people, and I've noticed it. They are very temperamental. They are extremely so uptight about things. When something happens they say, well, if you don't like it, you can go, but I'm not saying that about my children. And I think that is one of the worst things you can say to a man or say to a woman. If you are together in a house and you are trying to make things match, and you are trying to put things together and you are trying to have a happy moment, why do you have to talk so adversely? Why do you have to say such ugly things to each other? See, I never felt that way. Now, when things got quieted down and I was unhappy, I spoke up, but if we were both speaking at the same time, I don't think he'd know what I was saying, and I don't think I'd understand what he was saying.

In this dialogue, the husband admits that they have nothing in common and she says nothing about it. They do not talk to each other, they consistently talk to the interviewer. They rarely validate each other's stories, and there is no continuity in their storytelling. Each tells his or her own story, and the other moves in a different direction. They rarely talk at the same time like other couples who appear more connected. This couple's storytelling reflects a high degree of separateness. For example, he says they had dissention around the children, and she says it worked out beautifully. It is as if they are talking about different events and unaware of the invalidation of the other's perspective. There is no warmth or laughter in their storytelling, only a great deal of distance. They don't tell stories *together.*

Expression of Emotion

Another interesting finding that emerged from this study is that men appeared to present a wider range of emotions than women when telling stories. Men tended to validate their spouses more than women did, and men talked more about feelings and regrets than women did. The women appeared to be neutral and detached when telling many of their stories or listening to their spouses discuss events or talk about feelings.

In the next example, the couple is discussing overall feelings. In this dialogue, it is the husband who is disclosing feelings about his insecurity during the early marriage years and in the present. His wife actually learns new information about her husband and does not react. Even when he is discussing painful feelings he has about himself, she offers no support or empathy. His expressiveness alone is unusual for a man of his generation. However, he continues even though he does not receive support from his wife.

H: Well, I have always been myself, a little bit insecure even when I was a child. Being raised, I didn't quite meet up to the expectations of my parents, I don't think. And my sisters, they were always on the honor roll, and here I came along and I wasn't, and I was just a little bit better than an average student, but they was some of the top students in their classes. And I was, and I think that has followed through, and I think Sarah will agree with me, all my life. I still at times feel a little bit insecure, and when Sarah was

out there with her folks, well, is she leaving me or is she going to come back. (pause) I think that it is, ah, different things have happened when I was a little kid, I have always felt a little insecure.
(silence)

I: Sarah, when you went to go see your family did you realize that Jerry was afraid you wouldn't come back?

W: I hadn't realized it till later. At the time I didn't realize it, to me I was just going home. See my friends and my parents, didn't think too much about it. I didn't think he was upset about it.

I: When did you find out that it was stressful for Jerry?

W: I don't think I even knew.

H: Maybe I just didn't express my feelings to her about that. I know that you know that I am a little bit insecure.

W: You always have been and you always will be.

Typically, women are more expressive and emotional than men, but that trend did not appear in this study. Tamir and Antonucci (1981) also discussed this phenomenon in older couples, suggesting that as men age, they become more expressive and affiliative, whereas older women become more self-centered and individualistic than they were in previous life stages. The question is: Is this an individual developmental change, a product of the relationship, or something resulting from the combination?

How and Why Did These Couples Stay Together for 50 Years?

When we asked couples how they stayed together so long, we found three common characteristics across couples that were happy and stayed together for more than 50 years. First, couples emphasized the importance of mutual respect and treating each other with dignity. Consistent with this, some couples reported that it was important to put their spouses before everything else in their lives. Second, couples agreed on a comfortable level of closeness that was embodied in their relationships. Our data, however, do not indicate that there is a generalizable ideal here, for some couples were happy with relatively low closeness (the functional separate couples), and others needed and desired a higher level of closeness or intimacy in their marriages (the connected couples). One is not better than the other; the point is that the couples negotiated levels of closeness that were mutually satisfactory. Finally, it appears that successful couples shared a vision of life or had a "plan" of the course they wanted their lives to take. Many times the vision had to be readjusted or changed, but it still existed and was shared. Some couples reported actually discussing the "plan" or "vision," whereas others acknowledged that it existed but was rarely discussed. One couple said that they just knew what they both wanted out of life and for their family, and they both worked toward that goal.

The characteristics of unhappy couples are somewhat different. As stated earlier, unhappy couples display a great deal of individual storytelling, criticism, lack of empathy, and lack of interest in their relationships. So the issue is: Why and how did this type of couple stay together? First, the unhappy long-lasting couples reported, as other couples did, that divorce was not an option, so they just had to make it work. Second, they maintained high levels of distance in their relationships. The distance may have helped them stay together. By limiting time and interaction, they also limited the potential for conflict and the salience of the relationship in their overall (individual) lives. Third, these couples are highly committed to the relationship even though they are unhappy in the relationship. Fourth, some of these couples have developed stories that have a high level of fantasy and romance. It appears that this phenomenon is most apparent in couples whose families may have experienced high levels of dysfunction.

One of the perplexing questions that has emerged from this project is: Which couple should be commended—the happy long-term couple or the unhappy long-term couple? Both types of couples have stayed in a marriage for more than 50 years in a time when one out of three marriages ends in divorce.

Maybe the following dialogue will help us to understand the phenomenon of the long-lasting marriage.

I: So what would you say, overall, statements about your life together to end this?

H: It's been great.

I: Great?

H: Fantastic. Couldn't have been better. Look at this jewel I still have. Pretty, smart . . .

W: Oh, brother . . .

H: Sexy.

W: Hah!

H: That's not so laughable.

W: Well, if you'd asked this question every decade of the 52 years of marriage, I think the answer would have been different along the way, so here we are at the end and I'm supposed to say how it was? You know, and . . . (laughs)

I: It would have been different every step.

W: And the thing I think, um, perhaps psychologists and psychiatrists and counselors realize today, um, that you can actually change yourself. You cannot change the other person, but you can change yourself if you want to, if you want to, and life changes you along the way. Um, it's kind of . . .

H: She didn't say how it was, you've been talking all around it.

W: . . . like the ocean wave hitting this rock all the time and then there'll be a little reaction to it.

These narratives provide us with a framework in which we can analyze and understand the processes involved in long-lasting relationships. The data from this research program suggest that enduring relationships are marked by processes defined by themes of connectedness and separateness. These conclusions are supported by earlier research conducted on couples in earlier stages of their life together (Baxter, 1988, 1990; Fitzpatrick, 1988; Hess & Handel, 1959). In addition, these findings demonstrate the influence of context on the relationship (e.g., the Depression and World War II framing

couples' expectations and patterns of relating to one another).
This chapter argues that background historical events, such as
World War II and the Depression, are not simply contextual experiences fitted onto an otherwise standard way of doing relationships. These contextual experiences are fundamental experiences that shape people's view of themselves, partnership,
the world, the future, life, and family. These are not just events
that happened while life went on, but events that shaped the
way these couples think, the way they do and did life, and the
way they act in their relationships and everyday life. The contextual experiences are not something that their relationship
formed within, they are experiences that had a direct impact on
the way these people *did* their relationship.

This chapter also has an impact on the way in which we view
traditional relational paradigms. The processes addressed here
are hard to account for within the traditional paradigms based
on exchange theory. These people did not stay married because
of the many rewards they received from the marital relationship;
they stayed married because divorce was not an option for
them, within the contextual framework of their life and relationship. Many couples had the attitude that you had to make do
with less and did not have high expectations of their partner or
life.

The exploration of under-studied relationships helps us to
draw a more clear and accurate descriptive map of relationships. When you are thinking about the couples described in
this chapter, I would like you to frame your thoughts in the
bigger picture of what we know and do not know about relationships. Overall, this study demonstrates that long-lasting relationships involve changes and adaptations and that the happiest couples seem to be those who develop patterns that
encourage awareness and validation of one another throughout
the ongoing evolution of personal relationships. I believe that
this chapter also highlights the need to explore in great depth
those under-studied and overlooked relationships. These types
of relationships open us to uncharted and unknown territories.

3

Relationships Between
Members of Cultural Minorities

Stanley O. Gaines Jr.

I n this chapter, I focus on how the cultural values of particular minority ethnic groups are enacted within personal relationships between members of those groups. I use the term *culture* to refer to "the way of life [that a group] hold[s] in common" (Berry, Poortinga, Segall, & Dasen, 1992, p. 167), and I use the term *ethnic group* to refer to "an identifiable set of individuals who socially interact and who maintain themselves over time . . . [and who are bound together by] some social structure and some system of norms governing [their]

AUTHOR'S NOTE: Preparation of this chapter was facilitated by a postdoctoral fellowship from the University of North Carolina at Chapel Hill (1992-1993) and by institutional funds from Pomona College to the author. The author wishes to thank Katrina Bledsoe, editors Steve Duck and Julia Wood, the members of Caryl Rusbult's Close Relationship Discussion Group at the University of North Carolina at Chapel Hill (Christopher Agnew, Victor Bissonnette, Chante Cox, Lowell Gaertner, John Martz, Shelley Peterson, Bryan Reardon, and Caryl Rusbult), and especially Diana Rios for providing insightful comments during the preparation of this chapter.

conduct" (Berry et al., 1992, p. 293). Using blacks and Hispanics as examples, this discussion probes the character and influences of non-Anglo values, such as collectivism and familism, on relational processes. In particular, I present conceptual models that trace how participation in minority cultures influences interaction between spouses; the models reflect social scientific literature on (a) familism among Hispanics and (b) collectivism among blacks because virtually all of the extant research on cultural minorities and personal relationships has emphasized these as central values among those ethnic groups (Staples & Mirande, 1980). Familism and collectivism represent values salient in two particular minority cultures; as such, they are intended to illustrate, not exhaust, the influence of minority cultural status on processes in personal relationships.

Along the way, I shall attempt to debunk the notion that mainstream research in the field of personal relationships ever has been "value free" by identifying a central value (i.e., individualism) that has consistently surfaced as a theme in research on personal relationships. Finally, I propose a model of culture, personality, and marital behavior that promises to transcend culture by *including* a variety of cultural groups and accompanying perspectives within an overall perspective on marriage and the influences that shape it. This analysis ultimately suggests that it is important for researchers to develop enlarged conceptions and models of personal relationships that reflect more than values of middle-class Western Anglos.

Conceptions of the Self:
Culturally Constructed, Relationally Manifested

As Kenneth Gergen noted in *The Saturated Self* (1991), the belief that the individual is the locus or center of human behavior is fundamental to Western science, and indeed to Western culture itself. This individualistic belief is so pervasive in the United States and other Western societies that psychologists and laypersons alike commonly attest to the "objective" reality of one's identity as self-constructed and as superseding one's relatedness to other human beings in importance. However, upon further inspection, the reality of the self is anything but objective. *Who we are* depends to a large degree upon the language we are taught (and therefore our capacity for describing ourselves, along with how particular culturally authorized vocabularies shape our experience of relationships with other persons), the social categories by which we define or do not define ourselves (and thus our definition of others as in-group or out-group members), and even the values imparted to us (and, in turn, the values we expect to see in others' behavior; see Allport, 1954; Sullivan, 1953). According to Gergen (1991), then, our personalities represent the intersection between prevailing cultural norms and processes of relational involvement with others (see also Schellenberg, 1978; Stryker & Stratham, 1985).

In their chapter on the social psychology of marriage, Levinger and Huston (1990) noted that social psychologists seldom have examined the impact of personality variables, particularly as reflective of individuals' cultural contexts, on interpersonal behavior in marital relationships (or, for that matter, on behavioral processes in personal relationships as a whole). Because psychologically trained social psychologists tend to deemphasize culture and sociologically trained social psychologists tend to deemphasize personality when studying the antecedents of social behavior (Stryker, 1991), it is not surprising that such a small knowledge base has emerged within the field of personal relationships regarding the degree to which culture and personality interact to influence processes and dynamics in marriage. Such inattention on the part of social psychologists to the interplay among culture, personality, and behavior in marital and other personal relationships is regrettable because the core values embraced by members of a given culture not only help shape individuals' personalities but also may influence interpersonal processes that in turn affect the long-term satisfaction, the stability, and even the character of personal relationships in general (Berry et al., 1992; Honigmann, 1954).

Some social scientists (e.g., Kantor, 1982) would question the utility of exploring conceptual (and, ultimately, empirical) links among culture, personality, and interpersonal behavior in personal relationships. After all, they might ask, isn't the behavior of husbands and wives determined by idiosyncratic values or transcultural values rather than by culturally specific values? In response to such a question, I contend that individuals' internalized values (i.e., guides to behavior; Welte, 1979) and resulting behavior in personal relationships are formed through interactions with others who are members of particular ethnic groups.

Some critics (e.g., Kantor, 1982) also might challenge attempts to link culture with ostensibly noncultural processes (e.g., marital behavior) as constituting scientific reductionism (Wallace, 1970). However, I argue that recognizing how membership in particular cultures influences dyadic-level behavior can help researchers avoid the reductionistic tendencies toward individual-level analysis of behavior (Berscheid, 1986) that have plagued much research and theory in the field of personal relationships. Although it is true that culture and personality are separable as concepts, considerable overlap exists between those concepts and their pragmatic embodiments (Honigmann, 1954). Furthermore, although not all aspects of personality are relevant to interpersonal behavior, certain key aspects of personality that are sculpted in interaction *are* important to the study of behavior in marriage and other personal relationships (Wiggins, 1979).

Although in this chapter I stress the impact of cultural value orientations on individuals' personalities and couples' relational processes at a given point in time, it also is conceivable that as time passes, the relationship processes of members of a particular ethnic group help to sustain the very cultures in which those relationships initially arose. This latter perspective has been championed by leaders of the structuralist movement (e.g., Althusser, 1976; Foucault, 1988; for critiques, see Chiari, 1975; Poster, 1975) that arose in France during the 1960s. That is, structuralists would contend that in the processes by which individuals relate to others, those individuals serve a vital function for their respective cultures by affirming the existence of the cultures. Without individuals engaged in social relationships in which cultural values presumably are expressed, neither the abstract ideas nor the social organizations of a given culture could endure. Therefore, the histories of personal relationships cumulatively are interwoven with the histories of entire ethnic groups and their corresponding cultures.

Culture and Personality

Before examining how culturally shaped personal values affect personal relationships between members of particular cultural minorities, the concepts of *culture* and *personality* must be defined in greater detail. Honigmann (1954) provided an especially thorough definition of each concept, emphasizing the high level of correspondence between the two:

> In its technical sense "culture" is a short way of saying many things. The word points to two classes of phenomena, namely (1) to the socially standardized behavior—actions, thought, feelings—of some enduring group and (2) the material products of, or aids to, the behaviors of that group.
> Furthermore, the term means to designate that these referents are bound together in some kind of a system as a whole. (p. 22)

> In its present technical sense the word *personality* refers to the actions, thoughts, and feelings characteristic of an individual. We may also speak of personality patterns in the sense that people evidence regularities of behavior which, however, are usually situationally expressed. . . . Because personality comprises recurrent behavior it follows that knowledge of personality furnishes a basis for predicting individual behavior.
> . . . Personality patterns also constitute part of the socially standardized behavior patterns of an enduring group. The personality concept overlays the culture concept. In part at least personality means culture reflected in individual behavior. . . . As a matter of fact, it is from concrete regularities of individual behavior that the

anthropologist derives the cultural patterns of the community
which he studies. (p. 28)

According to Honigmann (1954), then, much of "who individuals are" can be traced to the culture(s) in which they were
born and raised. This basic point also has been made by Wood
(1993c; see also Allan, 1993; Baxter, 1993) in her chapter on
gender and communication in personal relationships in Volume
3 of this series (which focuses on social contexts of personal
relationships). If we apply Honigmann's logic to the study of
personal relationships, it follows that the behavior of individuals in marriage and other personal relationships can be understood largely in terms of individuals' "social heritage" (see
Welte, 1979). Honigmann's conceptualization of culture and
personality also allows us to identify certain interpersonal
needs (i.e., desired end states; McClelland, 1987) as more or less
reflective of cultural values and thus as relevant to the study of
personal relationships.

Consider Aronoff's (1967; Aronoff & Wilson, 1985) assertion
that the hierarchy of needs proposed by Maslow (1954) may be
either satisfied or thwarted by prevailing societal institutions.
Two of the needs (i.e., physiological and safety) in Maslow's
hierarchy are crucial to individuals' physical survival and can
be met through interaction with strangers or acquaintances
(Brown, 1965; Foa & Foa, 1974). The other needs, in contrast,
do not necessarily affect physical survival directly but are important to individuals' psychological well-being (which, in turn,
may affect physical well-being; Brown, 1986). This is not to say
that physiological or safety needs can be taken for granted, especially among Hispanics or blacks. The dire social, political,
educational, and economic conditions that Hispanics and blacks
in toto have confronted throughout their respective histories in
the United States still have not been eradicated (Commission on
Minority Participation in Education and American Life, 1988)
and have prevented disproportionately large numbers of Hispanics and blacks from fulfilling even those "lower order" needs, let
alone the "higher order" needs that Maslow identified.

Of the remaining needs in Maslow's hierarchy, two (i.e., love/ belongingness and esteem) must be met via interaction with significant others and, as such, may be linked with values (e.g., orientation toward one's family, toward one's ethnic group, and/or toward oneself; see Braithwaite & Scott, 1991) that persons learn regarding interpersonal relations—and that vary from culture to culture (Laudin, 1973; Welte, 1979). (The third need that is not related explicitly to physical survival, namely self-actualization, is highly idiosyncratic in nature and rarely is achieved; see Bellah, Madsen, Sullivan, Swidler, & Tipton, 1985, for a discussion of self-actualization as an individualistic goal that not only is unmistakably American but can be reached only by the socioeconomically privileged.) In other words, the members of a given culture may be taught, either implicitly or explicitly, that a particular source of love and esteem (e.g., the family, the ethnic group, oneself) is more critical than other sources. In turn, the degree to which individuals give and expect love and esteem in personal relationships, as well as what they count as representing love and esteem, may depend in part on the value orientations that prevail in their particular cultures.

The social/psychological needs (i.e., love/belongingness and esteem) defined by Maslow (1954) and linked by Aronoff (1967; Aronoff & Wilson, 1985) specifically to cultural conditioning are related conceptually to personality traits (i.e., expressivity and instrumentality; Spence, 1985), interpersonal resources (i.e., affection and respect; Foa & Foa, 1974), and motives (i.e., intimacy and power; McAdams, 1985) that appear throughout the personality/social psychology literature (see Wiggins, 1991). Later in this chapter, I shall make use of resource exchange theory (Foa & Foa, 1974) in postulating not only that affection (i.e., emotional acceptance of another person) and respect (i.e., social acceptance of another person) are reciprocated by spouses in fulfillment of each other's love and esteem needs, but also that the character of both reflects the influence of distinctive cultural values. Emphasizing resource exchange theory does not imply that a rational or economic account of interpersonal behavior necessarily represents the "best" way to

illustrate the potential impact of culture and personality on behavior in personal relationships (Brown, 1986; see also Bellah
et al., 1985; Welte, 1979). Rather, it illustrates how a conceptual
model of culture, personality, and marital behavior treats the
particular processes of exchange and opens inquiry into a variety of other social/psychological processes in personal relationships.

Manifestation of
Cultural Values in Relationship Processes

Prior to the 1960s, psychological masculinity (defined by
Spence, Deaux, & Helmreich, 1985, as an instrumental or "me-
oriented" orientation) was perceived by many psychologists as
the standard for mental health (French, 1985). In the aftermath
of the Women's Rights Movement, however, a new standard for
mental health was promoted by some psychologists: *androgyny,*
or the simultaneous possession of masculine and feminine personality characteristics (the latter of which reflect an expressive or "we-orientation"; Brown, 1986). Although masculinity
and femininity were shown to be orthogonal personality traits
and thus not mutually exclusive (e.g., Bem, 1974; Spence, Helmreich, & Stapp, 1974), some research has suggested that masculine and feminine qualities may not coexist peacefully but instead may "compete" for recognition incessantly within and
between individuals (Spence et al., 1985)—and that, in the end,
the "male" or masculine relational style predominates in male-
female interactions (i.e., partners exchange respectful—or,
more correctly, *dis*respectful—behaviors; Gaines, 1994a; see
also Foa, 1973).

In *Habits of the Heart,* Bellah et al. (1985) observed that individualism (i.e., prioritization of one's own needs over those of
other persons) is the predominant American cultural value, a
value that ostensibly encourages self-sufficiency but discourages
the very social obligations that (a) make genuine self-awareness
possible and (b) make enduring and satisfying personal relationships possible as well. *Utilitarian individualism* (i.e., an

emphasis on maximizing one's interests), manifested primarily in terms of devotion to one's vocation, clearly can inhibit the formation of close interpersonal ties. *Expressive individualism* (i.e., an emphasis on maximizing one's inner psychic goods), manifested primarily in terms of devotion to one's avocations, may facilitate the development of short-term personal relationships but also may promote the dissolution of those ephemeral ties when personal sacrifice is required of one or both partners. According to Bellah and his colleagues, both forms of individualism help define the "American character," yet neither form is sufficient to sustain long-term relationships in modern society. Indeed, both utilitarian and expressive individualisms are manifested largely in egocentric terms and, as such, can promote genuine companionship only to a limited degree (for a discussion of related concepts such as autonomy needs and connectedness needs, see Baxter & Simon, 1993).

Bellah et al. (1985) believed that social obligations to family (in both extended and nuclear forms) and to community (conceptualized broadly as a "lifestyle enclave") promote long-term commitment to marriage by rooting individuals in their culture and thus transcending the self-other dichotomy that, ironically, socialization helped foster in the first place (see also Foa & Foa, 1974). According to Bellah and his colleagues, obligations to family and community—which will be designated as *familism* and *collectivism,* respectively, throughout this chapter—remind individuals that their individuality is defined only in relation to the larger social context. In turn, the subjective sense of commitment leads individuals to display affection (e.g., by saying "I love you," expressing trust in partner, sharing with partner) and respect (e.g., by saying "I admire you," expressing faith in partner's abilities, challenging partner to achieve full potential), not out of an expectation that their partners will repay them in kind, but rather out of a conviction that their partners' welfare is at least as important as their own welfare (for an extended discussion of commitment processes in personal relationships, see Johnson, 1991a; see also Johnson, 1991b; Levinger, 1979, 1991; Rusbult, 1991; Rusbult & Buunk, 1993). The *relational culture* (Wood, 1982) sculpted by these values thus begins to take on a life of its own and helps ensure that the relationship will stand the test of time. Moreover, this relational culture reflects and perpetuates the particular values, rules, and interactional dynamics that partners have imparted from their ethnic cultures as well as other sources.

Through the process of cultural transmission, individuals within a given ethnic group learn the core norms and values of their culture actively and passively, through formal training and casual observation (Berry et al., 1992). Individuals thus internalize cultural values and manifest those values in their behavior toward significant others, usually within their own ethnic group. It is no accident that personal relationships frequently serve to affirm individuals' cultural values; after all, each culture orients individuals toward particular relational styles in the first place (Duck, 1988). This is not to say that all individuals internalize cultural values to the same degree; as with any other personality characteristic, individual differences in value orientation inevitably must be acknowledged in any attempt to understand the impact of culture on relationship processes (Berry et al., 1992; Gergen, 1969). Moreover, each personal relationship is to some extent a unique entity, created by two specific individuals within a specific historical context (Altman & Taylor, 1973). Yet the fact that one-of-a-kind individuals join together to build one-of-a-kind relationships in no way prevents cultural values from entering or shaping partners' relational styles. If anything, we may conceive of partners as the *mediators* of the impact of cultural values on relationship processes (see Jacobson & Margolin, 1979). Because relational cultures are established and maintained directly by individuals and only indirectly by the norms of the larger or "big-picture" culture, relational cultures reflect the influence of "big-picture" cultural values only to the extent that those values are embraced and displayed by women and men in personal relationships (Berry et al., 1992).

Bellah et al. (1985) admitted that their conclusions regarding cultural values and relationship processes were based on interviews with exclusively white, middle-class participants. Given that the existing literature on marital relationships among Hispanics, blacks, and other cultural minorities consistently reveals that the "me-orientation" of individualism is eclipsed in favor of "we-orientations" such as familism and collectivism (i.e., precisely those values that Bellah and his colleagues singled out as crucial to relationship commitment and mutuality in giving affection and respect), it is unfortunate that the boom in ethnic studies research that began during the 1970s (Omi & Winant, 1986; Sollors, 1986) and continues to this day has gone largely unacknowledged in the field of personal relationships. The study of nonmajority groups might not only enlarge researchers' understanding of relationships between members of minority social groups but might also clarify the values, rules, identities, and so forth of *majority* social groups as long as those are misspecified as universal.

In tandem, these two outcomes of research on minorities' relationships might yield important insights into personal relationships in general. Moreover, genuinely immersing oneself in cultures outside of one's immediate experience (as opposed to adopting the tourist mode of exposing oneself only to "safe," albeit unchallenging, aspects of other cultures) invariably heightens awareness of one's own culture. For example, as a consequence of challenging prevailing social scientific views regarding cultural values and relationship processes, we might find that the categorization of male-female interactions as inherently individualistic is no more accurate than the classification of Hispanic or black male-female interactions in such terms. Because this seems likely, I will now elaborate on the relevance of ethnicity and the cultural values promoted by specific minority ethnic groups to the study of relationship processes. In so doing, I shall consider the ways in which minority relational styles may differ from those of majority relational styles.

Ethnicity and Minority Status

Ethnicity must be defined more fully because it is central to a thorough examination of culture, personality, and relational processes. As Mindel, Habenstein, and Wright (1988) pointed out, ethnicity and culture are linked intimately as concepts:

> In [a] general sense, an ethnic group consists of those who share a unique social and cultural heritage that is passed on from generation to generation. . . . In America, the core categories of ethnic identity from which individuals are able to form a sense of peoplehood are race, religion, national origin, or some combination of these categories. . . . It is these categories, emphasizing substantively cultural symbols of consciousness of time, that are used to define the groups. (p. 5)

> Ethnicity usually is displayed in the values, attitudes, lifestyles, customs, rituals, and personality types of individuals who identify with particular ethnic groups. (p. 1)

Mindel et al. (1988) also noted that the concept of *minority group* is related to, though not identical to, the concept of ethnic group:

> "Minority," in the sociological rather than statistical sense, refers to a power or dominance relationship. Those groups that have unequal access to power, that are considered in some way unworthy of equally sharing power, and that are stigmatized in terms of assumed inferior traits or characteristics are minority groups. To be a member of a minority group, therefore, is to share a status relationship, and to act as a minority group member is to express power consciously. To be a member of an ethnic group, on the other hand, is to share a sense of cultural and historical uniqueness, and to act as a member of an ethnic group is to express feelings or call attention to that uniqueness. It should be understood that the same individual at any moment may act in either capacity. (p. 8)

Scholars within the field of ethnic studies disagree as to whether the terms *ethnic group* and *minority group* are synonymous. For example, Roucek and Eisenberg (1982) defined the term *ethnic group* as "a distinct cultural minority that wishes to protect its identity and promote its interests within the larger society" (p. 1), whereas Frisbee and Bean (1978) stated flatly, "An ethnic group may or may not be a minority" (p. 4). Moreover, some social scientists confine their usage of the term *ethnic group*, as applied to cultural affiliations in the United States, to white/European American groups, others limit the term to include only "racial" minorities such as blacks/African Americans and Indians/Native Americans, and still others argue that white as well as "nonwhite" persons may qualify as members of ethnic groups (Dinnerstein, Reimers, & Nichols, 1979).

Although it is possible to distinguish between ethnicity (which connotes certain social processes operating *within* a group) and minority status (which connotes the relation of a particular group to the larger social order), certain groups—specifically Hispanics/Latinos and blacks/African Americans—clearly constitute distinct ethnicities as well as historically disadvantaged minorities (Commission on Minority Participation in Education and American Life, 1988; Dinnerstein et al., 1979). Consequently this chapter focuses on the experiences of Hispanics and blacks, respectively, as members of cultural minorities and as partners in personal relationships that are shaped, in part, by distinctive ethnic values. With that focus in mind, let us examine more closely certain fundamental values associated with each group that might be expected to influence the socioemotional processes between husbands and wives in each group.

Familism and
Socioemotional Behavior Among Hispanics

As a whole, Hispanics currently make up the second-largest cultural minority in the United States (after blacks; Dinnerstein & Reimers, 1988) and probably will become the nation's largest cultural minority during the 21st century (Marin & Marin, 1991). In stark contrast to the mythology of the United States as a "nation of immigrants" (Dinnerstein et al., 1979; Dinnerstein & Reimers, 1988; Mindel et al., 1988), the history of Hispanics in the United States does not conform to the ideals of voluntary immigration or of the "melting pot" that frequently are invoked in accounts of the experiences of Anglos (e.g., Mexicans were designated as "foreigners" only when the United States annexed most of the land that formerly had belonged to Mexico and thus displaced the Mexicans; Mindel et al., 1988). Nonetheless, although Chicanos/Mexican Americans, Puerto Ricans, Cuban Americans, and other Hispanics have come to the United States from disparate lands and via many routes (Mindel et al., 1988), Hispanics as a group are linked culturally by language (i.e., Spanish), by religion (i.e., Catholicism), and by a set of values, most notably *familism,* which prioritizes the welfare of one's immediate and extended family by biology and marriage (Becerra, 1988; Sanchez-Ayendez, 1988; Szapocznik & Hernandez, 1988). Although familism is by no means the sole province of Hispanic culture (Schaefer, 1988), accounts of Hispanic marriages invariably turn to familism as a central value shared by spouses and reflected in the relationships that they create (Mindel, 1980; Padilla & Lindholm, 1984).

The emphasis on family well-being that often is cited by scholars and laypersons alike as a central value of Hispanic culture has its roots in Mexico and other Latin American countries. Familism not only has survived the trek to the United States but seems to have evolved and facilitated Hispanics' endurance, both physically and psychologically, as members of a cultural minority (see Becerra, 1988). Given that a particular culture must meet the psychological as well as the physiological needs of its members in order for the culture itself to remain viable (Honigmann, 1954; Laudin, 1973; Skinner, 1972), it is not surprising that familism has assumed such significance among Hispanics. As a cultural value, familism has helped perpetuate the very culture that spawned it. In fact, the prominence of familism in Hispanic culture helps explain why most Hispanics have held onto their social heritage with such tenacity: Giving up familism and other major features of their culture would amount to a loss of identity for a majority of Hispanics (Dinnerstein & Reimers, 1988).

To what extent is familism reflected in the processes of personal relationships between Hispanic men and women? Following the theoretical lead of Mirande (1977), I suggested (Gaines, 1993) that familism promotes mutual displays of affection and respect among Hispanic spouses. Using concepts derived from resource exchange theory (Foa & Foa, 1974) and from personality theory (Wiggins, 1979), I argued that familism as a cultural value is internalized to varying degrees by individual Hispanic men and women. As such, higher levels of internalized familism among individual Hispanic husbands and wives should be predictive of higher levels of affection-giving and respect-giving behavior toward spouses. Furthermore, although individual differences in internalized familism would not explain all of the variance in socioemotional behavior within a given sample of Hispanic couples, the relationship between familism and socioemotional behavior would be linear in nature and significantly greater than zero even after accounting for the impact of partners' behavior on each other's behavior. The resulting conceptual model, based on my previous account of familism as an influence on relationship processes among Hispanic couples, is shown in Figure 3.1.

To the extent that Hispanic partners incorporate familial values into their personal relationships, we would expect husbands and wives to make major decisions jointly, support each other emotionally, and bolster each other's confidence when necessary. In addition, we would expect husbands and wives to place the needs of their offspring—and, possibly, of kin such as elderly relatives—above their own needs when warranted. Notice that this conceptualization of familism as reflected in relational processes does *not* equate prioritization of the family with rigidity in gender-role arrangements; if anything, genuine adherence to familistic values may be antithetical to the concept of patriarchy (Cromwell & Ruiz, 1979; Hawkes & Taylor, 1975; Mirande, 1985).

Some evidence of familism as an influence on the quality of Hispanic marital relationships comes from a study in which

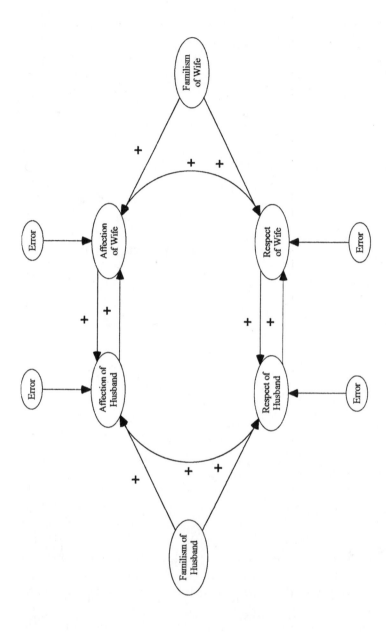

66

Figure 3.1. Conceptual Model Linking Familism and Socioemotional Behavior Among Hispanic Couples

Frisbie, Bean, and Eberstein (1978) used data from the 1970 1/100 (5%) Public Use Samples for the entire southwestern portion of the United States. Results from the data set, which included responses from 6,601 Mexican Americans and 59,469 Anglos, provided support for the hypothesis that the effect of age of first marriage on marital instability would be greater for Anglos than for Mexican Americans (i.e., younger couples were more likely than older couples to divorce among Anglos but not among Mexican Americans). Frisbie et al. (1978) interpreted the results as consistent with Mexican Americans' greater emphasis on familism (i.e., familism acts as a buffer against marital adversity for Mexican Americans but not for Anglos). It must be noted, however, that support for a similar hypothesis concerning level of education and ethnicity was not obtained. In addition, the data set used by Frisbie et al. did not specifically measure internalized familism or socioemotional behavior; therefore these authors relied heavily upon circumstantial evidence in drawing their conclusions. Unfortunately, some of Bean's own work (e.g., Bean, Curtis, & Marcum, 1977)—which also depends substantially upon indirect indices of familism—contradicts that of Frisbie et al. regarding the importance of familism in Hispanic couples' relational processes.

Two studies by Triandis and his colleagues (Triandis, Hui, et al., 1984; Triandis, Marin, et al., 1984) addressed cultural values and socioemotional behavior somewhat more directly than did Frisbie et al. (1978). In the Triandis et al. studies, Hispanics' behavioral intentions toward fellow Hispanics were more consistent with a familistic orientation than were Anglos' behavioral intentions toward fellow Anglos (or, for that matter, perceivers' behavioral intentions toward target persons belonging to out-groups). As in the Frisbie et al. study, however, Triandis et al.'s research did not include actual measures of internalized familism. Moreover, Triandis and his colleagues chose to measure the behavioral *intentions* of individual Hispanics toward *hypothetical others,* rather than the actual behavior of Hispanics toward real-life relationship partners. Thus the conceptual model that I advanced regarding relationship processes among

Hispanic couples has received only indirect support and has yet to be put to a formal empirical test.

The potential impact of familism on socioemotional behavior (and, in turn, marital satisfaction and stability) among Hispanic couples takes on added importance when one considers that Mexican American and Cuban American couples' divorce rates (i.e., less than 30%) are so much lower than the 50% divorce rate for the United States as a whole (Becerra, 1988). Despite the fact that Hispanics' socioeconomic status on average is lower than that of Anglos (Becerra, 1988), Hispanics' marriages are at least as durable as, if not more durable than, Anglos' marriages. Moreover, some research on family satisfaction (Schumm et al., 1988) suggests that Hispanic spouses are at least as satisfied as, if not more satisfied than, their Anglo counterparts.

To what degree can a familistic model of interpersonal behavior be applied to Hispanics representing diverse national origins and current geographic locales? Although I noted that divorce rates for most Hispanic couples are far lower than the corresponding rates for Anglo couples, Puerto Rican divorce rates are similar to those for Anglos (Becerra, 1988). Thus one might wonder whether the concept of familism is embraced differently depending upon which Hispanic group is considered. However, the relatively high divorce rates for Puerto Ricans can be explained largely on the basis of Puerto Ricans' low socioeconomic status relative to that of Cuban Americans and, to a lesser extent, of Mexican Americans (Becerra, 1988). The existing literature on Hispanic personal relationships suggests that familism is no less critical to Puerto Rican culture than to any other Hispanic culture (see Marin & Marin, 1991).

The statistics just described lend credence to the hypothesis that familism exerts substantial influence upon the behavioral dynamics of Hispanic marriages in general. It seems appropriate, then, for researchers in the field of personal relationships to incorporate this and other hypotheses into their work and to include Hispanics and other cultural minorities in their studies. In making this suggestion, I am not advocating merely including minority people within research framed by Anglo values and assumptions. Instead, conceptions of relationships must be re-framed to reflect the values, goals, and the like of multiple cultural groups.

Collectivism and
Socioemotional Behavior Among Blacks

At the present time, blacks constitute the largest cultural minority in the United States (Staples, 1988). Like Hispanics, blacks cannot be described properly as voluntary immigrants, having been subjected to American colonialism throughout their history in the United States (Mindel et al., 1988). Unlike any other cultural minority, however, the ancestors of many (if not most) blacks in the United States were subjected en masse to the dehumanizing institution of slavery. Even after the "peculiar institution" was abolished in the aftermath of the Civil War, segregation and other forms of discrimination continued to plague black Americans (Dinnerstein et al., 1979). Nevertheless, most African Americans have retained aspects of African culture to a greater degree than has generally been acknowledged by social scientists (Dinnerstein et al., 1979; Staples, 1988). Examples of the perseverance of African culture among black Americans include "Africanisms" in speech (i.e., words from African languages that were integrated into blacks' use of English), an oral storytelling tradition (evident in ancient folklore and contemporary music), and an emphasis on *collectivism* (i.e., an orientation toward the well-being of the entire ethnic group; see White, 1984; White & Parham, 1990).

Just as familism accompanied the ancestors of modern Hispanics, so too did collectivism survive the Atlantic Passage from Africa (especially West Africa, the area from which most slaves were uprooted) to the United States (Dinnerstein et al., 1979; Staples, 1988). Collectivism as a core value enabled blacks to adapt to the harsh reality of life in the United States, particularly in the antebellum South, where members of slave families frequently were sold to different plantation owners—and where no state court was obligated to accept slave marriages as legally binding (White, 1984; White & Parham, 1990). In fact, Dorman (1979) maintained that some form of collectivism is necessarily for any ethnic group to retain its identity: "If there is no sense of *ethnos,* no sense of we-ness, with at least some vague perceptions of cultural similarity among members; if there is no sense of collective norms, there is no ethnic group" (p. 33).

But how does collectivism influence the socioemotional behavior of blacks in their marital relationships? Asante (1981; see also Aborampah, 1989; Bell, Bouie, & Baldwin, 1990) asserted that collectivism was related directly to spouses' giving of affection and respect: That is, the greater the individual's internalization of collectivism as a psychocultural value, the more often that individual would display love and esteem toward his or her marriage partner. Similarly, by merging concepts derived from resource exchange theory (Foa & Foa, 1974) and from personality theory (Wiggins, 1979), I developed (Gaines, 1994b) a conceptual model of the influence of collectivism in black marriages. Hypothesizing that higher levels of collectivism would be associated linearly with higher levels of socioemotional behavior, I reasoned that collectivism ideally should be reflected in black spouses' affectionate and respectful behavior toward each other even after controlling for reciprocity between husbands' and wives' displays of each type of socioemotional behavior. This is not to say that a one-to-one correspondence between collectivism and socioemotional behavior ever would surface, or that collectivism would emerge as the only value manifested in socioemotional behavior (see Honigmann, 1954). My model does suggest, however, that a collectivistic personal orientation is a generally significant, albeit not singular, influence on black couples' affectionate and respectful behaviors.

Relatedly, Bellah et al. (1985) suggested that the *lack* of collectivistic values in white, middle-class, North Americans may lessen closeness and durability in their marriages. The influence of collectivism, then, may be germane to personal relationship processes in general. The resulting model of collectivism as an influence on relationship processes among black couples is shown in Figure 3.2.

What are some of the interpersonal implications of the collectivistic model? In terms of husband-wife relationships, we might expect that collectivistic values would promote egalitarian decision-making processes, mutuality in spouses' provision of nurturance, and mutuality in spouses' votes of confidence (see Dietrich, 1975; King, 1969; Melton & Thomas, 1976; Scanzoni, 1975). At first glance, the predictions that might be made regarding black couples' socioemotional processes, assuming that collectivistic values infuse their relational cultures, may appear identical to those that might be made using a familistic framework (which, as noted earlier, tends to be invoked more commonly when Hispanic couples are the subjects of investigation). However, if collectivistic norms foster the strengthening of *nonbiological* relationship ties such as those between adults and children whom they have adopted (whether officially or unofficially), we might expect the social networks of blacks and Hispanics to differ qualitatively (for a comparison of the unique sociohistorical forces that have helped shape the respective family patterns of blacks and Hispanics, see Zinn & Eitzen, 1987). That is, Hispanics' social networks might contain a proportionately higher number of biological kin outside of the nuclear family, whereas blacks' social networks might contain a proportionately higher number of nonbiological family members (though the practice of *compadrazgo* or godparenthood traditionally has brought close friends into *la familia* among many Hispanics; Williams, 1990). Given that black couples are more likely than any other couples to serve as adoptive parents (Kephart & Jedlicka, 1988), this hypothesis certainly seems plausible.

Past research on black marital behavior often has overlooked adaptive cultural values not salient in Anglo culture. As a result, many of the findings from research on blacks have been misinterpreted and/or ill explored. For example, in a study of solidarity among black and white married couples, Scanzoni (1975)

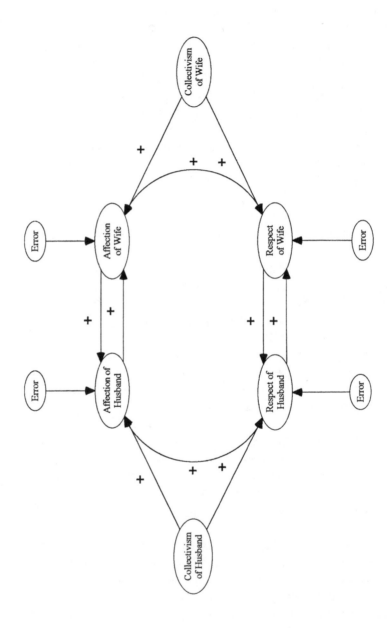

Figure 3.2. Conceptual Model Linking Collectivism and Socioemotional Behavior Among Black Couples

concluded that "Blacks emerge as more egalitarian on the more innovative and behavioral measures of sex roles. . . . Blacks also tended to score as more instrumental *and* as more expressive than Whites" (p. 143). Although blacks' greater tendency to embrace androgynous ideals and to share in decision-making processes than whites would seem to support the claim that the "we-ness" fostered by collectivism is reflected in high levels of affection-giving and respect-giving behavior (White, 1984; White & Parham, 1990), Scanzoni (1975) interpreted the results as signifying greater *individualism* among blacks than among whites. In the absence of a nonindividualistic basis for explaining the ethnic differences in marital relations, it seems as if the only recourse for many researchers is to assume that any interpersonal advantages must be attributed to individualism (Bellah et al., 1985).

Further support for the hypothesis that collectivism facilitates mutuality in reciprocity of love and esteem among many blacks was provided, if indirectly, by Triandis, Weldon, and Feldman (1972). Triandis et al. included affection-giving and respect-giving responses among a variety of behavioral intentions on the part of black and white males and females toward (a) persons of the same ethnicity and sex, (b) persons of a different ethnicity and sex, (c) persons of the same sex but different ethnicity, and (d) persons of the same ethnicity but opposite sex. Results suggested that trust, a key component of affection (Foa & Foa, 1974), was more likely to be displayed toward members of the opposite sex among blacks than among whites. As was the case for their work on Hispanic behavioral tendencies, however, the study by Triandis et al. did not attempt to gauge the actual behavior of black husbands and wives toward each other. Thus, this work does not test directly the model of collectivism and socioemotional behavior among blacks that I have advanced.

This is not to say that all blacks uniformly embrace the collectivistic ideal, or that collectivism always serves as a buffer in blacks' personal relationships. Some research (Willie, 1985; see also Kami & Radin, 1967; Phinney, 1991; Willie & Greenblatt,

1978) suggests that black middle-class couples may be in a better position than black lower-class couples to put collectivistic ideals into practice. That is, freed of at least some of the socio-economic obstacles that threaten the very survival of marital relationships among many lower-class blacks, many middle-class black couples are afforded the opportunity to draw upon their cultural heritage as a source of socioemotional strength and to relate in a loving, respectful, egalitarian manner. Despite the pressures to conform to individualistic norms that black middle-class couples undoubtedly face (Aldridge, 1991), such couples often are steadfast in retaining collectivistic values even as they climb the socioeconomic ladder and, at least to some extent, internalize individualistic goals.

The role of socioeconomic status in providing many blacks sufficient freedom to practice collectivistic values also may help explain why the aforementioned tendency of blacks to display higher levels of trust toward members of the opposite sex (Triandis et al., 1972) was more pronounced among men than among women. Given that black women are not inherently less affectionate than black men (Asante, 1981), and given that sex categorization is confounded with socioeconomic status among blacks as well as all other ethnic groups in the United States (French, 1985), any observed sex differences in displays of collectivism among blacks must be considered in light of differing levels of socioeconomic constraints.

The importance of anchoring one's marital relationship within a culturally supportive context has been voiced by Bellah et al. (1985), who also stated that genuine relational commitment must be rooted in an awareness of one's place within the larger community. Although such a view is not the unique province of black couples, collectivism certainly is prominent as a core value in black culture. Collectivism should not be regarded as the only value of importance to black culture and marriages, just as it would be wrong to assume that familism is the only value of importance in Hispanic culture and personal relationships (e.g., Marin & Marin, 1991; McAdoo, 1978; Padilla, 1985).

Although many blacks, Hispanics, and members of other cultural minorities can shift physically and psychologically from one cultural context to another quite readily (Ramirez, 1984), for some blacks the "we-orientation" of collectivism may come into conflict with the "me-orientation" of individualism emphasized by Anglo culture (Billingsley, 1968; Willie, 1985). Thus, it would be premature to conclude that operationalizing collectivism as an influence on black couples' socioemotional processes would allow researchers to explain *all* variance in displays of affection or respect by husbands and wives across different classes and other groupings.

The collectivistic value of black culture cannot be reconciled easily with contemporary trends in marriage and divorce. For example, the divorce rate for first marriages between black men and women (in excess of 60%; see Staples, 1988) is higher than that for first marriages between Anglo men and women, although the stability of *second* marriages is higher for blacks than for whites (Aguirre & Parr, 1982). Furthermore, the divorce rate for first marriages of blacks all but dwarfs that for first marriages of Hispanics in general, although Puerto Rican divorce rates rival those of blacks (Becerra, 1988). In fact, comparisons of black and white marital instability reveal significant differences even after accounting for socioeconomic status (Whyte, 1990), though it must be noted that blacks tend to earn less than whites in every social class throughout the United States (Staples, 1988)—and the negative impact of perceived lack of economic resources on marital quality is pronounced especially among the black lower class (Clark-Nicolas & Gray-Little, 1991). Existing theoretical and empirical work indicates that personal relationship researchers should attend to collectivism as one influence on socioemotional behavior (and, consequently, marital satisfaction) among "intact" as well as "fragmented" black families. Models such as the one that I have proposed could help direct scholars' attention toward the adaptive influence of collectivism and other core African values on black spouses' behavior.

Acknowledging (and Transcending) Ethnicity in the Study of Personal Relationships

Within any field of scientific endeavor, theoretical mind-sets often dominate the intellectual landscape, recede in importance, and even reenter the forefront much more often than many researchers realize (or, perhaps, more often than they admit; see Jones, 1985, for examples of "waxing and waning" of theories in social psychology). According to Shweder (1991), the much-trumpeted "cognitive revolution" in psychology already is passé, owing largely to the resurgence of *cultural psychology*—that is, the focus on the ways in which cultures and individuals influence each other. In a sense, psychology slowly is returning to the emphasis on the dynamic interchange between self and society that neo-Freudians such as Harry Stack Sullivan, Karen Horney, Erich Fromm, and Alfred Adler described prior to the emergence of the Cold War (Hall & Lindzey, 1978; Schellenberg, 1978; Wiggins, 1991). Such a development undoubtedly will sensitize increasing numbers of personal relationship researchers to individuals' incorporation of cultural values and norms, not only into their sense of who they are but also into their sense of the form that individuals' personal relationships will take (Wood, 1982). To the extent that social scientists in the field of personal relationships deny the importance of culture in individuals' relational lives, those social scientists will remain ignorant at best (Taylor & Rogers, 1993) and arrogant at worst (Harris & Majors, 1993) with regard to relationship processes between minority group members *and* between majority group members.

Although broad, generalizable models of personality and social behavior (Mook, 1983) perhaps can be developed and applied to the study of personal relationships, social scientists in general—and personal relationship researchers in particular—must acknowledge ethnicity if ever they expect to transcend ethnicity. As it stands, the field of personal relationships contributes little to the understanding of intersections among culture, personality, and interpersonal processes (Levinger &

Huston, 1990), depending as it does upon virtually all-white samples and value orientations characteristic both of those samples and of the researchers engaged in the scientific enterprise. Nowhere are the conceptual and methodological blinders in this field more obvious than in the prominence of individualism as a core value among white Americans—a value privileged in their relationships and falsely generalized to *all* relationships.

As many social scientists have noted (e.g., Bellah et al., 1985; Dinnerstein et al., 1979; McClelland, 1987; Szapocznik & Hernandez, 1988; Triandis, 1990; White, 1984), individualism as advocated centuries ago by the Puritans not only has facilitated continuity between European and European American culture but also has served as the standard against which all other cultural values have been measured. Whyte (1990) observed that the focus on individualism concurrent with the diminution of other value orientations is increasingly characteristic of research on personal relationships. That is, in spite of evidence that a "me-orientation" often runs counter to productivity in an array of academic and work settings (e.g., Helmreich, Spence, Beane, Lucker, & Matthews, 1980) and is not nearly as beneficial to satisfaction in ongoing relationships as was previously thought (Ickes, 1985; Spence et al., 1985), individualism is continually depicted in personal-relationships research as "good." Yet individualism cannot be presumed to work in favor of, and actually may work against, long-term mutuality in affectionate and respectful behavior, marital satisfaction, and marital stability. Further, individualism cannot be assumed a priori to be uniformly esteemed by people socialized within different ethnic groups.

Let us assume, for the moment, that internalized individualism—at least of the expressive variety (Bellah et al., 1985)— is related positively to Anglo spouses' socioemotional behavior. Suppose, furthermore, that our goal as researchers is to explain as much variance in the behavioral patterns of white, black, and Hispanic married couples as possible. Whyte's (1990) commentary on the field of personal relationships hinted that many (if not most) researchers in the field would take individualism as the only "worthy" value and examine its influence as a function of spouses' cultural/ethnic background. Such a procedure would probably result in the pronouncement that (a) individualism is not as influential in Hispanic and black spouses' behavior as it is in white spouses' behavior and (b) that consequently Hispanic and black behavioral dynamics are "dysfunctional." In much of the pre-Civil Rights Era literature on Hispanics (e.g., Lewis, 1963, 1966) and on blacks (e.g., Frazier, 1939; Parker & Kleiner, 1966), social scientists explicitly depicted cultural minorities as low in achievement orientation and, not coincidentally, as suffering from low-quality marital relationships. Despite post-Civil Rights Era scholarship that empirically refutes such claims (e.g., Cromwell & Ruiz, 1979; Davis & Chavez, 1985; Dietrich, 1975; Willie & Greenblatt, 1978; Zeff, 1982), future generations of researchers in the field of personal relationships well may repeat the errors of previous generations unless the field itself is expanded to include multiple cultural perspectives.

Now let us suppose that individualism is but one of a multitude of cultural values that might be reflected in (if not invariantly related positively to) affectionate and respectful behavior in marital relationships. The literatures on Hispanic, black, and white cultures together suggest that familism and collectivism should be included along with individualism as predictors of socioemotional behavior in marriage and other personal relationships. Following such a line of reasoning, we might postulate that all three value orientations would be found among all three cultural groups (see Dubos, 1974) but that the influence of each specific value would be moderated by ethnicity (e.g., familism would be strongest in influence among Hispanics, collectivism would be strongest in influence among blacks, and individualism would be strongest in influence among whites). Moreover, we might expect that the "we-orientations" of familism and collectivism would be positively correlated. The resulting conceptual model, which (like the two previous models in this chapter) could easily be tested via structural equation modeling (Joreskog & Sorbom, 1979; see Reis, 1982), is shown in Figure 3.3.

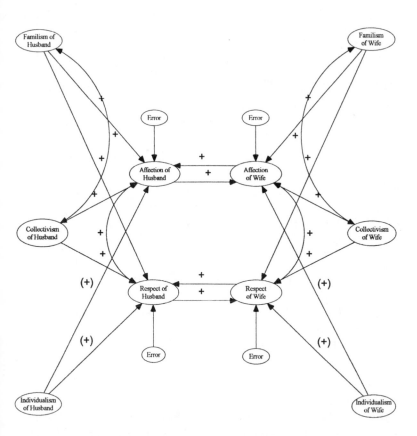

Figure 3.3. Conceptual Model Linking Familism, Collectivism, Individualism, and Socioemotional Behavior Among All Couples

Culture, Ethnicity, and Relationship Processes: An Exercise in "Balkanization" and "Political Correctness"?

The inclusive model specifying causal relations between cultural value orientations and relationship processes (as moderated by ethnicity) is essentially multicultural in scope. Implicit in the inclusive model is the assumption that two or more sets of cultural values may coexist within the same society. In addition, the model implies that a particular individual—regardless of his or her minority/majority status—could conceivably internalize values associated with his or her "native" culture (as the result of enculturation) *and* could internalize values associated with one or more "foreign" cultures (as the result of acculturation; Berry et al., 1992).

Some critics might contend that in real life, multiculturalism (as articulated in the inclusive model) amounts to a brand of "Balkanization" in which competition among varying ideologies is inevitable. That is, over the long run, individuals will reveal their biases in favor of values associated with their "in-group" and against values associated with all "out-groups" (e.g., Stephan, 1985; but see also Gaines & Reed, 1994, 1995). For example, even though Shweder (1991) was sympathetic to the ideal of multiculturalism (which he referred to as "relativism"), he believed that specific cultures either were dominant or were dominated:

> Relativism is consistent with a kind of pluralism or cognitive egalitarianism—a definite benefit, at least for some observers. Relativists provide us with a charitable rendition of the ideas of others, placing those ideas in a framework that makes it easier to credit others, not with confusion, error, or ignorance, but rather with an alternative vision of the possibilities of social life.
>
> Ironically, however, despite its egalitarian intentions relativism lends support to a world based on intellectual domination and power assertion. The relativist views the understandings of others as self-contained, incommensurate, ideational universes ("paradigms"); *across* these universes there is no comparability, no common standard for rational criticism. . . . Consequently, people's changes of ideational worlds (which do happen) can be examined by the relativist only in terms of domination, force, or nonrational conversion. And for disagreements between two or more peoples (which often happen) the only means of adjudication is force of arms—there is nothing to discuss. When consensus is the final arbiter of what is real, numbers count, and the powerful and/or the masses have their way. (p. 121)

In response to such a critique, I contend that the "dominate or be dominated" assumption regarding ethnicity and cultural values is just as erroneous as the now-discredited belief that "masculinity" and "femininity" within the context of gender and personality are mutually exclusive (e.g., Bem, 1974; Spence et al., 1974). Just as it is possible for an individual—whether male or female—to be androgynous (i.e., "me-oriented" as well as "we-oriented"), masculine (i.e., "me-oriented" but not "we-oriented"), feminine (i.e., "we-oriented" but not "we-oriented"), or undifferentiated (i.e., neither "me-oriented" nor "we-oriented"), so too is it possible for an individual—whether Hispanic, black, or white—to be integrated (i.e., in-group oriented as well as out-group oriented), separated (i.e., in-group oriented but not out-group oriented), assimilated (i.e., out-group oriented but not in-group oriented), or marginalized (i.e., neither in-group oriented nor out-group oriented; see Allport, 1954, Berry et al., 1992; Ramirez, 1983; Rios, 1993). To the degree that individuals learn about cultural values associated with ethnic groups other than their own, we may speak of *acculturation;* to the degree that individuals learn about cultural values associated with their own ethnic group, we may speak of *enculturation* (Berry et al., 1992).

Exactly how some persons come to be integrated, separated, assimilated, or marginalized is not clear (any more than it is clear how some persons come to be androgynous, masculine, feminine, or undifferentiated). However, we can state confidently that such differences exist within ethnic groups. Furthermore, although the United States never has lived up to its own "melting-pot" ideal (Allport, 1954; Gordon, 1978; Myrdal, 1944), it nonetheless is true that the United States is a society that houses a multitude of ethnic groups and accompanying cultural values that cannot help but exert some influence upon each other even while retaining some level of resilience (Berry et al., 1992). Therefore, I maintain that within individuals and within an entire society, the coexistence of two or more sets of cultural values is not inherently problematic at all. In fact, I would go so far as to argue that relationship processes often involve partners' efforts to find a basis for cultural common ground even when conventional wisdom would predict that no such common ground exists (e.g., among interethnic couples).

Still other critics (e.g., Bloom, 1987; D'Sousa, 1991) might dismiss the inclusive model as yet another example of "political correctness" in academia (Gergen, 1991). However, if the model is correct—and indeed the companion chapters in this volume on under-studied relationships indicate that we are on the right track, however untraveled it may be—the payoff for researchers in the field of personal relationships is enhanced ability to predict the course of socioemotional behavior in marital relationships. Such an accomplishment would advance understanding of intersections among ethnicity, culture, and personal relationships.

In turn, future researchers might opt to expand the focus of the inclusive model (Figure 3.3) beyond the confines of marital relationships. Lest we assume that marital relationships are the only personal relationships that reflect cultural values, many personal heterosexual relationships—including those in which offspring are produced—never result in marriage. Black women, for example, are less likely than white women to marry at all (Tucker & Taylor, 1989). This does not mean, however, that relationships involving black women are less important socially or psychologically than relationships involving white women. In fact, a collectivistic framework might anticipate a larger percentage of ongoing black male-female than white male-female relationships occurring outside the traditional sphere of marriage (either because the couples never married or because the marriages ended in separation or divorce) precisely because such nontraditional relationships are less likely to be censured by the black community (see Billingsley, 1968; Brown, Perry, & Harburg, 1977; Lammermeier, 1973; Miao, 1974; Pope, 1969; Staples, 1972, 1985; Willie & Greenblatt, 1978).

A corollary point also is in order regarding the use of marital satisfaction and stability as indices of relational well-being: Although such indices might seem reliable as far as white middle-class relationships are concerned, exclusive reliance on such indices may lead researchers to assume erroneously that because the relationships between members of cultural minorities (e.g., blacks, Puerto Ricans) do not "measure up" according to existing (i.e., Anglo-oriented) standards of marital quality, the relationships between members of cultural minorities somehow are deviant and/or deficient (see Zinn & Eitzen, 1987). Perhaps marital satisfaction, marital stability, and other individualistic success/failure indices could be supplemented by collectivistic and/or familistic barometers of relational closeness (e.g., amount of time spent together with children, degree of overlap in partners' social networks). I suspect that black and Hispanic relationships would look significantly less "deviant" if such steps were taken to avoid cultural biases in research on personal relationships.

Strengths and
Limitations of the Inclusive Model

The inclusive model of cultural value orientations and socioemotional behavior that I have introduced in this chapter offers several distinctive features that recommend it as a conceptual and methodological framework for studying relational processes among various ethnic group members. First, the model explicitly identifies three value orientations (i.e., familism, collectivism, and individualism), each of which has traditionally been associated with a particular ethnic group, that theoretically should allow researchers to explain a significant portion of between-group and within-group variance in affectionate and respectful behavior. Second, the model specifies that the couple, rather than the individual, ideally should serve as the basic unit of analysis for research on relational processes. Third, the model lends itself exceptionally well to sophisticated analytic techniques such as structural equation modeling, cluster analysis, and discriminant analysis. Fourth, the model acknowledges that at least some portion of variance in socioemotional behavior is influenced by factors not measured in a given study. Finally, the model can be adapted easily and tested among a multitude of relationship types and samples (e.g., friendships between men and women, romantic homosexual relationships, interethnic marital relationships) in addition to, or instead of, romantic heterosexual relationships among members of the same ethnic group.

Nevertheless, as is the case with any conceptual representation of real-world phenomena, certain limitations inevitably can be identified in this model. For example, even though values such as familism and collectivism certainly can be found among cultural minorities other than Latinos/Hispanics or blacks/ African Americans (e.g., Asian Americans, Native Americans; see Lin & Rusbult, in press; Triandis, 1990), perhaps greater attention to the social and historical experiences of such numerically smaller cultural minorities would uncover additional critical values (e.g., spiritualism, environmentalism; see Cook & Kono, 1977; Ramirez, 1983) associated traditionally with those groups. In the same vein, although I alluded earlier to the relevance of studying interethnic couples, intensive analyses regarding such couples (for examples, see Porterfield, 1978; Spickard, 1989) might yield still other core values (e.g., feminism; see French, 1985) that should be specified in any truly inclusive model.

Beyond considerations of the value and ethnicity dimensions that have yet to be dealt with explicitly in the inclusive model that I have proposed, by no means have I exhausted the possibilities regarding those relational processes that might be influenced by cultural values. For example, relationship processes include instrumental as well as socioemotional behaviors (Rusbult, Insko, Lin, & Smith, 1990); furthermore, the concept of exchange can be taken to include forms of reciprocity that partners perceive as obligatory (Clark & Mills, 1979) in addition to forms of reciprocity in which partners willingly engage.

Therefore, researchers who are interested in applying the model should attend carefully to the limitations as well as the strengths of the model.

Concluding Thoughts

On the basis of post-Civil Rights Era scholarship devoted to the United States' two largest cultural minorities (i.e., Hispanics and blacks), I have identified two sets of values (i.e., familism and collectivism) that potentially may explain substantial variance in married couples' socioemotional processes. Both sets of values attest to the fact that marital and other personal relationships occur within a broader social and cultural context than that of the Anglo majority. Unlike individualism, the values of familism and collectivism explicitly encourage relationship partners to deemphasize self-interest for the sake of significant others and for the sake of larger social units (e.g., the extended family, the entire ethnic group). Familism and collectivism certainly are related in that both inherently are social in orientation; in fact, it is difficult to imagine either value manifested outside of interpersonal contexts. Individualism, in contrast, well may be reflected in *alienation* from personal relationships (Bellah et al., 1985).

Yet it is possible for individuals to embody individualistic as well as familistic and/or collectivistic values (Berry et al., 1992), and the "we-orientation" of familism is not identical to the "we-orientation" of collectivism (Marin & Marin, 1991). Thus I suspect that (a) collectivism and familism, albeit strongly and positively correlated, are not correlated perfectly, and (b) individualism is weakly (and, perhaps, negatively) related, if at all, to either collectivism or familism. Of course, all of the hypotheses that I have advanced in this chapter still await the scientific rigor of data collection and hypothesis testing.

If we consider the marital dyad per se, we might not find that cultural values make the socioemotional processes of couples

from various backgrounds look very different from each other;
after all, the need for love and esteem is a basic part of the human condition that most individuals hope to fulfill in their personal relationships. However, the causes of ostensibly identical
behaviors (e.g., consulting each other regarding major pur-
chases, listening to each other's problems, reassuring each
other that net income is not a valid indicator of personal competence) might differ according to the cultural perspectives of the
partners in particular personal relationships. Exactly how behaviors and couple processes are experienced by partners may
well vary along lines influenced by ethnicity. Furthermore, by
expanding our focus to include relationships involving biological as well as nonbiological kin, we might succeed in uncover-
ing qualitative differences in relational behavior as a function of
culture and ethnicity (e.g., the affective tone of grandparent-
grandchild relationships among Hispanics might be especially
pronounced, as might the affective tone of unofficially adoptive
adult-child relationships among blacks; see Billingsley, 1968;
Schmidt & Padilla, 1983).

   This chapter suggests that culture is a macro-level influence
on socioemotional processes in personal relationships. Moreover, I have aligned culture primarily with ethnicity to render
culture more concrete as an entity (see Skinner, 1972). Of
course, the concept of culture need not be linked exclusively
with ethnicity; Whyte (1990), for instance, alluded to a "dating
culture" in his study of marital relationships. In addition, culture may be viewed in micro-level as well as macro-level terms;
as I mentioned earlier in this chapter, Wood (1982; see also
Phillips & Wood, 1983), for example, has referred to "relational
cultures" as unique influences created by partners that in turn
influence couples' behavioral dynamics. And many social scientists (e.g., Sullivan, 1953; Tannen, 1990; see also Gaines, 1994a;
Ickes, 1993; Wood, 1993a) have reasoned that gender-segregated
patterns of socialization are so entrenched in American society
that, effectively, distinct "male" and "female" cultures can be
identified. By the same logic, the present chapter argues that

ethnic cultures vary and that the distinctive character of any particular ethnicity influences processes in personal relationships. Ethnicity represents a great deal more than "demographics" or "bean counting" (see Whyte, 1990); ethnicity is essential to our understanding of culture and personality because it is implicated in the dynamics that create and reflect personal relationships.

As Allport (1954) noted several decades ago, ethnicity encompasses much more than shared genetic lineage. In fact, most between-group differences in social and psychological processes are attributable, not to DNA as such, but instead to differences in *socialization* (Berry et al., 1992). Although it is possible to classify individuals according to a seemingly infinite number of characteristics (e.g., gender, age, socioeconomic status), no other individual-difference variable has approached the salience of ethnicity in entrenched patterns of residential, educational, or vocational segregation in the United States from colonial times to the present (DuBois, 1986; Gaines & Reed, 1994, 1995).

Even if the cultural values historically treasured by Hispanics and blacks somehow had been stamped out by Anglo dominance, the very fact that members of those ethnic groups were obliged to form their social and personal relationships primarily with fellow group members suggests that Hispanics and blacks effectively have been prevented from joining the cultural mainstream of white America (Goffman, 1963). However, because it is now clear that the cultures of Hispanics and blacks were not completely dismantled, we would be wrong in assuming that members of those ethnic groups either embraced Anglo culture or embraced nothing at all. The idea that many Hispanic and black couples have been bound together by prevailing cultural values such as familism and collectivism more overtly than have many white couples may appear to be novel (if not counterintuitive for those social scientists who are immersed in Anglo culture so deeply that they do not even know that they are part of that particular culture). However, by no means are familistic or collectivistic values new in and of themselves. What *is* new is the explicit recognition that those values may be manifested in relational cultures (Wood, 1982) by way of individuals' active internalization of those values.

4

The Relationships of
Lesbians and of Gay Men

Michelle Huston

Pepper Schwartz

lthough interest in gays and lesbians has increased and diversified
in the last two decades, the ma-
jority of research has primarily concentrated on drawing a broad
descriptive and demographic picture of this under-studied
population. Early work in the 1960s and 1970s generally centered on "normalizing" gays as people and providing ethnographic accounts of their lives and sexual preference (e.g.,
Warren, 1974; Wolf, 1979). In recent years our knowledge has
begun to grow more sophisticated, with new attention to relationships, internal states, experiences, community organization
and mobilization, and the impact of race and gender differences. However, in-depth and multivariate studies are still
scarce, and although the growth of gay and lesbian studies looks
promising, much of the information about same-sex relationships that should inform students of personal relationships is

either unintegrated into the relationship literature or not yet systematically studied.

Still, it may seem to those most familiar with the same-sex literature that our knowledge of gays and lesbians is too comprehensive for their inclusion in a volume whose focus is understudied relationships. We believe, however, that much more needs to be done to bring the type of research to the level of current knowledge about heterosexual relationships. For example, we know little about gay courtship in serious relationships, norms of equity, or methods of maintenance and commitment. Our intent in this chapter is to show what we do know and highlight what is missing.

The first issue that must be addressed when studying gays and lesbians is exactly who we are talking about. Over the course of their lives, many men and women who consider themselves to be heterosexual have physically intimate same-sex experiences. Some homosexuals fall in love with members of the opposite sex; some marry early in life before they know or act on their "true" orientation. In short, sexuality is much more fluid and harder to categorize than many researchers and most laypeople assume. This makes researching this topic difficult; definitions become tricky, and we must resist the temptation to make unwarranted assumptions, overgeneralize, or reify data.

We must also realize that traditional models of relationships (all of which assume heterosexuality) may not be the only viable models of intimacy. To apply models derived from and appropriate for heterosexuals to homosexual relationships not only leads to questionable conclusions but also obscures a wealth of information about ways couples organize and conduct their relationships (Harry & DeVall, 1978; Peplau, 1991).

Likewise, notions of "competence" and "success" in relationships are often different for heterosexuals and gays and lesbians. In marriage, "success" is usually (at least partially) defined in terms of endurance. Because homosexuals do not use "lifetime" marriage as their model—nor place the length of the relationship above other factors—gays and lesbians measure "success" by other factors, such as equity, satisfaction, and happiness. This difference has profound effects on how lesbians and gay men conduct their relationships and how they evaluate them.

This chapter introduces issues, processes, and factors that have been identified as important for lesbian and gay relationships. We cover influences on finding partners as well as on the maintenance and dissolution of already established couples.

Throughout, it is important for readers to realize that the data on which most of our conclusions are based are affected by the limitations placed upon any research about a hidden community. It is impossible to get a truly representative sample, and findings may be skewed because they exclude people who are not "out," underrepresent people who live in rural or isolated settings, and usually miss older, more conservative couples who do not want to talk about their private life. These limitations notwithstanding, existing research indicates that gay and lesbian relationships are very similar to heterosexual relationships in some ways, and quite distinct in others.

Beginning a Relationship

Like most people, the majority of gay men and lesbians value long-term, committed relationships. In the pre-AIDS years, more lesbians than gay men reported being in committed relationships, partially because the gay subculture of that time period endorsed singlehood over couplehood for most gay men (Hoffman, 1968; Silverstein, 1981; Tuller, 1978). Most researchers agree that this finding underrepresents older gay men who did not frequent gay bars and who were probably coupled in marriage-like relationships. More recent work indicates a growing desire among gay men to commit early and monogamously (Davidson, 1991; McWhirter & Mattison, 1984). In this case, when individuals do get ready to look for a committed relationship, how do they find partners? In a society that, in general, stigmatizes homosexuality, how do gays and lesbians identify others who share their sexual preference, and how do they communicate their interest? How is the intricate courtship process leading from casual acquaintance to a more serious involvement negotiated? Furthermore, how is this process affected by gender, sexual preference, community, and ideology?

Gendered Dating Patterns and Preferences

Traditionally, men and women in Western society grow up having different values about when sex is appropriate. More women than men are taught that only love legitimizes sex. More men than women are taught that it is justifiable to have sex for its own sake. Hence lesbians usually seek emotional connection before having sex with their dating partner (Wolf, 1979), whereas gay men frequently have sex first and develop feelings of attachment and emotional closeness later (Warren, 1974). These gendered styles of viewing love and sex influence the dating styles of lesbians and gay men, just as they shape the styles of heterosexuals.

The subculture of gay men fosters the "sex first" view of courtship, and many conventions in the gay community streamline the process of getting from "hello" to sexual contact. A great deal of the early research on gay men (e.g., Humphries, 1970) dealt with institutions that enabled quick and uncomplicated sex: gay bath houses, "tea rooms" (rest rooms known to accommodate homosexuals looking for impersonal sex), and gay bars. For men, finding another man with whom to have a one-night stand is relatively easy. More difficult is learning to identify, in a glance, the men whom one can trust: trust to be disease-free, to not be undercover policemen, to not be "bashers." In the pre-AIDS era, there were few institutions designed to promote more long-term relationships; today, more varied gay and lesbian meeting places and organizations help bring people together. A growing number of cities have gay ghettos in which men and women easily meet potential partners at the grocery store, the library, and church groups. However, these opportunities remain rare in rural areas and many cities.

Not all gay men are comfortable with or desire only casual sex. In the past decade, the fear of AIDS has made impersonal sex a frightening part of the gay male sexual culture. In the 1970s, writers who studied partner-oriented men referred to them as "nest builders" (Silverstein, 1981) and "the hidden segment of the gay world" (Tuller, 1978). More recent writers are aware of a growing number of partnership-oriented gay males (Davidson, 1991; Kelly, St. Lawrence, Hood, & Brasfield, 1989). However, finding a partner is still difficult: A man must not only determine who is homosexual, but also try to find someone who shares similar desires and definitions of a committed relationship. This search is made more difficult by the institutions that perpetuate an orientation to and acceptance of casual sex rather than emotional intimacy and the possibility of a lifelong partnership.

Lesbians, in part because of their distinctive emotional agenda, have traditionally had fewer institutions designed to promote the development of casual sexual relationships. Furthermore, whereas men have been trained to be sexually aggressive, women are taught to be more reactive than proactive. For lesbians, this can result in an impasse in which neither woman is comfortable making the first move—even, for example, to ask another to dance. Nonetheless, most lesbians overcome or work around their gender socialization and form relationships. Although the exact mechanism by which this is accomplished is not well studied, ethnographic accounts of the lesbian community suggest that some women adopt more assertive roles, whereas for others, mutual friends play matchmaking roles. This question of how lesbians defeat gender patterns that inhibit dating is ripe for inquisitive minds who wish to understand not only this portion of lesbian experiences, but how people (in general) accomplish tasks for which they had little or no training as children or adolescents.

Gendered Preferences for Partners

Gender also influences the characteristics that lesbians and gay men look for in partners. Data gathered both from interviews and from personals advertisements lend credence to this assertion (Gonzales & Meyers, 1993; Laner, 1978). Gay men tend to desire a very specific "type" of man for both recreational sex and more serious relationships. This standard includes an extremely attractive face, an athletic body, and a well-groomed appearance. Some men have specific demands that place extreme importance on particular parts of the body—most commonly the buttocks, but also the penis or chest. Gay men also value many of the "status symbols" that go along with "manliness" in this culture: a well-paid or "masculine" career, and the material accoutrements of the "good life" (Davidson, 1991; Silverstein, 1981). Lesbians are much more likely to emphasize socioemotional characteristics, and less likely to concentrate on physical characteristics or dress. However, many lesbians admire an androgynous or "butch" look—which signifies rejection of male-derived standards of beauty and weakness. Recently, more traditional standards of female attractiveness have also become acceptable. By virtue of their involvement in the women's movement, many lesbians also value self-sufficiency and strength in a long-term partner; however, job status or prestige is not as important to them as it is for gay men. This is pragmatic as well as ideological: Few women have high-prestige, high-paying jobs, and prioritizing status and money would make finding a partner more difficult.

A more detailed analysis of the gay community helps contextualize the ways in which gender affects the dating relationships of lesbians and gay men. For men, bars have provided a relatively secure pickup spot: a place to meet other men interested in casual sexual encounters. Occasionally these one-night stands result in long-term relationships, but this is the exception rather than the rule (Silverstein, 1981). Indeed, there is some stigma attached to men who go to bars and overromanticize a given sexual encounter. Therefore, men who are interested in finding a potential partner may find little encouragement at gay bars. In rural areas or smaller cities, this problem is exacerbated by the fact that there may be only one gay bar to serve the needs of the entire homosexual community. The result is that the clientele of any one bar will probably be so diverse that meeting someone with similar interests, experiences, and beliefs is difficult. In short, highly educated professional and uneducated working-class men are equally likely to be gay, but their sexual preference does not mean they will have something mutually interesting to discuss over breakfast. Furthermore, upper-class white-collar professionals in rural settings or small cities may not be able to afford being seen in a gay bar (Moses & Hawkins, 1982). Hence finding a partner with similar interests, experiences, and beliefs is difficult.

Larger cities (in general) offer gays and lesbians a much wider variety of bars and meeting places. Bars accommodate differing styles and sexual tastes: There are leather bars, working-class bars, stylish yuppie clubs, country-western dancing places, and so on. Resources such as *The Gay Yellow Pages* and *Inn Places* enable traveling men and women to know in advance what various cities have to offer gay people.

Outside the big cities, lesbian bars are even more rare than gay bars, mostly due to the fact that lesbians do not have the large disposable income available to many gay men, but perhaps also due to the fact that more lesbians are "closeted" and infrequently visit bars or other public lesbian places. Hence it is hard to keep lesbian bars financially stable and able to stay in business. Partially because of many women's desire to know a person before having sex, lesbian bars are rarely "pickup" spots. Although it is possible to meet unattached women there, most are already partnered. Therefore, lesbian bars are more oriented to socializing within well-defined acquaintanceship circles than toward finding new love interests. In the last few years, however, several cities in the United States have been home to a new form of the lesbian club that is modeled after gay baths. Partially a conscious rejection of traditional (and confining) definitions of female sexuality and partially a natural outgrowth of one wing of the lesbian movement, these "sex clubs" give lesbians a place to meet other women who are interested in impersonal sex. It is not uncommon for these sex clubs to have separate areas designated solely for the purpose of providing a safe space in which women can have impersonal sex. Research about this new form of bar would tell us a great deal about the emerging "sex-positive" movement that is affecting many women: straight, lesbian, and otherwise. (Sex-positive women are attempting to redefine sexuality in broader terms than those typically used by conventional notions of "proper" female sexuality including the creation and use of nonexploitative pornography, as well as by broadening the boundaries of "acceptable" sexual behavior to embrace such formerly taboo activities as sadomasochism and anonymous sex.) Thus far, however, this topic has remained relatively unaddressed in academic literature.

Although bars are a mainstay of gay culture, it is not surprising that the majority of homosexuals meet their future partner by some other means. For both lesbians and gay men, it is most often mutual friends who do the matchmaking (Peplau, Cochran, Rook, & Padesky, 1978; Tuller, 1978; Vetere, 1982; Warren, 1974). This usually promotes a greater degree of similarity between potential partners in terms of interests and backgrounds. However, this also means that couples who break up have to renegotiate relationships with mutual friends and may have to deal with loyalties. This puts additional pressure on the ex-couple because they are likely to run into each other at social events, dinner parties, and celebrations that bring the friendship circle together (Becker, 1988; Clunis & Green, 1988).

For lesbians, the second most common meeting place is political functions (feminist and/or lesbian). As with matchmaking by mutual friends, this method emphasizes similarities—in this case, political activism. This is extremely important because matching on certain characteristics is highly predictive of lesbian satisfaction and stability (Howard, Blumstein, & Schwartz, 1992). For example, a great deal of research has pointed out that lesbians usually value both dyadic attachment and autonomy. Partners try to balance a high degree of emotional closeness and intimacy with a high degree of independence and freedom. Although these characteristics are not mutually exclusive, tension between needs for intimacy and autonomy causes conflict (Andrews, 1990). Starting out mismatched complicates the beginning of a relationship and lessens the possibility of relation-

ship longevity. Research indicates that lesbians who value autonomy quite highly may prolong the dating process and may fore-
go monogamous commitment altogether (Peplau et al., 1978;
Vance, 1984). Although most lesbians value autonomy, those
who seek it above all else are also most likely to be the most
politically active. Paradoxically, therefore, meeting a potential
partner through political activities predisposes desirable similar
ideologies, yet simultaneously makes it more likely for partners
to have qualms about commitment.

What neither very many young gay men or lesbians can do is
court openly. They cannot go to the high school prom (although
a few couples have made newspaper headlines trying to do so)
or openly discuss their latest crush with their predominantly
heterosexual peer group. It is even less likely that they can confide in their parents. Deprived of these early experiences common to heterosexual teens, initial homosexual exploration is
generally confined to furtive and hidden impersonal sex or a
taboo relationship with a peer that must be concealed. Thus
most gay men and lesbians begin courtship and dating experience after high school, sometimes even after college. These
days, there are more gay teen clubs or college homosexual associations, but these are usually confined to larger cities and
schools or elite smaller high schools and colleges. Many gay students, not yet comfortable with or ready to take on the burdens
of social stigma, avoid these places even if they would clearly
love to go. Thus, for many gay men and lesbians, serious courtship starts much later than it does for their heterosexual peers.
This means that they may have fewer social skills than comparable heterosexuals, less practice at knowing who is right for
them, less awareness about available choices, and fewer opportunities to check reality and make social comparisons with
peers.

This whole research area of how individuals go about finding
other gays and lesbians, as well as what they do once they find
them, needs much more attention from researchers. What effect
does the smaller pool of eligible people have on relationships?
To what extent does the fact that lesbian and gay youth enter

serious relationships later than most heterosexuals affect those (and subsequent) relationships? How do homosexuals overcome their more circumscribed set of experiences and limited practice at knowing what they want in a partner?

Maintaining a Relationship

Once begun, which factors contribute to stability and satisfaction in lesbian and gay relationships? In general, relationships of lesbians and gay men are strengthened by a variety of factors. For lesbians, an equitable balance of power, a high degree of emotional intimacy, and high self-esteem all contribute to satisfying relationships (Eldridge & Gilbert, 1990). For gay men, little conflict, high appreciation of partner, stability, and cooperation are important for satisfaction (Jones & Bates, 1978). For both types of couples, the frequency of "destructive arguing" is negatively correlated with satisfaction (Kurdek, 1993b), Beyond these rather static correlates of relationship quality, several processes are associated with maintaining a homosexual relationship.

Communication

The large body of literature about communication between men and women suggests several interesting points relevant to relationships of gay men and lesbians. In general, women use conversation as a springboard to intimacy and are skilled at playing a supportive role in communication to further this goal. Men, on the other hand, frequently see conversation as a competitive endeavor, with the most powerful partner "winning" points while asserting his status for his conversational "opponent." These basic styles of communication form the underpinnings on which couples base problem-solving and decision-making efforts: In general, women seek consensus when faced with a hurdle, whereas men tend to expedite decision making by allowing the more powerful partner to get his own way (Kollock, Blumstein, & Schwartz, 1985; Tannen, 1990).

Researchers who study communication and gender have a variety of explanations for the different styles or definitions of communication used by men and women. One branch of this field emphasizes the degree to which men and women are socialized into different communication cultures in this society (Wood, 1994a). This perspective explains gender differences as the result of distinct cultures created by the different social positions occupied by men and women. A different school of thought focuses instead on power as the pertinent explanation of gendered communication. Researchers from this tradition believe that male and female differences in communication styles are actually reflections of relative degrees of power. Power mediates gender differences. Male communication styles are in actuality the styles of the privileged and dominant. When we control for the unequal distribution of power in the communication process, "gendered" styles of communicating disappear, and we are left instead with "powerful" and "less powerful" styles (Kollock et al., 1985).

In heterosexual couples, the "dominant-supportive" model of conversing is somewhat preprogrammed. The male, traditionally the more powerful member of a couple, also plays a dominant role in communication. He interrupts more, uses fewer tag questions (a supportive device used to show interest and ask for others' opinions and input), and reveals less of his emotional state than his partner (Blumstein & Schwartz, 1983; Fishman, 1983). Women, on the other hand, tend to play a supportive role in conversations. They interrupt less often and less successfully, use more tag questions, and reveal more of themselves than their male partners (Fishman, 1983; Lakoff, 1975; Thorne & Henley, 1975). Although some claim that this dominant-supportive pattern is functional for relationships, other researchers believe it is not necessarily desirable. Gay and lesbian couples, by virtue of the sex composition of their relationships, are not prompted to automatically fall into this gendered style of communication. Nonetheless, gender socialization does affect the goals and styles of gay and lesbian discourse, and it is not without its own pitfalls and dangers.

Some researchers have argued that it is often power, and not gender, that determines the style of communicating used by partners in intimate couples. A study by Kollock et al. (1985) found that the more powerful partner often uses conversational privileges not available to the less powerful partner. These tactics include using minimal responses ("hmmms" and "uh-huhs" used to avoid having to do the work of formulating a verbal response), interrupting more often, and not seeking other opinions through the use of tag questions. Other elements of conversational style seem related more to the gendered goals of partners than to power alone. For example, women in general desire greater emotional disclosure from themselves and their partners than men do (Tannen, 1990). Also, women often see the use of challenges as running contrary to the intent of conversation (the building of intimacy), whereas men view challenges as an excellent way to spar for dominance (Tannen, 1990).

Communication for lesbians and gay men is thus shaped by power and gender in different ways. Because most lesbians are very conscious of power imbalances in their relationships, they try to avoid most of the dominant conversational techniques discussed above. They usually have a common goal (the creation and maintenance of emotionally close and fulfilling conversations), and the power differentials that are somewhat unavoidable in heterosexual relationships are not usually played out in the communication styles of lesbian partners. For example, for most partners, the less powerful member uses more tag questions; this effect is much smaller in lesbian couples. Although power is an important determinant of the use of questions for all other types of couples, it is not significant for lesbians. They also have the lowest rates of attempted interruptions of all intimate couples (Kollock et al., 1985), and issue few challenges (Clunis & Green, 1988; Tannen, 1990).

Although gay men also tend to share a conception of how conversation is to be used, and what its goals are, their notion is less

conducive to the creation of intimacy, at least as it is traditionally defined. Communication, for many men, is a tool by which
power is accumulated and displayed. More than any other type
of couple, gay men use minimal responses as a way to fill conversational gaps. Unlike heterosexual couples, for whom the use
of tag questions is correlated with less power, the most powerful
partner in a gay relationship uses the most tag questions. This
could be due to an effort on the part of the couple to equalize
the power imbalance in the conversation, with the more powerful trying to draw the less powerful into the discussion. Negotiations over power also influence the success of interruptions.
Although attempts are made, gay couples have the lowest successful interruption rate of all couples. Furthermore, like most
men, gay men perceive challenges as a normal part of dialogue
(Tannen, 1990), and use them as a reasonable way to assert their
own authority within the conversation.

Many homosexual couples aspire to egalitarian relationships,
but not all couples accomplish this goal. The conversational
styles used by partners affect and reflect the power differential
within the couple. Furthermore, the unique combination of
power and gender, even in balanced relationships, creates potential problems of its own. For lesbian couples, the intensity
with which they pursue emotional familiarity may sometimes
leave them spinning their wheels in endless conversations about
their relationship and how they feel. This preoccupation with
matters of intimacy can leave one or both of the partners feeling
claustrophobic and less satisfied. Furthermore, the discomfort
some lesbians have with open conflict over difficulties in the
relationship may lead them to be unable to produce effective
modes of resolution (Becker, 1988; Clunis & Green, 1988).

Gay men have different issues to resolve when it comes to
communication. The style of communicating learned during
boyhood does not lend itself to disclosure and mediation. Conversations sometimes take on the character of little wars, in
which partners challenge and attack one another without ever
really listening to the points their partner is trying to make
(Berzon, 1988). Finally, because compromise is a solution that

connotes a loss of power to many men, the resolution of even little issues may become problematic when neither partner is willing to negotiate a middle ground (Berzon, 1988). Consequently arguments can escalate into full-fledged breakups.

Sex

Sexual intercourse is more than a physical release for most people. It affects and is affected by other parts of a couple's relationship, and it is laden with symbolic meaning for both partners. Some people have a lot of sex, others have no sex; some couples have a large repertoire of behaviors and techniques, whereas others have relatively limited variety. No matter what the mechanics are, sex is rarely devoid of import, and it is the impact this has on the relationship that makes sex interesting and important to understand when studying gay (and heterosexual) couples.

Before the mid-1970s, gays and lesbians had few, if any, models of gay sexuality. Since that time, a growing number of books have been written that not only detail the techniques and positions of homosexual acts, but also sanction attitudes and beliefs surrounding gay sexuality in general. Therefore, readers of this literature may not only learn more about the mechanics of sex but may also become more comfortable with it (and their own sexuality) as well. However, not all homosexuals read this literature, and there may be a substantial proportion of gays and lesbians who never have access to it.

Initiation and Frequency

In general, lesbians have sex less frequently than any other type of couple (heterosexual or homosexual), at least partially because women in this culture have been raised to believe that they are less sexual than men and therefore sex can appropriately be a less central characteristic of lesbian relationships. Furthermore, women are generally taught that initiating sex is something left to men; hence lesbians often do not learn the skills needed to comfortably launch sexual experiences. There-fore, an inability to initiate sex, because it is not part of the female sex role or because it is seen as a dominating, unwelcome part of the male sex role, deters some lesbians from having sex as often as they would like. Furthermore, many lesbians believe that snuggling and other forms of physical affection are ends in themselves, whereas for most men these are viewed as precur-sors to sex. (Although women in heterosexual couples may see hugging and petting as ends to themselves, the presence of a male partner usually results in these activities' concluding in sexual intercourse.) Hence behavior that often culminates in in-tercourse for heterosexual and gay male couples does not lead to sex (as often) for lesbians.

In the first 2 years of their relationship, gay men have sex the most often of all couples who live together. This is not surpris-ing, given that men in this society are encouraged to be sexual, and having a potent sexual appetite is considered an important part of the male sex role. Although at first glance it would seem that the initiation problems that plague lesbian couples would not surface in gay men's relationships, this is not always the case. Because initiation is part of the male sex role, the partner who begins sex is also asserting his manhood. Two men can therefore turn initiation into a competition, with the noninitiat-ing partner feeling "one-upped" by his companion. At that point, the partner who is placed in the receptive role can only assert his own control over the situation by refusing his partners advances. Refusal is also a "power move" that is not congruent with male sexual norms. This symbolic tug of war can wreak havoc as power dynamics in the bedroom spill over into other elements of the relationship.

Sexual Activity

Despite the association in many people's minds of lesbian sexuality with oral sex, cunnilingus is not the mainstay of most lesbians' sexual activity; in one study, only 39% of the respon-dents reported usually or always having oral sex, and nearly a quarter said they rarely or never engaged in it (Blumstein & Schwartz, 1983). Although lesbians have more oral sex than heterosexual women, a surprisingly large minority are uncomfortable with oral sex for a variety of reasons, including shyness, embarrassment about sex in general, and uneasiness with intimacy. In most couples, oral sex is performed by both partners. If this reciprocity becomes unbalanced, some lesbians may feel guilt or resentment (either for always receiving or for always being responsible for performing) and will engage in oral sex less often.

The symbolism of oral sex is not lost on women, although it is interesting that the meanings associated with it vary greatly. Some women report that being the receiver of oral sex makes them feel powerful, in control, and worshipped by their lover. Paradoxically, those same feelings are reported by women when they are the performers of oral sex. In any case, the intimacy achieved through this sex act appears to be valuable to many relationships, and as the frequency of oral sex increases, so does a lesbian's satisfaction with both her sex life and the relationship in general (Blumstein & Schwartz, 1983).

Gay men have more oral sex than lesbians, although this act is just one of many they perform with their partners. As it is for lesbians, oral sex connotes feelings of power and control, and a lack of reciprocity is generally resented. Anal sex, however, has different parameters. One large study reports that only 27% of gay men both receive and insert during sex (Blumstein & Schwartz, 1983), whereas in another study just over half the respondents play both roles during their lovemaking (Spada, 1979). For most men, sexual position can become intertwined with images of power, dominance, and "manliness." In many situations, the "penetrator" can be seen as the more manly and more powerful, and the "penetratee" as more effeminate and submissive. Although none of these traits is necessarily correlated with sexual position, the meanings men bring to bed with them can affect their enjoyment of sex and the relationship in general. Position preferences can also affect the ritualized dance that gay men often perform when looking for a sex partner. If a man has a very specific desire to play one and only one role in sex, it is helpful to advertise this desire to his potential lovers. Some men try to signal their preferences using a variety of cues (keys worn on the left or right side of the belt, bandannas, leather clothing, etc.) to avoid an unhappy discovery of incompatibility when the two men are in bed,

One of the most frequently studied variables of gay and lesbian sexuality is monogamy. Traditional views of love and marriage frown upon extramarital sex and equate it with unfaithfulness, lack of commitment, and absence of love. For homosexual couples, however, at least among gay males, nonmonogamy was traditionally a preferred lifestyle (Silverstein, 1981; Spada, 1979). In the 1970s, some researchers attempted to redefine extrarelationship sex in less moralistic terms in order to reflect more accurately the feelings and experiences of heterosexuals. More recently, some lesbian literature has insisted that discussions of nonmonogamy not be cast in a heterosexual paradigm.

Early in relationships, homosexuals may continue to see others before they decide to commit themselves to just one partner. Sometimes people have clandestine affairs of varying duration. Another form of nonmonogamy involves agreement that one or both partners will have sex with other people; these affairs can either be long-term or "one-night stands." The sexual revolution of the 1960s and 1970s experimented with new ways of organizing relationships, including nondyadic sex and living arrangements; however, it has also complicated both negotiation and discussion of these issues.

Although marriage is laden with norms governing extramarital affairs, gays and lesbians are excluded from this formal institution. Therefore, they must individually and in collaboration with partners generate their own definitions and norms. Although the gay subculture has established some widely shared understandings (which will be discussed shortly), they lack the universal, monolithic character of marriage. Gay and lesbian couples' negotiation of the meanings of fidelity and acceptable behavior is facilitated when partners have similar backgrounds, values, morals, and beliefs about fairness. It is also helpful for partners to have complementary notions about love and the importance of safeguarding the relationship, In other words, if a couple is highly mismatched on commitment to the relationship, discussions about monogamy may not have mutually satisfying resolutions.

The definition of love most women in this society are trained to endorse views sexual activity outside the relationship as a violation of the partnership. For decades, lesbians followed the norms of a feminized version of love, and most, if not all, tended to desire monogamous relationships (Tuller, 1978), although a surprising number were unsuccessful in achieving this ideal (Blumstein & Schwartz, 1983; Peplau et al., 1978). More recently, a growing number of lesbians have been reconceptualizing the meanings of monogamy. Seen now as an extension of the patriarchal control of women, monogamy is defined as an unnecessary and limiting factor to be avoided or at least renegotiated within lesbian relationships.

Although monogamy is a norm for all people in this culture, men's extramarital affairs have been less stigmatized than women's. In essence, although relationships are supposed to be exclusive, men can generally break this rule more easily than women, in part because sex for men is less personal and hence is seen as less dangerous to the primary relationship. Furthermore, sex for men is supposed to be more instinct driven and less controllable than for women; this understanding of men's sexuality makes trespasses easier to forgive. Gay men in particular have traditionally ignored monogamy in favor of a less monopolistic version of couplehood. Before AIDS was a recognized threat to men who had many (which could literally mean thousands of) sex partners, most young gay men tended to have multiple lovers, often concurrently; it was unusual to find a man who was monogamously committed. As men aged, however, they tended to move toward committed primary relationships (with or without monogamy as a component). Interestingly, even before the onset of AIDS, there was a growing trend toward monogamous relationships in the gay community (Davidson, 1991; Silverstein, 1981). This is probably due largely to the age structure of the society: The baby-boomers were getting older and were already starting to "settle down." Although gay men still have the highest rates of nonmonogamy of all types of couples (heterosexual married, heterosexual cohabiting, gay, and lesbian), there is an increasingly visible minority who seek and maintain exclusive relationships (Davidson, 1991; Kelly et al., 1989).

Because men and women hold different views of monogamy and its relevance to relationship satisfaction and success, lesbians and gay men have very different rates and types of nonmonogamy experiences. The exceptions already noted notwithstanding, most lesbians involved in a committed bond see outside sex as both a betrayal of and a threat to the primary relationship (Peplau, Padesky, & Hamilton, 1982). Perceptions of threat and betrayal are intensified because the person with whom the infidelity occurs is usually a close friend rather than a stranger. The emotional component of the affair heightens the risk that a "fling" will turn serious and end the first relationship. Perhaps that is why most intact lesbians couples only have one experience with infidelity; most relationships do not recover from more (Blumstein & Schwartz, 1983). The subsection of the lesbian community who view monogamy as an unwanted or harmful form of control tend to replace a primary commitment with sexually active singlehood. In other words, these women have several sexual partners, none of whom are considered a "life partner" or "mate."

Gay men have developed several different styles of nonmonogamy. Some remain single and sexually active with other single or nonmonogamously coupled men. Others are involved in enduring primary relationships that allow sex with casual (nonemotional) partners. Still others are serious about maintaining an exclusive relationship with one other person, and react to a partners affair in much the same manner as heterosexuals do.

Nonmonogamy affects relationships by establishing ground rules and boundaries. For some gay men this is a relatively easy task, and the relationship is enhanced by the excitement and variety of numerous sex partners. For others (especially those who agreed against their better judgment to allow their partner to have other lovers), nonmonogamy entails stress and tension. Some of these couples will eventually reach an impasse and break up over the issue, whereas others either renegotiate or learn to live with their arrangements.

A new element, however, has been added since the early 1980s and the horrific impact of AIDS. Today, negotiation of nonmonogamy is often regarded as a matter of life and death; forsaking the rules is potentially lethal. Some gay men who would have heretofore paid no attention to a partner's non-monogamy now demand strict adherence to fidelity; others want strict adherence to safer sex guidelines. Partners negotiate what is allowed with another man: masturbation, sex with a condom, no anal sex, or maybe just "telephone sex." The desire to stay alive has made gay men's already frank discussions of sex even franker.

Less is known about the process by which lesbians reach understandings about outside affairs; however, some research indicates that under certain conditions outside sex does not detract from the satisfaction of both women in the primary relationship (Peplau et al., 1978), whereas other research has found that a third person is a significant factor in the dissolution of lesbian relationships (Tuller, 1978).

Power and Equity

Because the vast majority of gays and lesbians strive for egalitarian relationships, the distribution of power is almost always an issue of negotiation. Power imbalances manifested in unequal influence in decision making, an unfair division of household labor, or biased allotment of rights, resources, and privileges usually create conflict. Among heterosexual couples, some of these imbalances are expected and tolerated parts of life: Men earn the money, women care for the home and children. Each partner (traditionally) has his or her own sphere of influence and responsibility. Because gays and lesbians do not have gender differentiation to guide a division of labor, they must find new ways to design their relationships and distribute responsibilities within them.

A good deal of research indicates that lesbian couples go out of their way to minimize power differentials. Lesbian couples guard equality and, in fact, are more likely to share duties and decision making than any other type of couple. This may account for the fact that for them, in contrast to heterosexual women, the level of housework performed does not correlate with depression (Kurdek, 1993a). Nonetheless, a large minority of lesbians are unsuccessful in achieving this equality (Lynch & Reilly, 1985/1986). In general, the partner who works fewer hours outside the home will be responsible for more of the housework. Although such imbalances are practical, most couples are attuned to them and define them as temporary ("just until she finds a better job," or "just until she works fewer hours"), or the partner who is doing less explicitly concedes she is not doing her fair share.

For most heterosexual and gay male couples, the person who makes more money has more power relative to his partner, in terms of both decision making and getting out of housework. Money does not serve the same function in lesbian relationships, where it is not correlated with power (Blumstein & Schwartz, 1983; Lynch & Reilly, 1985/1986). This could be due to the fact that women in this society are not trained to judge their worth by the size of their paycheck and hence do not apply that criterion to their partner or to other women. Or it may, in some cases, be a conscious rejection of the heterosexual model that accords husbands more power and privilege because they provide the greatest income to the family. It is also true that most women never have a lot of money, so that the idea of using it as a bargaining tool is foreign to them. Finally, most lesbians endorse independence, so the notion of using money as an instrument of control is ideologically repulsive. In general, lesbians view money as a means to avoid dependence on one's partner. Even in relationships that are characterized by unequal

incomes, lesbians very rarely see themselves as financially dependent, and most pay their bills either proportionately or
equally (Lynch & Reilly, 1985/1986).

For gay men, money remains a yardstick by which to judge
one's own and one's partners worth. Income is more directly
related to power—and to proprietary rights in the relationship.
The man with the higher income has more power over decision
making (Blumstein & Schwartz, 1983; Harry & Devall, 1978),
and this inequality can cause serious problems for gay male relationships, particularly when the income difference is quite
large and the power differentials are quite obvious. These problems may be exacerbated by the fact that gay men tend to compare themselves to their partners in this respect, and the more
affluent partner will actually feel more successful if his partner
makes less money. Thus competition and hard feelings are not
uncommon. Furthermore, gay men tend to be more career oriented and less relationship oriented than lesbians (Blumstein &
Schwartz, 1983); they may be less willing or less able to work
on interpersonal problems.

Norms operating in both the larger society and the gay and
lesbian subcultures suggest that we look to other areas besides
money to explain the distribution of power in homosexual relationships. For example, gay men tend to place a high value on
physical attractiveness; hence if one man is much more attractive than his partner, he can use this to his advantage. In couples
with a large age difference between the partners, it is not uncommon for a young, attractive man to "trade" his beauty for the
experience and financial resources of an older and less physically attractive man (Harry, 1982)—a trade quite common among
heterosexuals as well. However, more heterosexuals seem to
find partners who are age mates, and attractiveness is but one
variable when selecting someone to parent with and marry. The
male homosexual bar culture intensifies the salience of beauty
as a sorting characteristic, and because so many men meet in
bars, looks may predominate over other important traits and
personal resources. A "resource" that may be used by lesbians is
children. Recent research, however, indicates that children are

highly valued by the mother's partner in lesbian couples, perhaps more so (or at least differently) than by the mother's partner in heterosexual couples. This attachment gives the biological mother more power in the intimate relationship because she
controls access to her children. The nonbiological parent has no
legal rights and must remain in the good graces of the biological
parent. Compromises, such as staying "closeted" in order to protect custody, further erode the nonbiological caretaker's independence of choice and action (Moore, Blumstein, & Schwartz,
1993). This is quite a contrast to heterosexual couples. In these
relationships, women experience diminished power due to in-
terrupted work histories, reliance on male income for family
support, and perceived and real decreased attractiveness upon
reentry in the marriage market (England & Farkas, 1986). Arguably, someone else's children are seen as a cost to heterosexual
men, whereas lesbians see them as a relationship benefit (Moore
et al., 1993).

In conclusion, lesbians and gay men strive for egalitarian relationships, and the power differences found in heterosexual couples do not manifest themselves as often or as dramatically in
homosexual couples. Because it is common for both partners to
have jobs and for people of the same sex to have equal opportunity in the job market, financial differences are generally not as
large as they are for heterosexuals. Furthermore, the fact that
housework is consciously negotiated (rather than assumed to be
settled automatically by sex) means that the distribution of
chores tends to be more fair, either by sharing all tasks equally,
dividing the responsibilities equitably between the two partners, or recognizing imbalances and trying to compensate for
their unfairness.

Again, our narrow knowledge about the allocation of rights
and responsibilities in gay and lesbian relationships reflects
the relative newness of this field of research. We can say with
relative assuredness what lesbians and gay men *do* and the correlates of outcomes (i.e., how power and income relate to decisions about chores), but we know very little about how they go

about doing it. The processes remain under-studied, and more research in this area is warranted.

The Impact of the Larger Society

Relationships do not exist in a vacuum, and the social environment plays a complex role in the formation and sustenance of gay and lesbian relationships. At the local level and in relation to various levels of involvement, the gay community provides both support and legitimation for homosexuality and homosexual couples. On a broader scale, the general society has profound effects on homosexual couples by denying them many of the freedoms, rights, and recognitions routinely afforded heterosexual couples.

The gay community is both a blessing and a threat to lesbian and gay relationships. On the one hand, it provides common meeting places for homosexuals, general support for homosexuality, and a network of information about everything from job and housing opportunities to political organizations to yoga classes. For many, the gay community is an essential component of life. However, the same reasons that make the community so valuable also make it dangerous for many relationships. It is here that couples meet other lesbians and gay men; Blumstein and Schwartz (1983) found that lesbians who were heavily involved in the gay community were more likely to break up. They surmised that this was due to women's falling in love with friends who were also active in the community. Other researchers have suggested that it is possible that women who are active in the lesbian community are also likely to value autonomy more highly and hence may break up more (Peplau et al., 1978). Fifteen years ago, it was suggested that gay men face much the same strain because most of the men in the community were either single or nonmonogamously partnered (Harry & DeVall, 1978). However, the growing trend among gay men toward monogamy and long-term relationships may point toward a change in the way in which community affects ongoing couples. The norms of the community are increasingly supportive of couple-hood, and fewer men in the community are "available." Hence the lure of other men—or the dangers of succumbing to it—may differ from 15 or 20 years ago.

Historically, neither the United States nor any other country has been supportive of its gay and lesbian population. Many states have laws that make most sexual acts between people of the same sex illegal, and the U.S. Supreme Court ruled in 1986 (*Bowers v. Hardwick*) that breaking into a gay couple's house to arrest them for committing "sodomy" was not an invasion of their civil rights (Hunter, Michaelson, & Stoddard, 1992). It is also still possible for gays and lesbians to be denied housing, jobs, loans, and insurance in many areas. Institutionalized homophobia, though not universal, is common enough to prompt the exodus of many homosexuals to larger cities in the Northeast and on the West Coast (creating "magnet" cities such as New York, Chicago, Los Angeles, San Francisco, Portland, and Seattle).

Individual homophobia, which can cause everything from minor insults to property damage and even death at the hands of "gay bashers," also takes a daily toll on the comfort and peace of mind of lesbians and gay men. Some gays and lesbians try to avoid discrimination, danger, or humiliation by remaining closeted. However, this makes finding a partner and pursuing a social life very difficult. Furthermore, having a partner also increases the chances that someone will find out about this secret. This is especially true for two men who wish to live together. Traditionally, women have found acceptance as "roommates" much more often than men.

Research indicates that disclosure and being out are directly related to psychological well-being; hence being closeted creates extra pressure, although the degree of disclosure does not affect relationship satisfaction directly (Eldridge & Gilbert, 1990; Jones & Bates, 1978). Also, if two people have very different ideas about the degree to which they should be "out," the relationship may be imperiled. In general, living with the possibility of oppression (even if it has not been apparent in one's own life) makes life as a homosexual (and homosexual couple) more stressful.

The lack of institutional recognition and regulation for homosexual couples also plays a very powerful role in their stability. Heterosexual unions are sanctioned by the church and the state through the marriage ceremony. The state rewards such unions with family health insurance, property rights when breakups occur, and institutional prerogatives such as untaxed inheritance and the right to distribute property after a partner's death. Although many gays and lesbians and gay organizations actually seek these rights, it is the simple recognition of their relationships that is most desired. Should this acknowledgment be bestowed upon them, the unions made by lesbians and gay men might resemble heterosexual marriages more (for good or ill). The ties that bind heterosexuals are not only emotional, but legal as well. If gays and lesbians had these legal bonds, their "divorce" rate might resemble marital breakup rates more closely.

In some states, petitions have been made to ask the courts to grant homosexual couples marriage licenses. Only one state, Hawaii, has recognized any "right" of gay people to have a legal union. Whether this will stand up against the appeals process is unclear (Leo, 1993). In the meantime, some states have set up legal counsel for "domestic partners" who wish to dissolve their relationship and require litigation to work out who gets how much of the couple's combined resources. A few cities, such as Seattle and San Francisco, recognize "domestic partnerships" (same-sex and mixed-sex cohabiting couples) and provide health plans, bereavement leave, and so forth. However, for the most part, governmental agencies steadfastly refuse to give gay and lesbian couples institutional recognition.

Finally, because gay men and lesbians are not immune to the pressure from society to be in a heterosexual relationship, some attempt to form relationships with members of the opposite sex. Sometimes this occurs before the individuals recognize or accept their homosexuality, whereas at other times people simply fall in love unexpectedly. For men, the male sex role is so intrinsically tied to heterosexuality that giving in to this pressure sometimes may seem easier than following personal desire. Although gender norms for women follow these same lines, lesbians may also marry men because such a marriage (at least traditionally) would probably increase their standard of living and free them from the need to work full time if they did not want to (Ross, 1983; Whitney, 1990).

The End of the Relationship

In general, gay and lesbian relationships are not as durable as heterosexual marriages. Even though there are a significant minority of couples who break this rule, Blumstein and Schwartz found that nearly 48% of their lesbian respondents and 36% of their gay male respondents (compared to 29% for heterosexual cohabitors and 14% for married couples) broke up within 2 years of the original study (Blumstein & Schwartz, 1983). Among all types of couples, several variables affected the likelihood of breakups. First are individual-level variables—perceived barriers to leaving the relationship and alternatives outside the relationship. For example, heterosexual marriages have many barriers to leaving, including the cost of a divorce and the negative effects it could have on children. Wives in particular are hampered by their usually lower earning power, which makes it difficult to exit bad marriages. Alternatives most often present themselves in terms of one's perceived chances of finding a better partner. Hence attractive young women or very successful, well-off men may feel they have more alternatives outside their marriage because their ability to find another (possibly better) mate is quite good. In general, lesbians and gay men have no kin or parents who reinforce the relationship and support its viability. Lesbians also report having fewer alternatives to their relationships than heterosexuals and gay men (Kurdek & Schmitt, 1986b). This is partially due to the fact that more lesbians are already partnered, whereas most gay men are single or available (Harry & DeVall, 1978). Furthermore, whereas heterosexual

women may find it harder to find a mate as they age (because
many heterosexual men place a premium on youth and physical
attractiveness), lesbians may find it even harder to find a partner
because single lesbians are rare and tend to be sparsely distrib-
uted, and older women tend to be more closeted, making them
that much harder to find. Most gay men, on the other hand, have
few barriers and many alternatives, which may explain why a
smaller percentage of gay men than lesbians are in a relationship
at any one time. Coupled lesbians, however, are at risk if they
are part of a large or intense lesbian network. Alternatives become real and do in fact account for many breakups.

Another variable that has been shown to play a part in all relationships is the length of time the couple has been together.
Kurdek and Schmitt (1986a) found that all relationships experience a stage effect, with the first year and post-third-year stages
exhibiting higher satisfaction than the "nesting stage" in the second and third years. He suggests that it is during this middle
stage that a couple loses the first blush of being in love and gets
down to the serious work of finding compromises for problems
and adjusting to one another's differences. If successful, the
later years of the relationship yield more satisfaction for each
partner; the couple reaches a state of comfortable predictability
and, though not totally stable, remains dynamic around a mutually agreeable consensus.

Research about the reasons gays and lesbians break up has
shown that there are distinct patterns among each group that
correlate with relationship dissolution. Among lesbians, couples who argue about sex are more likely to report being dissatisfied with their relationship (Blumstein & Schwartz, 1983;
Kurdek, 1991b) and break up more than those who do not, although the frequency of lesbian sex is not correlated with relationship longevity (Blumstein & Schwartz, 1983). Arguments
about money, kin, friends, or unequal power also correlate with
higher chances of breaking up (Eldridge & Gilbert, 1990; Peplau
et al., 1982). As with heterosexuals, homosexuals who are higher
earners—and more powerful partners—are most likely to leave

(Blumstein & Schwartz, 1983). Lesbians have no training or affection for the provider role; thus if they have this role, their resentment may push them out of the relationship.

According to therapists who work with lesbian couples, the most common source of strain results from the combination of unrealistic expectations and outside pressures. Women in this society are usually expected to be empathetic and relationship oriented. However, most lesbians also have responsibilities outside the couple, including a career and political involvement. This sets up a no-win situation for some lesbians who expect a great deal from themselves and their partner in terms of time and energy spent on the relationship.

Finally, lesbian relationships are susceptible to affairs and jealousy (Becker, 1988; Wolf, 1979). Usually it is the woman who had the affair who ends the relationship, probably because she has fallen in love with the other woman (Becker, 1988). Also, if one woman moves away to pursue educational opportunities or a career, the couple may break up. Because lesbians need their jobs to survive, the option of following a partner is not always available. Distance makes it hard to maintain the relationship, especially if the couple cannot afford frequent trips or high phone bills (see Chapter 7 of this volume).

Gay men often break up over large and unresolvable power differences. Whereas for lesbians this is usually due to the discomfort arising from supporting a partner who is (ideally) supposed to be independent, for gay men it is probably more due to an ego-based tug of war that one partner is losing. Other literature about the dissolution of gay couples simply cites "personality differences," whereas ethnographic accounts point to the trend among gay men that they simply fall out of love and move on.

Although these correlates of dissatisfaction and dissolution are interesting, they tell us nothing about the processes and consequences of terminating a relationship. For most people, ending a relationship is rarely easy, especially if it was long-term and the couple lived together. For gays and lesbians, this process may be aggravated by the fact that they do not have access to the culturally accepted symbols that mark the demise of a marriage or institutional regulations to protect partners' rights: They do not legally separate, sign divorce papers, and so forth. Furthermore, a heterosexual going through a divorce can usually expect sympathy and advice from family, friends, and coworkers. Depending on how closeted they are, lesbians and gay men may not have these outlets and must therefore carry the burden of their turmoil alone (Becker, 1988). Sometimes parents who are not accepting of their child's orientation further complicate a breakup by using it as proof that the child should be heterosexual. This denies the individual validation for the good parts of the old relationship, as well as adding emotional strain at a time when it is neither helpful nor needed (Becker, 1988).

Individuals experiencing a breakup must also deal with issues of equitable division of property. Partners have to decide who moves out, which possessions go and which stay, and how mutually held financial investments will be split up. Even for couples who make these decisions peaceably, physical belongings take on an emotional content. For those who can afford to, it is sometimes easier to just walk away with nothing than to face the painful process of dividing the tangible symbols of the couple. For those with children, this ran be an especially difficult process, including discussions about visitation rights and custody that have no protections in law.

Emotional trauma aside, breakups can have a positive effect on the individuals involved. Many people report feeling more free, and feeling welcome relief from conflict after a relationship has ended (Kurdek, 1991a). Furthermore, a growing number of lesbians and gay men have come forward about their experiences in relationships that were physically and emotionally abusive. Although an exact figure is impossible to find, most research indicates that between 10% and 20% of homosexual relationships experience violence of some sort (a number roughly equivalent to that found in research about heterosexual relationships) (Renzetti, 1992).

Conclusion

The study of gay and lesbian couples teaches us about a wide variety of topics, including the effects of community, gender, and relationship values and norms of intimate relationships and the processes needed to initiate and maintain them. However, researchers should be alerted to certain obstacles that make research on homosexual couples complex, and access tricky.

Homosexual individuals and homosexual communities and organizations are exposed to certain risks if they reveal their identity, sexual preferences, and experiences. Real and perceived threats of political or popular backlash make it virtually impossible to obtain a truly representative random sample. No matter how well-funded or credible the study, some, perhaps many, homosexuals remain closeted. In fact, getting any type of sample requires a large investment of time and energy. Many investigators begin by immersing themselves in local organizations (formal and informal) that cater to gays and lesbians. Personal relationships build on mutual trust, which takes time to create. Researchers also need to go to some lengths to deserve this trust, including taking extra precautions for the protection of confidentiality and anonymity (including, for example, encrypted data sets that eliminate identifying data from each case). People who are interested in pursuing research agendas that focus on people with "alternative" sexual practices or orientations must also prepare themselves for several pragmatic problems. Funding is scarce (necessitating smaller scale work), and it is not uncommon for researchers interested in this topic to be stigmatized (either for their interest in sex, which is derided as either prurient or trivial, or by the assumption that the researcher is homosexual and therefore engaged in ideological self-justification rather than pure science).

Furthermore, analyses can be difficult because most of us have been raised with heterosexual models of relationships, and we must resist the tendency to apply these models unthinkingly to homosexual couples. As noted before, for example, "success" in a homosexual relationship might be defined very differently from "success" in heterosexual relationships. Also, the conceptualization of "power" is often formulated in terms of what a stereotypical male would want to accomplish: getting his way, winning a point, and so forth. However, if we use women's communication as a standard, *power* might instead be defined as the ability to create consensus, to build rapport, or to communicate difficult or highly personal ideas with ease. Researchers used to thinking about heterosexual norms need to be aware of the implicit assumptions they make when they ask questions and conduct analyses, and try instead to rework their previous models to include same-sex issues, problems, and innovative solutions.

Despite these hurdles, scholars have begun producing a formidable body of academic research; however, we still know much less about homosexual couples than we do about heterosexual relationships, and they remain one type of under-studied population. The relationships formed by lesbians and gay men are in many ways very similar to heterosexual ones; in other ways, distinct factors influence relationship formation and survival. Institutional recognition is one important difference; above all else, the lack of a marriage contract frees lesbians and gay men to form their relationships as they see fit, although it also contributes to a higher attrition rate and the possibility of less equitable breakups. Gender is also an important variable because it contributes to the shape of the power structure within heterosexual couples, and by holding it constant in homosexual couples, we can begin to see to what extent gender is (and is not) a fixed determinant of behavior and organization within the relationship. For example, women in heterosexual couples tend to do the bulk of housework even when they work as many hours as their husbands. Gay men, however, manage to find ways to take care of those chores that often fall to women in heterosexual couples. Men can and do take up their fair share of housework when they couple with one another; the fact that men coupled with women do not usually do this suggests some interesting questions and leads us to pursue with greater diligence the "undoing" of many myths about men's and women's roles in the home vis-à-vis one another.

Finally, it is important to note that the sociopolitical climate in the United States is changing. Lesbians and gay men are growing more vocal about expanding their civil rights; furthermore, they have an increasingly sympathetic audience. Demographically, the average homosexual is growing older, and because of this combined with the impact of AIDS is much more interested in maintaining an exclusive relationship. The numbers of gay-oriented therapists, counseling groups, and self-help books are increasing in response to this need and there is a growing number of gay and lesbian mental health professionals. Also, long-term, satisfying relationships are coming out of the closet within their communities: People now have role models and norms to legitimize their desire to be in a relationship. Therefore, the study of these relationships and the processes involved in their initiation and maintenance teaches us a great deal not only about sexuality and individuals but also about all relationships, and the ways in which they are affected by gender, power, and broad social practices and structures that impinge on private arrangements.

Bosses and Buddies: Constructing and Performing Simultaneously Hierarchical and Close Friendship Relationships

Theodore E. Zorn

Readers would normally expect a chapter on relationships in organizations to be about the relationships between managers and subordinates—and this one is—but they will also recall that there is already a huge literature on that sort of relationship. The present chapter looks at a version of that relationship that is almost never studied: the types of relationships between close friends who are also at different levels of hierarchy in an organization. For example, I am living the focus of this chapter. In 1991 one of my closest friends, who had been my coworker,[1] became my supervisor, the chair of our department. The change in roles affected my feelings and thoughts about our relationship, as well as communication between us. We have remained close friends, yet there have been times when I resented his power over me or hesitated to tell or ask him something because of his position.

Many managers experience similar situations. In the management and supervisory skills workshops I conduct for organizations, I am recurrently asked, "How do I deal with subordinates who used to be my friends and coworkers?" Underlying this question are many others, such as: "How do I earn their respect when they're used to treating me as a colleague?" "How do I continue to be a friend when I have to make demands, evaluate performance, and decide on raises?" "How do I deal with their testing to see how far their relationship will let them push me?" "How do I deal with expectations that I'll give them preferential treatment or the 'inside scoop'?"

Like the other "under-studied" relationships addressed in this volume, close relationships between supervisors and subordinates, especially nonromantic relationships, have received little research attention. However, close friendships and romantic involvements between people linked by hierarchical relationships in the workplace are commonplace, perhaps even ubiquitous (Dillard & Witteman, 1985; Henderson & Argyle, 1985).

The limited research on personal relationships in organizations may be due in part to the perceived functionality of personal relationships. As many scholars have noted (e.g., Burrell & Morgan, 1979; Pacanowsky & O'Donnell-Trujillo, 1983; Putnam, 1983), traditional functionalist research has focused almost exclusively on topics that serve managerial purposes in accomplishing organizational goals such as productivity and profitability. Personal relationships, when addressed at all, have been viewed primarily as dysfunctional (e.g., Collins, 1983; Kets de Vries & Miller, 1984). However, as Trujillo (1985) suggested, "Managers do not merely engage in social cosmetics [with subordinates], but they also play together, 'bitch' together, and share confidences with others—others who come to be called 'informants,' 'work acquaintances,' and even 'friends'" (p. 208).

The purpose of this chapter is to examine personal relationships in hierarchically linked dyads. Specifically, I explore the tension between hierarchy and closeness and the nature and effects of one type of personal relationship between supervisors and subordinates: close friendship. Research on simultaneously personal and hierarchical relationships is scant, and what exists is largely atheoretic and unmindful of the processual dynamics of relationships. Reflecting the positivist paradigm, it has tended to focus analysis on individuals and to embrace a variable-analytic model. After reviewing this body of research, I propose a perspective that is grounded in interpretive theories and, in line with the focus of this series, is mindful of relational processes. To illustrate the fruitfulness of interpretive studies of processes in personal and hierarchical relationships, I then discuss exploratory interviews I conducted with supervisors and subordinates who were formerly coworkers and close friends.

Research on Personal and
Hierarchical Relationships in Organizations

A central feature of hierarchies in modern bureaucratic organizations is the supervisor- (or manager-) subordinate dyad. Although it is conceivable that other, more egalitarian forms of organization could emerge, the supervisor-subordinate dyad has traditionally been endemic in organizational life. Currently, organizations are experimenting with team-based organizational designs that encourage employee self-direction (Barker, Melville, & Pacanowsky, 1993; Tompkins & Cheney, 1985). Still, even these organizations typically rely on "team leaders" whose roles carry some supervisory responsibilities. Organizations and researchers have spent considerable energy attempting to improve the interaction between supervisors and subordinates, assuming, like Kets de Vries and Miller (1984), that "the quality of superior/subordinate interaction is one of the cornerstones of successful organizational functioning. Short circuits in this interaction process will seriously impair organizational effectiveness" (p. 95). One reason for the importance placed on this dyadic relationship may be the amount of time supervisors and subordinates spend interacting. Jablin (1979) concluded from his review of literature that supervisors spend from one third to two thirds of their time interacting with subordinates. According to his review, most supervisor-subordinate communication is face to face, and most interaction focuses on impersonal (e.g., task-related) rather than personal issues.

Many organizations discourage personal relationships between supervisors and subordinates because they assume that such relationships threaten organizational efficiency. It is often assumed that supervisors' objectivity in decision making will suffer. Larson (1984), for example, suggested that positive affect toward subordinates makes managers less likely to give them negative feedback about poor performance. He suggested that this occurs for two reasons. First, supervisors have more to lose in giving negative feedback to a liked subordinate than to a subordinate they dislike or toward whom they feel neutral. Second, evidence indicates that personal feeling can bias attributions, making supervisors less likely to view liked subordinates as being personally responsible for negative outcomes. Similarly, DeCotiis and Petit (1978) argued that interpersonal relationships between supervisors and subordinates are a "potentially powerful contaminant" (p. 640) of performance appraisal ratings.

A great deal of research has focused on "effective" supervisor-subordinate relationships (e.g., Dansereau & Markham, 1987; Jablin 1979, 1985). For example, Lamude, Daniels, and Graham (1988) summarized a number of studies reporting that supervisors and subordinates often have greatly divergent perceptions of their communication. Typical of these studies is Webber's (1970) study, which found that supervisors see themselves talking to subordinates on more occasions than subordinates see. Of interest to the present chapter is the question of how the development of a close personal relationship between supervisor and subordinate might affect these behaviors and perceptions of them. Some research suggests that perceptual divergence may be less extreme in such relationships (Byrne, 1971; Wexley, Alexander, Greenwalt, & Couch, 1980; Wexley & Pulakos, 1983).

Trust and openness seem to underlie effective communication in supervisor-subordinate relationships (Jablin, 1979;

Mellinger, 1956; Roberts & O'Reilly, 1974). Personal relationships have the potential to enhance or jeopardize trust and openness between supervisors and subordinates. Some studies (Collins, 1983; Quinn, 1977) report negative effects on relations between a supervisor and other subordinates when the supervisor develops a romantic relationship with one subordinate.

Some types of organizations may actually depend on close personal relationships coexisting with hierarchical relationships. Byron (1976) described 12 widely scattered North Atlantic fishing communities, representing a broad range of technologies, in which members are recruited into fishing crews almost exclusively on the basis of kinship or friendship ties. Although tradition underlies this system, Byron maintained that it is also rational, because the nature of the work requires close, trusting relationships among crew members. Byron suggested that the kinship values of trust, solidarity, the equivalence of siblings, and mutual aid translate into organizational cultures valuing voluntary cooperation, equality, and mutual reliance at a team level. Coaches of college and professional athletic teams similarly encourage friendship formation among players—for example, by requiring them to room together—for similar reasons. It is possible that large, bureaucratic organizations, especially those changing to team-based structures, might also encourage and benefit from personal relationships among employees.

So although organizations have typically frowned on the development of personal relationships between supervisors and subordinates, positive effects may accrue from such relationships in some work situations. There may be greater understanding between the two persons involved, and the subordinate may be more satisfied and communicatively open. However, other subordinates may respond negatively to a personal relationship between a supervisor and one of her or his subordinates. Because little research to date has focused on concurrent friendships and hierarchical relationships, we cannot yet assess the advantages and disadvantages they might yield, nor can we identify conditions and contexts that influence their effects.

Although close friendships between supervisors and subordinates seem to be common, some characteristics of hierarchical organization may decrease the likelihood of forming these friendships. Citing Hall's (1974) finding that managers prefer soliciting feedback to disclosing interpersonal information, Laurent (1978) suggested that hierarchical organization may discourage self-disclosure, which is often considered a prerequisite for intimacy. Similarly, Feldman (1985) demonstrated that demands for conformity necessitated secrecy and avoidance of self-disclosure at one of the Bell telephone companies. However, Haaken and Korschgen (1988) found that individuals' backgrounds moderated the relationship between hierarchy and disclosure. They found that adolescent workers from working-class backgrounds were wary of expressing feelings to managers, but middle-class respondents were often more gratified by the opportunity to express feelings to managers regardless of concrete results of their requests or complaints. These researchers further found that the middle-class workers were more likely to look favorably toward management and develop friendships with supervisors. Those with working-class backgrounds were more likely to see managers as adversaries and view the promotion of a peer to a management position as a fundamental shift in allegiance.

There is some reason to suspect that close friendships develop more often at upper than at lower levels of organizations. First, Jablin (1982) found that subordinates at lower levels perceived less openness in their relationships with supervisors than did subordinates at higher levels. Second, Lieberman (1956) found that workers promoted to supervisory positions developed more favorable attitudes toward management, perhaps increasing the likelihood of close friendships between supervisors and subordinates when both parties are in supervisory roles. Third, Schutte and Light (1978) found that proximity was a stronger influence on friendship choice at lower levels of the hierarchy, whereas status was a stronger influence at upper levels. They reasoned that higher levels of organizations are typically composed of ambitious, mobility-minded people who regard higher status persons as instrumental to their own advancement. This evidence suggests that subordinates at upper levels may be more likely than subordinates at lower levels to view supervisors as attractive.

The research summarized above offers some useful insights into simultaneously hierarchical and personal relationships. It suggests that supervisors and subordinates interact extensively, thereby increasing both the opportunity for and the consequences of friendship. It also suggests that many organizations have assumed that close relationships threaten organizational effectiveness, and indicates some reasons this assumption may be justified: For example, close relationships may bias supervisors' evaluations of subordinates' job performance. Finally, this research hints at some factors that increase the likelihood that friendships will form between supervisors and subordinates. It seems, for example, that being relatively high in the organizational hierarchy, being proxemically close, having a middle-class background, and having strong self-serving motives enhance the likelihood of supervisor-subordinate friendships.

However, as is clear from the preceding pages, little previous work has even recognized, much less addressed, friendships between supervisors and subordinates. Those studies that have been conducted are atheoretic, tend to subordinate interpretive and processual dynamics of relationships to individualistic variables, and generally accord priority to managerial interests, such as identifying means of increasing worker effectiveness. Further, consistent with much social science work, previous research has decontextualized relationships by ignoring the historical, cultural, and situational environments within which they are embedded.

Given the lack of research on simultaneously personal and hierarchical relationships, and the limitations of the research that exists, a challenge is to articulate a theoretical perspective that focuses on the symbolic and interpretive processes through which such relationships are created, maintained, and altered.

In what follows, I suggest one theoretical perspective within which such relationships might be viewed and studied. Following this, I report an exploratory study of simultaneously close and hierarchical relationships.

Theoretical Foundation:
A Constructive-Dramaturgical Framework

The theoretical perspective I propose begins with Delia and colleagues' constructivism (Applegate, 1990; Burleson, 1987; Delia, O'Keefe, & O'Keefe, 1982) and is embellished by concepts from McCall and Simmons' (1978) role-identity model, Goffman's (1959) dramaturgy, and Baxter's (1988) research on dialectical processes in relationships. This perspective embraces an interpretive orientation, assuming that humans are actional, interpreting, meaning-seeking, and meaning-creating beings. One's meanings are the dynamic products of personal and interpersonal sense-making processes that are influenced by social-cultural structures and processes. Consistent with the constructivist view of communication as the simultaneously psychological and social process of creating shared meaning (Delia et al., 1982), this perspective places a dual emphasis on understanding the ways individuals make sense of situations and the ways their sense-making processes and structures contribute to and are influenced by communicative performances.

Epistemologically, I assume that although we may usefully identify statistical trends in human relationships or in factors that contribute to various aspects of them, such relationships are cultural and historicized products and processes. Therefore, many statistical relationships that usefully describe particular types of relationships in one culture or era may not apply in other temporal and/or cultural contexts. In addition to or instead of noting statistical relationships among variables influencing human relationships, it is useful to examine individuals' sense-making and communicative practices through "thick description" (Geertz, 1973) and to examine such practices in light of the social forces that operate within them. Of particular significance, given a focus on interpretation and recognition of the cultural and historical influences on sense-making and communicative practices, are cognitive and communicative schemata that are shared by members of a culture within an historical period. Not only are similarities among individuals of interest, but so are differences in meanings, structures, and practices.

Delia's constructivist theory of communication borrows heavily from Kelly's (1955) personal construct theory, fusing it with concepts from symbolic interactionism (Blumer, 1969; Mead, 1934; Wood, 1992a), Bernstein's (1974) theory of position-centered and person-centered speech, and Werner's (1957) theory of cognitive development, among others. Constructivism focuses on the ways in which social cognitive structures and processes interact with communicative practices, particularly the sophistication, or complexity, of messages. The centerpiece of this theory is the notion of interpersonal constructs, which are assumed to be the most basic social cognitive structure or interpretive schema. An interpersonal construct is essentially a bipolar dimension of judgment, a cognitive "tool" individuals use to construe people and social situations.

Higher order cognitive schemata, which are constructed from personal constructs and reflect how an individual conceives relationships among constructs, seem linked to the concept of relationship dialectics, or opposing forces that are both interdependent and mutually negating (Baxter, 1988, 1990; Baxter & Simon, 1993; Goldsmith, 1990; Rawlins, 1989; Wood et al., 1994). Baxter (1988) identified three primary dialectics that operate across personal relationships: autonomy-connection, novelty-predictability, and openness-closedness. She conceptualized these as forces operating in the relationship rather than as cognitive structures. Although I agree that these are relational forces, I contend that these dialectics may *influence* individuals' cognitive schemata. From a constructivist perspective, dialectics may suggest primary or socially shared constructs that individuals use to make sense of their personal relationships and guide choices within them. Dialectics have been studied primarily in dating relationships and marriages. It remains to be seen to what degree they are useful in understanding simultaneously personal and hierarchical relationships in organizations, and whether such relationships might include additional dialectics.

Dialectical theory provides a way to theorize the tensions intrinsic to these relationships and thus the dimensions likely to be prominent in thinking about them. Also needed is a means of theorizing relational partners' communicative practices. This gap is filled by McCall and Simmons' (1978) role-identity model.

McCall and Simmons argued that each of us enacts a variety of roles and that we have preferred ways of thinking of ourselves, or identities, in each role. A role identity is "the character and role that an individual devises for himself as an occupant of a particular social position" (McCall & Simmons, 1978, p. 65). From a constructivist perspective, a role is a higher order schema made up of a variety of constructs. Some role identities are more prominent in our minds than others, and for these we continually seek support or legitimation. Legitimation is largely accomplished through what McCall and Simmons call role performances, by which they mean symbolic actions that embody the role identity, as described by Goffman (1959), among others. Although many factors may influence the relative position of a role identity in one's "prominence hierarchy," McCall and Simmons (1978) argued that "perhaps paramount among these determinants . . . is the degree to which the individual has committed himself to the particular contents of his role-identity, has gambled his regard for himself on living up to certain imaginations of self" (p. 75).

McCall and Simmons' model is particularly useful in exploring relationships that are simultaneously personal and hierarchical because it highlights the particular feature of these relationships that makes them special as well as problematic: the fact that they feature prominently for each participant two roles and therefore two identities, as well as two analytically separable relationships. That is, the central characteristic of simultaneously hierarchical and personal relationships is the tension created by two prominent role identities (friend and supervisor/ subordinate), both of which may be salient in the same context, but which often suggest quite different role performances.

Relational dialectics suggest dimensions, or constructs, along which one's role performances may vary and along which role performances—one's own or those of one's relational partner—may be interpreted by interactants. Thus, for example, a supervisor-friend, in interacting with a subordinate-friend, may want to be open (e.g., by disclosing information about another member of the work group), consistent with his or her conception of the role performance for "friend," and alternatively want to be closed (e.g., by not disclosing the same information) to fulfill the supervisor identity. People do not necessarily associate appropriate or competent performance of each role identity with one pole of each dimension. So a supervisor-friend may value openness in performing both roles at times, and may see closedness as characterizing desirable performance of both roles at other times. However, if relational dialectics are important relational forces that suggest primary constructs, they should figure prominently in how relational partners conceive the relationship and their performances in it. The constructs they suggest should guide interactional choices as well as individuals' judgments about the competence, appropriateness, or desirability of particular role performances.

Baxter and her colleagues (Baxter, 1988, 1990; Baxter & Simon, 1993) identified a number of communication strategies, or communicative performances, used by partners in close relationships—specifically, romantic or intimate relationships rather than friendships—to manage dialectical tensions. Following O'Keefe and Delia (1982), Baxter (1988) suggested that partners use the general strategies of selection, separation, and integration. However, the strategy of separation appeared to dominate in a study of how dialectics were managed (Baxter & Simon, 1993). Separation involves enhancing each pole of the dialectic, either in alternating cycles or in compartmentalized relational domains. Baxter and Simon further suggested that when a particular pole is dominant in a relationship at a given time, symbolic acts enhancing the other pole will be desirable.

Thus partners in a closedness-dominated moment will respond more favorably to openness-enhancing strategies. Baxter and Simon found mixed support for this contention.

The hypothesis that the dominance of one dialectical pole prompts a desire for actions that enhance the other pole is interesting and intuitively appealing. However, to assume that the dominant pole of the moment alone will make desirable a strategy that enhances the other pole seems to suggest a linear causality that is counter to a conceptualization of relationships as processual. Baxter and Simon's (1993) findings that novelty-enhancing strategies correlated positively (though not significantly) with novelty-dominated moments and that closedness-enhancing strategies were not significantly correlated with openness-dominated moments also argue against assuming that the opposite of a dominant pole is automatically desired. The theoretical framework I propose suggests that individuals' role identities may make one or the other pole of a dialectic more desirable, perhaps continuously. That is, an individual's imagined self in a particular contextualized role may include a strong preference for one pole. For example, if Baxter and Simon's speculation that we have a strong cultural preference for openness is correct, many people's identities—for friend, supervisor, or subordinate—will include a preference for openness that will make openness-enhancing strategies desirable even in openness-dominated moments. This assertion does not deny that at some point closedness will become desirable, even to someone having a general preference for openness.

In sum, the framework being developed here attempts to integrate several theoretical perspectives to explore individuals' and relational partners' joint constructions of (a) the self in the relationship, (b) the relationship, (c) the relational partner, and (d) the communicative choices made in situations. The following exploratory study was conducted to examine (a) the degree to which this framework is useful in explaining the tensions inherent in simultaneously personal and hierarchical relationships, (b) how individuals employ the primary constructs suggested by relational dialectics to understand and manage such relationships, and (c) how these primary constructs surface in participants' communicative actions.

Exploratory Study

I interviewed five people who claimed to be either currently or in the recent past in a relationship that was both personal and hierarchical. All interviewees described friendships, not romantic relationships; four were female dyads and one was a male dyad. Three of the people interviewed had been the supervisor in the dyad, and two had been the subordinate.

After small talk intended to develop rapport with the interviewee, as well as to learn about the context in which she or he worked, I asked each to simply tell me the story of the relationship with the other person, giving as many examples as came to mind to indicate what the relationship was like at each point. Rarely referring to my interview guide, I asked questions to probe for examples, as well as to learn what interviewees thought, felt, and said in various situations they had mentioned.

The transcribed interviews were then interpreted and analyzed to assess the prominent dimensions along which participants construed their relationships, their relational partners, and their relational actions. Their descriptions, evaluations, and explanations of these elements were isolated, and the construct or constructs that appeared dominant for the description were noted.

The dominant constructs for each segment were identified in an iterative fashion. That is, I began with the three bipolar pairs suggested by Baxter's (1988, 1990) dialectical research: connection-autonomy, openness-closedness, and novelty-predictability. I also included two other pairs in this initial guide because they stood out so prominently in the interviews: equality-superiority and privilege-uniformity. When a relationship-relevant description was not characterized by one of these five dimensions, the dominant construct was inferred and added to the list of dimensions. The constructs that were added were considered upon subsequent readings of the interview transcripts to see if they might best capture the dominant dimension on which a participant viewed a relational element. Because this study is exploratory, and because 86% of the interview segments were characterized by one of the five dimensions identified above, the discussion below is limited to these five.

Rather than being clearly distinct issues in the participants' discussion of their relationships, the dimensions often overlapped. Because constructs are regarded as the building blocks for more complex cognitive schemata, this is neither problematic nor surprising. It is also not surprising that participants differed in the emphasis they placed on various dimensions, with ones central to some hardly mentioned by other participants.

Connection-Autonomy

This dialectic entails the physical, psychological, and emotional closeness or connection characteristic of personal relationships as well as the distance, differentiation, or personal autonomy necessary to preserving personal identity. Baxter (1988) argued that this dialectic is so central to relationships that "it can be regarded as the principal contradiction" in close relationships (p. 259). Indeed, in these interviews, autonomy-connection surfaced more often in discussion than did any other dialectic.

The interviewees often mentioned physical closeness, such as working in proximity close to each other or doing things together, in explaining how their relationships began and how they became emotionally close. Rose provided examples of the role of physical closeness in forming her personal relationship: "We were in the trailer over there by the _____ Building and sat in the little bay area, maybe 5 feet away from each other. And . . . we just hit it off. It was instant." This closeness was manifest in being together and spending time together: "We were friends inside work and outside work. Her husband and my husband and I about every weekend went out together."

Several interviewees mentioned that distance emerged after the promotion of one friend to a supervisory position. Speaking of Kate, who was promoted while Debra was on maternity leave, Debra said,

> You know, our families got together and we did it right up until I had [my baby]. She came to see [the baby] when I came home [from the hospital] and pretty much after that, it started stopping. I called, and she couldn't talk to me. Beforehand she could talk all the time.

She went on to describe a nearly complete cessation of socializing with her former best friend. So although it may not have been a conscious strategy to manage the change in the relationship, the participants generally construed their relationships as becoming more distant once hierarchy intruded.

A particular manifestation of the autonomy pole was the differentiation of distinct, and sometimes seemingly incompatible, relationships and roles. That is, the participants clearly saw the duality of their relationships and roles, and struggled with the need to separate friendship from the work relationship, along with the need to see their connection in some holistic fashion. Rose and Sally even named this in their communication, by prefacing their communicative acts:

> What Sally and I would always do is I'd say, "All right, I'm talking to you Sally-friend not Sally-supervisor." Or she'd say, "I'm talking to you Rose-friend." . . . And that kind of meant when we said that, that that was never to come back and haunt us and we understood that with each other.

Differentiating the roles allowed autonomy, or greater freedom of action. That is, Sally legitimized, by the preface "I'm talking to you as Sally-supervisor," certain role performances that might not have been viewed as appropriate actions for "Sally-friend." Similarly, Elaine discussed how keeping roles distinct had enhanced their relationship since she first became T ammy's supervisor: "Sometimes we don't act like friends anymore when we're at work. . . . And then when we're friendship, when we're together outside of work, it's more like we're just friends, and so it's more distinct now than I thought it was before."

Connection-autonomy was thus a prominent dimension for all the participants in constructing and performing their relationships. Connection or closeness was evident in their discussion of being physically close, spending time together, and engaging in activities together. Spending time together and engaging in activities together were seen not only as evidence of connection but also as processes to create and maintain closeness.

Openness-Closedness

This dialectic involves the tension between the need or desire to talk openly to each other and the need to avoid disclosure on some issues at some times. This dialectic surfaced often in participants' comments. For example, Glenda said of her subordinate-friend Janet, "I was always very comfortable with her, as far as being able to confide in her. . . . She'd always be there any time I needed something." And Rose described Sally as maintaining closedness: "Even with me she kept pretty guarded on her personal life." However, the duality of the relationship and roles added some interesting twists to openness and closedness in relationships.

Talk about the supervisor-subordinate relationship when one person first became supervisor was prominent in four of five participants' stories. Rose and Sally, who both applied for the position Sally got, discussed the promotion very openly. Closedness was also evident, particularly in supervisors' need to keep some information confidential. Supervisors differed on how much they chose to disclose. Rose, for example, took great delight in the fact that Sally told her many things "she probably shouldn't have told me." Elaine, on the other hand, told of having to be cautious to avoid disclosing confidential information to her subordinate-friend.

Glenda's description of Janet's actions illustrated the dilemma faced by relational partners in managing this dialectic. The following excerpt suggests that the vulnerability created by being open with friends may be heightened if the friend is also a supervisor or subordinate:

> I was having personal problems, which I did leave out of work. But when I had to, you know, talk to her about some of her performance, late cases and that kind of thing, she would somehow manage to pull in the personal . . . who was doing this and that and just all sorts of things. And she knew I was just at a real bad point and that these little things would just, you know, send me away.

Thus, openness was clearly valued in these close relationships, and prompted a common role performance of openly discussing events and changes surrounding one partner's promotion. Openness was also frequently described by these participants as the source of problems or potential problems in their relationships, suggesting a role performance of avoiding disclosure or at least being cautious regarding what and how much to disclose.

Novelty-Predictability

Predictability and novelty in relationships were not prominent in interview texts. Although each of the interviewees mentioned novelty or predictability at least once, this was usually in response to direct questions about how the relationships had changed.

Rose and Sally shared an understanding that they would ask each other when they went to lunch or breaks. This shows how predictability was manifest in that relationship, and how it was intertwined with connection. Novelty was more often mentioned as a source of stress, as in Debra's description of Kate:

> One minute, she's your best friend. The next minute, you're nothing. She doesn't talk to you. . . . I mean, you've got to feel her

out to find out what kind of mood she's in. . . . I try to be as nice as I can, because I don't know what kind of mood she's in. . . . And it's like, "How are you this morning" type deal and try and feel her out, and I just try.

This is a good example of how a novelty-dominated moment—Kate's erratic behavior—prompted a predictability-enhancing strategy—Debra's "feeling her out"—just as Baxter and Simon (1993) suggested.

Although interviewees suggested that novelty or uncertainty was present in their relationships, and gave indications that predictability was desired, there was no evidence that novelty was sought. It may be that the dual roles and relationships make the novelty pole of this dialectic inherently dominant in these relationships. Thus, participants may have to work constantly to meet predictability needs. This suggests that dialectics may not always emerge in interaction nor be managed in interaction. Rather, in certain types of relationships, one dialectical pole may be a "given," so that partners' efforts may focus only or primarily on the other pole.

Equality-Superiority

Although the autonomy-connection dialectic may be the principal contradiction in personal relationships, the equality-superiority dialectic may be nearly as important in simultaneously personal and hierarchical relationships. The hierarchical structure of most organizations dictates that supervisors are privy to information to which their subordinates are not, are paid more than subordinates, and have other freedoms and benefits not allowed those lower on the organizational ladder. Also, the supervisor typically gives direction to subordinates, evaluates subordinates' performance, and makes and communicates a number of decisions that influence subordinates.

At the same time, in most personal relationships, partners downplay superiority and emphasize equality. As the work of Goffman (1967) and Brown and Levinson (1987) demonstrated,

giving direction, communicating evaluation, and other communicative acts typically performed by supervisors are inherently
"face threatening." As such, they imperil personal relationships.
Thus partners in simultaneously personal and hierarchical relationships often strive to create a sense of equality even as they
attempt to accept and perform their unequal positions.

One respondent, Debra, began looking for a new job as soon
as she heard of her best friend Kate's promotion: "I can't accept
the fact that she's in a supervisory role. . . . We've just been
equal for so long. . . . If I sit there and watch her sign my time
sheet, I feel ill." She also described how Kate acted out this tension: "One day she turned her little supervisor title at me,
. . . and ever since then she's just had this air like she's throwing
her 'supervisor' at everybody. *She* was supervisor, she said."

Equality-superiority was also central in Elaine's construction
of her relationship with Tammy. As a new, first-time supervisor
of a close friend and former coworker, Elaine was clearly uncomfortable with the notion of being "superior" to others. This tension led her to enact a communicative performance in which
she downplayed her supervisor role by giving instruction and
direction as if it were coming from her boss rather than her:

> Usually if I have to ask her to do something, . . . usually it's coming
> from [my boss], that he wants me to tell them to do this or that. I
> really don't ever have the need to tell them to do something
> coming from me. It's just not myself. So they usually know that.

In this example, Elaine used a communicative strategy of external justification. This allowed her to perform her supervisory
role while also honoring friendship norms, by attributing the
face-threatening request to a higher authority. In addition, it
suggests a way subordinates can justify and accept a friend's
enacting superiority, in that it essentially absolves the friend
from responsibility for the act. Alex described an alternative
means of softening the face threat inherent in performing the
supervisor role that involved framing his direction as a sugges-

tion and involving his subordinate-friend Dan in elaborating the direction.

Privilege-Uniformity

It became obvious in talking with the interviewees that the dual roles in these relationships created a significant tension between friends who expected to be "special" because of their friendships, and supervisor-subordinate dyads who expected to be fair and uniform in their treatment of relational partners. Friends want their friends to view them, and treat them, as special. Yet supervisors usually want to avoid charges of favoritism, and subordinates often want to avoid being labeled the "boss's pet." Thus, both ends of this bipolar dimension are sought while being mutually negating. Elaine gave an example of the tension this dialectic created for her: "[Tammy and I] went out to lunch the other day and . . . I always wonder what [the others] think, because . . . I don't want them thinking that [I'm] going to favor that person. . . . But then again, I don't think that you should stop being friends with someone because you're . . . their supervisor."

This dimension was in some cases closely connected to the openness-closedness dialectic, in that relational partners wanted to share information with each other, yet concerns about confidentiality and fairness to others created pressure to avoid disclosure. Rose described how this operated in her relationship with Sally:

> We were real close friends, and so I, probably more than any other staff, knew everything that was going on. Maybe not everything, . . . but she, we still held each other's confidence. I'm sure there were things that happened that she would like to have told me but didn't because of her role.

For Rose, the special treatment from her supervisor-friend was in tension with not abusing the privilege conferred by friendship:

It probably made my job more fun, because I did feel like I was in the know a lot. . . . But I always still, I tried really hard to keep the line there and not cross over it. . . . I tried to be careful about if I needed to be off, asking her rather than saying, I'm leaving at 3:00.

This tension was also evident in Glenda's reflections on evaluating her friend-subordinate:

I didn't treat her, you know, any differently as an employee than I did any of my other staff members. . . . As a matter of fact, I think I was probably a little more lenient with her because of our friendship, you know, than I would have been had someone else had been doing some of the things that she was doing.

The contradiction in Glenda's comment ("I didn't treat her any differently" versus "I was more lenient with her") points to the appeal of both poles of the dialectic and the struggle to satisfy both.

An interesting twist on this dimension was subordinate-friends being singled out for negative treatment by their supervisor-friends. That is, both Rose and Debra described situations in which their supervisor-friends had, in their minds, "picked on" them *because* of their friendship. Rose explained that she and several other employees were complaining about the arrangement of the office, and Sally singled out her for reprimand. "I remember being very surprised that she would come out and kind of publicly scold me for saying, we were all saying it, but it was me that she was saying something to." Similarly, Debra said, "I think [Kate will] get harder on me because, you know, I'm the closest thing. I'm there and she knows me better than she knows them." The privilege-uniformity dialectic seemed a major force in these interviewees' relationships and in the communicative choices they made.

Although simultaneously personal and hierarchical relationships have rarely been systematically investigated, if my own experience and those of the five participants in this pilot study are typical, they are apparently quite common. Several interviewees agreed with Glenda, who said, "Actually, it was pretty common in our office." Yet although these relationships are apparently widespread, they are experienced and managed in diverse ways.

Thus a framework for theorizing and investigating these relationships should identify generalizable dimensions and relational dynamics, and should also promote awareness of the substantial differences in how participants experience and manage such relationships. In order to understand real and important complexities and inconsistencies that are part and parcel of human relationships, the framework presented in this chapter focuses on sense-making and communicative processes and structures, yet the particular content and form such processes and structures take are assumed to vary considerably.

The theoretical framework presented assumes, consistent with constructivism and related social cognitive theories, that humans interpret and plan interaction using cognitive schemata. Cognitive schemata are seen as varying in complexity from constructs, or bipolar dimensions of judgment, to highly complex configurations such as role identities. Dialectics are relational phenomena: That is, they are forces in the relationship rather than cognitive structures within individuals. As significant forces, however, individuals must interpret and grapple with them in managing relationships. Thus dialectics probably prompt individuals to develop schemata for interpreting and planning communication in relationships. Particular types of relationships in a given culture and era, such as simultaneously hierarchical and personal relationships in the late 20th-century United States, are likely to be characterized by similar dialectics; these dialectics should in turn prompt many individuals to develop similar constructs for making sense of and managing the dialectics. Thus, for example, autonomy-connection appears to be a force in the relationships explored in this chapter, and many people in such relationships are likely to develop a construct very similar to this dimension.

The exploratory analysis of five relationships presented here may be seen as preliminary evidence for the viability of the proposed theoretical framework. The interviewees' accounts of their relationships suggested that interviewees employed several primary constructs that reflected dialectical tensions. Some of the dialectics characterizing the relationships have been noted in previous work on close relationships, and some may be unique to simultaneously close and hierarchical relationships. In addition, there was some evidence that relational partners employ these dimensions to interpret relational dynamics and plan their communicative actions.

In particular, these relationships, similar to personal relationships described in previous research, were construed by the interviewees as prominently characterized by the dimensions of autonomy-connection and openness-closedness. Autonomy-connection emerged as the dimension along which the relationships were discussed more frequently than any other dimension. This points to the need to differentiate the dual relationships and roles, thereby enabling freedom of action, while at the same time maintaining closeness or connection to valued friends. Openness-closedness was also prominent in the discussions, which suggests the importance and obtrusiveness of a major issue for people in these dual relationships: the simultaneous desire for open communication with close friends (as well as with supervisors and subordinates) and the difficulties and dangers that such openness creates.

Tension between novelty and predictability was not as prominent in these relationships as were many of the other dialectics, which suggests that it was not a primary construct for these participants. Yet the participants may still struggle with the tensions implied by this dimension: That is, the force of the dialectic may still be operative. It seems more likely, however, that the need for novelty is not nearly as great in these relationships as in some other types of relationships, such as romantic involvements. Alternatively, the ambiguity of two simultaneous and distinct roles may provide an inherent novelty that is sufficient.

Two prominent dimensions in the participants' discussions that appear not to characterize many other types of close relationships were superiority-equality and privilege-uniformity. Because of the unequal formal status and power of the two partners in these relationships, along with the discomfort of this inequality, participants talked extensively about issues characterized by the superiority-equality dimension. And, because of their special relationship with each other, contextualized within a network of other relationships with coworkers and other subordinates, participants struggled to reconcile the need to privilege each other with the need to appear (and be) fair and uniform in their treatment of others in the same role as their relational partners.

The present chapter has implications for constructivism, the conceptualization of relational dialectics, and the study of personal relationships in the workplace. First, constructivism's heuristic value is unquestionably extensive. Delia and colleagues' theory (Applegate, 1990; Burleson, 1987; Delia et al., 1982) has stimulated perhaps more research than any other in the field of communication studies. Furthermore, this research has enjoyed enormous success in supporting some of the major propositions of the theory. The present chapter provides further evidence of the heuristic value of the theory. As Burleson (1987) noted, further research is not needed to establish the link between interpersonal construct system development and person-centered communication. That link has been well established.

What is needed to advance the theory are conceptual and empirical explorations of other aspects of constructivist theory. I have attempted to show how constructivism can fruitfully guide research of a much different character than the typical study of cognitive differentiation and person-centered message production, and how constructivism might be integrated with other theoretical concepts to broaden the range of phenomena it might usefully explain. Both the concept of relational dialectics and the role-identity model augment constructivism to provide a more powerful means of conceptualizing certain social cognitive and communication processes. Dialectical theory suggests particular types of primary constructs likely to characterize individuals' constructions of relationships, and the role-identity model suggests a primary means by which situated constructions influence communicative performance.

This chapter also extends the relational dialectics perspective in three ways. First, finding evidence of the applicability of dialectics to relationship types to which it has not been applied previously increases its purview, and thus its explanatory power. Second, the preliminary finding of additional dialectics operative in simultaneously personal and hierarchical relationships is important. If particular types of relationships are characterized by different dialectics, this seems to buttress the claim that dialectics are relational forces rather than simply qualities of individuals. Third, I have proposed two extensions to dialectical theory: that dialectics are relational forces but may prompt the development of cognitive schemata, and that influences other than the dominant dialectical pole may drive communicative choices in relational interaction. Regarding the first extension, if dialectics are important relational forces, people will have to develop appropriate cognitive structures to make sense of and manage them. This view gives priority to the relational nature of dialectics, but recognizes that relationships are created by and managed by individuals in interaction and that individuals must develop the resources, including cognitive schemata and communicative strategies, to cope with them. The second extension has to do with the ways in which dialectics influence communicative choices. Baxter and Simon (1993) suggested that dominance by one pole of a dialectic prompts the desirability of the other; I have suggested that this general tendency is likely to be moderated by such influences as the individuals' values relative to each pole and perhaps by the extent to which particular contexts furnish or preclude one or the other pole in a dialectic.

Finally, the chapter begins to address a need to explore workplace relationships in ways that conceptualize them as important processes in and of themselves, and not merely as means or hindrances to organizational effectiveness. I have also attempted to create a framework that places importance on the interpretive, processual nature of these relationships rather than viewing them from the static, variable-analytic paradigm characteristic of traditional studies of supervisor-subordinate relationships.

Conclusion

One of the most important processes in organizations, at least from the perspective of organizational actors, is the formation of personal relationships. People create, manage, and terminate relationships with friends, lovers, and spouses at their workplaces, and doing so affects substantially the quality of life at work. Yet rarely has the topic of personal relationships between supervisors and subordinates been the focus of serious research.

In this chapter, I have offered a framework for investigating such relationships and employed this framework to explore how people in such relationships construct and perform them. The results are suggestive of the promise of this framework rather than conclusive. They indicate that an interpretive approach that simultaneously focuses on the ways that relational partners construct and perform their relationships can illuminate many of the major issues that emerge in forming, maintaining, and terminating such relationships.

Note

1. I use the term *coworkers* throughout this chapter to describe individuals who are on the same organizational level. Even though supervisors and subordinates are technically coworkers, for ease of understanding I am excluding them from this designation.

6

Current Trends in Nonmarital Cohabitation: In Search of the POSSLQ

John D. Cunningham

John K. Antill

By now it has become de rigueur for academic discussions of nonmarital heterosexual cohabitation to commence by noting the dramatic and continuing rise in the incidence of this institution over the past generation in Western industrialized nations. This includes (but is by no means limited to) Australia (Bracher & Santow, 1990; Carmichael, 1990; Khoo, 1987) Canada (Beaujot, 1990; Hobart & Grigel, 1992), France (Leridon, 1990a), Hungary (Carlson & Klinger, 1987), the Netherlands (Liefbroer, 1991; Wiersma, 1983), New Zealand (Carmichael, 1984), Sweden (Bernhardt & Hoem, 1985; Trost, 1979), the United Kingdom (Office of Population Census and Surveys, 1987), and the United States (Blumstein & Schwartz, 1983; Bumpass & Sweet, 1989; Thornton, 1988). These trends must not be allowed to obscure the fact that in some regions, particularly Africa (Bledsoe, 1990), Latin America (Fennelly, Kandiah, & Ortiz, 1989), and Sweden (Bradley, 1990), "consensual unions" and other forms of non-church-sanctioned marriage have been common for centuries, particularly among low-income couples. Indeed, the high incidence of heterosexual cohabitation and its increasing social acceptance make it plausible, following Bradley (1990) and Gwartney-Gibbs (1986), to define cohabitation as a societal institution. In order to limit the scope of this chapter, only heterosexual cohabitation will be addressed. Among other differences, gay and lesbian relationships suffer from strong social and legal stigmata that do not now apply to heterosexual cohabitation; these stigmata undoubtedly have vast ramifications for the nature of such relationships. These are large topics that deserve consideration in their own right (see Chapter 4 of this volume).

The popular press and subsequent academic interest began to focus on cohabitation only with the celebrated case of Linda LeClair, a Barnard College, New York, undergraduate, that hit the headlines in 1968 when it was revealed that she was living off campus with her boyfriend of the time. Loud moralistic voices demanded her expulsion from college for breaking in loco parentis rules. A certain amount of journalistic prurience was also betrayed by such headlines as "Linda the Light Housekeeper." Much was made of this apparently new manifestation of libertine excess; much less was made of wiser statements, such as that of anthropologist Margaret Mead (1966), who advocated "marriage in two steps" as an antidote to the divorce rates, which were rising even then.

Serious academic attempts to describe and interpret the cohabitation institution began in the early 1970s and continue today. Early studies focused on what appeared to be primarily a campus phenomenon and drew heavily on this convenient population for their samples. As well, the eagerness with which such studies were undertaken was undermined by their methodological weaknesses. Since that time, however, the methodological and statistical sophistication of empirical studies on cohabitation has risen enormously, and some firm conclusions can be drawn as to the antecedents, concomitants, and consequences of such relationships.

However, the topic is still relatively overlooked by academic researchers on relationships. Consequently understanding of its processes remains limited, and more research is needed. As it is one of the under-studied relationships examined in this volume, the primary purpose of this chapter is to update Newcomb's (1987) fine review of cohabitation research and hence his conclusions. Other useful recent reviews of the cohabitation literature have been produced by Buunk and van Driel (1989) and Macklin (1987, 1988). In particular we shall attempt (a) to record changes in popular attitudes toward cohabitation over the years, (b) to describe the incidence of cohabitation; (c) to identify the characteristics, beliefs, values, and behaviors that distinguish cohabitors from single and married people of a similar age, and—most important—(d) to examine the consequences of cohabitation for marriage and divorce. Along the way we shall identify important oversights in existing knowledge and thereby suggest directions for future work. By way of previewing what is to come, we note that perhaps the greatest gap in current knowledge concerns the actual processes at work in cohabiting arrangements.

As our review demonstrates, we know far more about the demographics and attitudes of those who cohabit than about the ways they weave their lives together, define the meaning of their relationship, and, in general, go about the business of enacting connection. Thus we are quite limited in our ability to focus on the series theme of relational processes, taking *process* to mean, in its simplest form, change over time. For instance, we believe that the study of process demands much more than drawing boxes depicting State 1 and State 2 and merely connecting them with an arrow, a practice that Duck (1990) cogently criticized. We can and shall, however, address processes in our concluding comments.

In order to promote comprehensiveness, an attempt was made to locate all journal articles, books, and book chapters on this topic published since Newcomb's (1987) review. Other than his own 1986 article, the latest reference he cited was published in 1984. Through our own database-assisted search, covering the period from 1985 to August 1993, 73 items were sought and obtained. Our aim is to examine this recent literature in order to confirm or revise the conclusions of earlier reviewers.

To promote comprehensiveness further, we did not exclude any references according to their definition of cohabitation. The U.S. Bureau of the Census uses the cute acronym POSSLQ to designate "Persons of Opposite Sex Sharing Living Quarters" who are otherwise unrelated to each other. Undoubtedly, this net catches an unknown number of people boarding together but not sexually or even romantically involved with each other. In fact, this definitional issue is central to the entire concept of cohabitation. The terms *common-law marriage, trial marriage,* and *de facto marriage* (the latter is particularly popular in Australia) carry a range of assumptions as to the nature of the relationship and the rights of partners that are inappropriate to the majority of cohabitors. For example, the key question in the 1984 Family History Survey conducted by Statistics Canada was, "Have you ever been a partner in a common-law relationship? By this we mean, partners living together as husband and wife without being legally married" (White, 1987, p. 642). In contrast, the Canadian Fertility Survey used, "Have you ever lived with a partner without being married?", a difference that led to a higher reported incidence of the latter in the same country and the same year (White, 1989). The latter is probably the broadest definition ever used in surveys; probably the most specific is that of "sharing a bedroom and/or bed with someone of the opposite sex to whom you are not married, for four or more nights a week, for three or more months" (Macklin, 1974). Even this restrictive definition does not request information on whether the couple are sexually involved, though the context may seem to imply it strongly. Rather than entangle ourselves in definitional thickets, we have, as noted above, elected to embrace all definitions of heterosexual cohabitation.

Attitudes Toward Cohabitation

In line with the rising incidence of cohabitation, attitudes toward this institution have been moving in a favorable direction for at least a generation. Data are not yet available to inform us, however, whether attitude change preceded behavior change or conversely, or whether both attitudes and practices changed in response to external forces, such as the large postwar "baby boom" generation's reaching the age of sexual maturity and survey respondenthood.

In any case, there are now nationwide U.S. and Canadian figures that support Macklin's (1987) conclusion, based on samples collected in the 1970s, that cohabitation is increasingly accepted, particularly by younger people. For example, agreement by first-year college students that "a couple should live together for some time before deciding to get married" rose (though not uniformly) from 45.3% in 1974 to 50.7% in 1989 (Smith, 1990); this figure is somewhat lower for Midwest U.S. college students but higher for London college students (Black & Sprenkle, 1991; Brooks & Kennedy, 1989). Condemnation of cohabitation among final-year high school students—that is, agreement that "a man and a woman who live together without being married are living in a way that could be destructive to society"—declined by half from 1976 to 1988, from 8.4% to 4.3% (Smith, 1990). Such clear change did not occur uniformly across the three other cohabitation beliefs in the Monitoring the Future survey, though students who considered it "a good idea" rose over that period. Younger generations proved more liberal or nontraditional than their elders in Canada (Wu & Balakrishnan, 1992). Beyond this, there was change even in the same individuals over time; mothers, sons, and daughters in the Detroit-based Study of American Families in the same panel (fathers were not surveyed) all became more positive toward cohabitation between 1980 and 1985 (Thornton, 1989). By 1987 more than half of 17- to 23-year-olds originally in the National Survey of Children regarded living together before marriage as making "a lot of sense" (Moore & Stief, 1991). Elsewhere, one third of students from India (presumably a traditional country regarding family life) attending a university in Texas agreed that "I want to live with someone before I marry" (Davis & Singh, 1989). Finally, whether fictitious couples were presented as cohabiting prior to marriage or not had no effect on U.S. undergraduates' predictions of their marital satisfaction (Tucker & O'Grady, 1991).

In Australia cohabitation was viewed more favorably than such "permissive issues" as abortion, censorship, contraception, extended pub hours, gambling, homosexuality, marijuana use, and prostitution even as early as 1975 (Hasleton, 1975), and given the rising tide of Australian cohabitation there is no reason to think that present attitudes would be less favorable.

What factors influence attitudes toward cohabitation? The often negative experience of parental divorce, singlehood, and possible remarriage may make the children of such divorces more skeptical of the benefits of marriage and perhaps more accepting of cohabitation as a prelude or alternative to marriage. In line with this reasoning, a majority of Midwest U.S. undergraduates who had experienced parental divorce wanted to live with their partners before marriage, but a majority of undergraduates whose parents remained married did not wish to cohabit (Black & Sprenkle, 1991). Similarly, Australians between ages 18 and 34 from divorced families were less likely than those from intact families to recognize problems with cohabitation (Amato, 1988); slightly more of the former (85%) than the latter (76%) also agreed that it was "all right to live together without planning marriage."

Perhaps the strongest individual-difference variable predicting both cohabitation experience and cohabitation attitudes is religiosity. In the 1984 Canadian Fertility Survey of women aged 18 to 49, church attendance was the strongest (negative) predictor of favorability toward cohabitation of the nine sociodemographic variables (Wu & Balakrishnan, 1992). However, this was not supported in a study of Canadian tertiary students in 1988, which found that only 3 of the 17 demographic, attitudinal, and experiential variables predicted these attitudes in all three geographical regions: mother's perceived attitude on

sexual permissiveness and number of own sexual partners (positively) and desired number of children (negatively); significant
positive predictors for two of the three regions also included
positive relationship with family, close friends being sexually
experienced, fathers' sexual-permissiveness attitudes, and parental divorce (Hobart & Grigel, 1992). Intriguingly, favorability
of attitudes toward cohabitation correlated positively with
favorability of attitudes toward marriage in Canadian tertiary
students (Hobart, 1993), suggesting that cohabitation and marriage are regarded as quite compatible with each other, rather
than as alternatives.

In conclusion, the substantial work on attitudes that promote
and inhibit cohabitation, though important in informing us
about individual cognitive variables that affect cohabiting, does
not shed much light on how such attitudes surface in interaction between partners and how they shape the unique qualities
of cohabitation as a relationship form. In short, what is lacking
is an understanding of how these attitudes translate into cohabitation processes.

Incidence of Cohabitation

Now that we know that younger cohorts are more favorable
toward cohabitation and that the same individuals are becoming
more favorable toward it over time, how many people have actually been cohabiting? Although the percentages of people currently cohabiting or having cohabited at some time vary across
Western societies, it is abundantly clear that the past generation
has seen a strong rise in their numbers everywhere. In Australia
in 1992, 8% of all couple families were cohabiting (Castles,
1993); this represented a rise from 4.7% in 1982 and 5.7% in
1986 (Carmichael, 1990). This compares with 4% of all U.S. couples in 1981 (Spanier, 1983), 8.3% of all Canadian couples in
1986 (Hobart & Grigel, 1992), and 14% of French couples aged
between 21 and 44 in 1985 (Leridon, 1990a). This proportion
varies greatly by age, with 8% of U.S. couples aged 19 to 29

cohabiting in 1987, compared with less than 1% of couples over age 60 (Bumpass & Sweet, 1989). The one exception in the literature to the youth-and-cohabitation nexus is Hungary, where one third of all female "partners in life" are divorced mothers, and the peak incidence of cohabitation for never-married women was 9.3% for the 45 to 49 age group in 1984 (Carlson & Klinger, 1987); this disproportion of divorced mothers is thought to be due to the special housing and other benefits that they receive but would forfeit if they remarried.

The incidence of current cohabitation masks the fact that many who are not currently cohabiting may have done so in the past. Thus, although 8.7% of Canadians aged 18 to 29 were in "common-law unions" in 1984, 23.4% had at some time been in such unions (Beaujot, 1990). In 1987, about 25% of U.S. people aged 19 or over had ever cohabited (Bumpass & Sweet, 1989); in 1983, 29.6% of never-married women aged 20 to 29 had cohabited at some time (Tanfer, 1987); and in 1985, one third of a Detroit-based sample had cohabited but not married by the age of 23 (Thornton, 1988).

Who Cohabits?

As noted above, age is a prime predictor of who cohabits, with younger people almost universally more likely to cohabit than older people. This is true only if *younger* is defined as those under about age 30; among Canadian tertiary students under age 27 the older students were more likely to have cohabited (Hobart & Grigel, 1992). What other demographic, attitudinal, and personality variables predict a greater likelihood of cohabitation? Opportunity to cohabit is an obvious but important predictor for young Canadians. Those currently living at home were much less likely to have cohabited in the past than those living independently (Hobart & Grigel, 1992); this was also true in the Netherlands (Liefbroer, 1991). It seems, then, that independence from parental influence enables students to practice their pro-cohabitation attitudes. In this Canadian sample, as in most others addressing this issue, the number of sexual partners was positively linked with cohabitation experience. Education is strongly but negatively related to cohabitation in the United States, contradicting the frequent opinion that it typifies tertiary students (Bumpass & Sweet, 1989). As with attitudes toward cohabitation, religiosity (but not religious denomination) predicts cohabitation experience. Both Detroit mothers' and their 18-year-old children's religious participation and ratings of its importance predicted (negatively) the child's cohabitational experience up to the age of 23 (Thornton, Axinn, & Hill, 1992). In turn, cohabitation led to lower levels of religious involvement. Similar results occurred when religiosity measured at age 16 predicted less cohabitation up to the age of 25 (Yamaguchi & Kandel, 1985). No relationship between religiosity and cohabitation was found in Canadian tertiary students (Hobart & Grigel, 1992), but in Canadian women aged 18 to 49, cohabitation strongly correlated with religiosity in the predicted direction (Balakrishnan & Chen, 1990).

In line with attitudes toward cohabitation, the experience of parental divorce increases the probability that the child will cohabit at maturity. Though null conclusions on this issue were drawn from earlier work comparing cohabitors with noncohabitors (Macklin, 1987), cohabitors are more likely than similar married couples to have parents who divorced, to regard their parents' marriage as unhappy, and to have poorer relationships with their parents (Cunningham & Antill, 1994; Newcomb, 1986b; Tanfer, 1987; Wiersma, 1983). Those who experienced parental divorce or widowhood as children were much more likely to cohabit than those from intact families (Thornton, 1991). Parental remarriage also accelerated the child's transition to cohabitation or marriage, for young women more than young men. As well, in about half of currently cohabiting couples one or both partners are separated or divorced (Buunk & van Driel, 1989).

As for personality and attitudinal variables, 18-year-old Los Angeles men who were low in congeniality, law abidance, orderliness, and religious commitment were more likely to cohabit

during the ensuing 4 years; women who were low in deliberate-
ness, diligence, law abidance, objectivity, religious commitment, and self-acceptance, but high in liberalism, were also
more likely to cohabit, when compared with others of their respective genders (Newcomb, 1987). Consumption of cigarettes,
alcohol, and illicit drugs at 18 also predicted cohabitation. Marijuana use at age 16 predicted the incidence of cohabitation over
the ensuing 9 years (Yamaguchi & Kandel, 1985). Indeed, lifetime prevalence of cocaine use by cohabitors was over three
times that of noncohabitors (Trinkoff, Ritter, & Anthony, 1990).
Replicating earlier findings, cohabitors had had their first sexual intercourse earlier, and had had sex with more partners,
than noncohabitors and, not surprisingly, were more favorable
toward cohabitation and premarital sexual intercourse and
less favorable toward marriage than noncohabiting couples
(Cunningham & Antill, 1994). From these and similar findings,
it is tempting to conclude that cohabitors have fewer internalized constraints on their behavior than those who do not cohabit (see Newcomb, 1981). However, despite earlier and greater
sexual experience for cohabitors generally, there were no differences between Montreal cohabitors and marrieds in the frequency of coitus when age and length of relationship were held
constant (Samson, Levy, Dupras, & Tessier, 1991).

A disturbing phenomenon that has been neglected in previous
cohabitation reviews is that of higher violence in cohabiting
couples than other types of couples (West, in press). On self-
reports of "conflict tactics," student cohabitors were less likely
to report (for themselves and their partners) using reasoning
and more likely to report using verbal aggression or violence
than noncohabitors were, but the differences were not statisti-
cally significant (Billingham & Sack, 1987). Cohabitors had a
higher rate of assault than dating and married couples, even after controls for age, education, and occupational status were included (Stets & Straus, 1989). Children were more likely to suffer sexual abuse from their mother's cohabiting partners than
from noncustodial fathers, but less likely than from their natural
fathers in intact families (Faller, 1989). In five reviewed studies,

cohabiting women reported from 1.5 to 2 times greater abuse than married women (Ellis & Dekeseredy, 1989); the authors interpreted this finding in terms of the high dependency, high availability, and low deterrence experienced by cohabiting men. Ellis (1989) argued provocatively that compared with married men, cohabiting men have low investment in the relationship, strong conflict between their high rates of unemployment and their patriarchal values, greater rates of previous marital breakdown (often involving violence) and normlessness—all of which may predispose them to violence.

Another problem in cohabitation concerns the mental health of children in such families. Compared with those whose mothers had remarried, were not involved with a new partner, or were seriously involved but not cohabiting, Philadelphia children whose divorcing mothers were living with a new partner had substantially higher behavior problem scores and lower social competence, suggesting greater maladjustment (Isaacs & Leon, 1988); older children were also affected more than younger children. Given that 27% of cohabiting couples have children from a previous relationship present (Bumpass, Castro Martin, & Sweet, 1991), this indicates a problem of great importance.

Relationship Quality

As for the quality of the relationship, cohabiting couples have lower relationship satisfaction than married, gay, and lesbian couples in some studies (Kurdek & Schmitt, 1986b), but no differences were found in others (Cunningham & Antill, 1994; Yelsma, 1986). American married couples who had cohabited beforehand reported less frequent activities with their spouse, greater amount and severity of conflict, slightly poorer communication, and lower perceived stability (Booth & Johnson, 1988; Thomson & Colella, 1992), but this was not confirmed in Australian couples (Cunningham & Antill, 1994). Cohabitors' satisfaction, job prestige, and androgyny scores correlated more highly with their partner's than in married, gay, or lesbian couples, indicating higher homogamy in cohabiting couples (Kurdek & Schmitt, 1987).

Cohabitors scored lower on the Rubin love and romanticism scales than married couples, especially those who did not cohabit premaritally (Cunningham & Antill, 1994); they also had lower Rubin love scores than married, gay, or lesbian couples (Kurdek & Schmitt, 1986b). The latter study also found that cohabitors perceived the fewest barriers of all four couple types, suggesting that they would have rather little difficulty in leaving the relationship. Once cohabiting couples did marry, no differences in marital satisfaction or happiness were found between those American, Australian, and Israeli couples who had or had not cohabited premaritally (Booth & Johnson, 1988; Crohan & Veroff, 1989; Cunningham & Antill, 1994; Shachar, 1991; Thomson & Colella, 1992), though black and first-marriage American couples who did not cohabit were more happy or satisfied than those who did (Crohan & Veroff, 1989; DeMaris, 1984).

Beyond the stark findings of significant or nonsignificant differences in happiness or satisfaction between cohabitors and other types of couples, little attention has been directed at the processes underlying these levels of happiness or satisfaction. For example, some cohabitors may be quite happy with the quality of their daily interaction with their partner but quite unhappy that their relationship is not progressing toward marriage. How these considerations translate into overall satisfaction with the relationship is anyone's guess.

Childbearing

Marital childbearing has declined sharply over the past generation in Western nations, particularly Europe, while constraints against nonmarital childbearing have faded. Hence a greater proportion of children are born out of wedlock in almost all Western nations than ever before. Does this mean that children are commonly born in cohabiting relationships?

The short answer is no, but with the notable exception of Sweden, where about half a sample of 111 cohabiting couples had had one or more children with each other (Lewin, 1982). In contrast, though 36% of Australian cohabiting couples had dependent children in 1992 (Castles, 1993), only 18% of 152 Australian cohabiting couples in 1982 had at least one child from their relationship (Khoo, 1988); in the United States the comparable percentage was 12% (Bumpass, Sweet, & Cherlin, 1991). Never-married U.S. women who cohabit tend not to have children. When age, race, number of children, and education were controlled for, the odds of practicing contraception were four times higher among never-married cohabitors than among currently married women (Bachrach, 1987). Few expected a birth within the next 5 years; this is consistent with previous research. However, cohabiting women were 2 to 5 times more likely to become pregnant than noncohabiting unmarried women (Yamaguchi & Kandel, 1987). In France the sharp rise in nonmarital childbearing since 1978 is due to both a rise in the childbearing of cohabiting couples (though still lower than in married couples) and the rising proportion of such couples in the population (Leridon, 1990a). How do cohabiting couples who have children in their relationship differ from those who do not? Australian cohabiting couples with "ex-nuptial" children were economically disadvantaged, with lower levels of education and income and higher levels of male unemployment than married couples with children and cohabiting couples with stepchildren only (Khoo, 1988). We know little about the reasons why some couples choose to have children while cohabiting and others wait until marriage.

Cohabitation and Marriage

No consideration of cohabitation can ignore its relevance to marriage. In Oregon, marriages preceded by cohabitation with the future spouse rose from 13% to 53% between 1970 and 1980 (Gwartney-Gibbs, 1986). Of most recent or only Australian marriages the proportion preceded by cohabitation rose from 15% to 57% between 1975 and 1991 (Castles, 1993); if this trend were extrapolated linearly (as only the rash would do), all Australian marriages would be preceded by cohabitation by the year 2007.

As noted earlier, laypeople and researchers have found it difficult to discuss cohabitation without likening it to marriage, whether as common-law, de facto, informal, "paperless," or trial marriage. There are obvious ways in which they are similar— among other things, the coresidence of a male and female with (usually) a sexual relationship. The similarity immediately falters, however, when we examine the motives that people have for living together. Rarely do they define their relationship as some type of marriage (except for New York City Puerto Rican women; Landale & Fennelly, 1992). A large majority of them expect to marry someone in their lifetime, but not necessarily their current partner. The desire for children is a prime motive for marriage; in contrast, Western cohabitors rarely expect to have children without marrying, except in Sweden. Although 40% of U.S. cohabiting households include children, they are mainly from previous relationships (Bumpass et al., 1991). Cohabitations also differ from marriages in their transience: The median length of U.S. cohabitations is estimated at 1.3 years, ending in eventual marriage for 59% of them (Bumpass & Sweet, 1989; see also Sarantakos, 1991, for longitudinal Australian figures).

Beginning in the late 1960s, optimists argued that cohabitation afforded partners the opportunity to live under marriage-like conditions and therefore to decide whether their potential marriage was likely to succeed, separating before the wedding if the partners regarded the risk as too high (Mead, 1966). Hence they predicted that marriages preceded by cohabitation would experience a lower rate of divorce than those not preceded by cohabitation. In support of this general argument, 95% of cohabitors who married and 80% of current cohabitors agreed that cohabitation prepared them for marriage (Kotkin, 1985). Unfortunately for this scenario, evidence in favor of it is sparse, but evidence for a higher rate of divorce among premarital co-habitors is large and growing. To anticipate our later conclusion, it seems that those people likely to cohabit are also the people more likely to divorce—this has become known as the selectivity or unconventionality hypothesis—but there are many qualifications to this, as noted below.

Important recent advances in investigating this idea include the drawing of large, representative national samples of individuals in Canada, France, Sweden, and the United States, the gathering of thorough sexual, cohabitational, and marital histories from them, and the consequent application of complex multivariate statistics, including logistic regression (logit/probit models) and hazard models. Logistic regression has enabled investigators to consider the covariation of many variables in predicting the odds that an individual or couple will cohabit, marry, or divorce. Hazard models, which are essentially multivariate life tables, are superior to logistic regression in that they are based on rates, not probabilities (Trussell & Rao, 1989). However, large longitudinal panel studies remain scarce, due to their high costs and high rates of attrition. This is the method of choice. Examples include the National Longitudinal Study of the High School Class of 1972 (Teachman, Thomas, & Paasch, 1991) and the Survey of American Families (Thornton, 1988).

To begin with, what is the overall higher rate of divorce that can be attributed to premarital cohabitation? Cohabitors who then married have from 46% to 144% greater likelihood of eventual divorce in Canada (Balakrishnan, Rao, Lapierre-Adamcyk, & Krotki, 1989; Halli & Zimmer, 1991), New Zealand (Ferguson, Horwood, & Shannon, 1984), Sweden (Bennett, Blanc, & Bloom, 1988), and the United States (Bumpass et al., 1991; DeMaris & Rao, 1992; Newcomb, 1986a). One exception to this finding was the Canadian study by White (1987), but Trussell and Rao (1989) demonstrated that White had inappropriately defined marital duration and that the correct model showed the usual increased rate of divorce for cohabitors; White (1989) concurred with this reanalysis. Also, a quasi-exception to this finding was found by Kurdek (1991b), who reported that husbands who had lived with their wives only briefly before marriage, if at all, showed rising levels of marital distress over the 3 years of the study.

At least six qualifications can be posed regarding the universality of this empirical generalization.

1. Regardless of empirical findings, it remains plausible to argue that without cohabitation, during which undoubtedly many potential poor-risk marriages dissolved before the wedding, the overall rate of divorce might have been even higher. Bumpass and Sweet (1989) argued that part of the plateau in U.S. divorce rates since 1980 may be due to the screening function of cohabitation. That is, we simply cannot know, in the theoretical absence of the cohabitation option, how much higher the divorce rate might have been. We know that those who divorce are also those more favorably disposed to cohabitation; even if by some means they had been prevented from cohabiting, they were likely to have divorced following an unhappy marriage. Stated differently, the breakup of an unhappy cohabitation prevents the unhappy marriage that might end in divorce.

2. Teachman and Polonko (1990) suggested that rather than count time since marriage as the beginning of couples' "union," time since the start of cohabitation should be used for premarital cohabitors, because they had a longer time than premarital noncohabitors within which to terminate their relationship. Once total length of union was accounted for, there was no difference in marital disruption between cohabitors and noncohabitors. However, using the same sample, Teachman et al. (1991) failed to replicate this result, which was most likely due to different model specifications; using different samples, Booth and Johnson (1988) and DeMaris and Rao (1992) also failed to replicate the finding. Teachman et al. concluded that cohabitations that become marriages do not attain the stability of direct marriages. Equally, however, the marriages of premarital cohabitors last longer than cohabitations do.

3. The longer cohabitors live together before marriage, the less successful their marriage will be (Bennett et al., 1988; Teachman & Polonko, 1990; Thomson & Colella, 1992). For example, Swedish women who cohabited for more than 3 years had 54% more marriage breakups than those who cohabited for less time. Perhaps cohabitation represented more of an alternative to marriage for the former and a prelude to marriage for the latter, or the former may have had more doubts about their partner or the institution of marriage all along.

4. Canadian premarital cohabitors dissolve their marriages at more than twice the rate of premarital noncohabitors up to the fifth year of marriage, but the latter then have higher rates of dissolution than the former (Halli & Zimmer, 1991); similar findings hold true in Sweden and the United States (Bennett et al., 1988; Schoen, 1992).

5. Serial cohabitors—those couples in which one or both partners had cohabited with someone other than the spouse—reported higher marital instability, compared with single-instance cohabitors and premarital noncohabitors (DeMaris & MacDonald, 1993). Serial-cohabiting men (but not women) are more likely to experience marital disruption (Bennett et al., 1988; Teachman & Polonko, 1990). This practice may make the individual more likely to dissolve a later relationship, whether it is cohabitation or marriage. Note, however, that marrying a previously married individual raises the probability of marital dissolution for both sexes. Thus it seems that the more cohabitations and/or marriages an individual has experienced, the more likely it is that his or her subsequent cohabitation or marriage will terminate.

6. In recent cohorts, in which cohabitation is more frequent, the differential in marriage dissolution rates between premarital cohabitors and noncohabitors has been declining and has even reversed slightly (Schoen, 1992). The fact that premarital cohabitation is now a majority practice in many Western nations is likely to have weakened any individual differences in beliefs and behavior that may have accounted for this differential.

Given that cohabitation increases the risk of marital dissolution overall, how can we account for this fact? Booth and Johnson (1988) proposed three general models of the way in which cohabitation might diminish marital quality. No support was found for the accelerated-marriage model, which posits that marriages "actually" begin when cohabitors move in together, and thus that the documented decline in marital quality over the years begins at that point rather than with the wedding. No data were available to test the argument that cohabitation causes a decline in marital quality. However, some cohabitors were poor marriage risks before they married, in terms of a higher incidence of drug problems, inability to handle money, trouble with the law, unemployment, and personality problems reported for self or partner. This lent support to the selectivity or unconventionality hypothesis—that those likely to cohabit differ from those who do not in ways that predispose them to eventual divorce.

Other evidence for the selectivity argument includes the fact that wives who had cohabited expressed more individualistic views of marriage than others (Thomson & Colella, 1992). Cohabitation led to more individualistic attitudes and values (Waite, Goldscheider, & Witsberger, 1986) and to increasing acceptance of divorce when attitudes were measured twice over 5 years (Axinn & Thornton, 1991). The latter study also found that cohabitation was selective of those who were initially less committed to marriage and more accepting of divorce, indicating reciprocal causality. That is, those who are favorable toward divorce are more likely to cohabit than others, and those who cohabit become more favorable toward divorce over time.

However, contrary to the selectivity argument, when *unconventionality* was defined as acceptance of eight nontraditional family beliefs, it had only a minimal impact on the cohabitation effect (DeMaris & MacDonald, 1993). It must be remembered, however, that the Axinn and Thornton (1991) study, supportive of selectivity, was based on a longitudinal panel—the method of choice—and that the Thomson and Colella (1992) and DeMaris and MacDonald (1993) studies were based on the same cross-sectional sample, with unknown changes in respondents' attitudes prior to the survey. Thus the selectivity or unconventionality hypothesis remains quite plausible, perhaps as regards personality and behavior rather than beliefs; see the previous section "Who Cohabits?" as to how unconventional cohabitors are. At the same time, as increasing normativeness robs cohabitors of their distinctiveness from the rest of the population, we expect that the difference between cohabitors and noncohabitors in terms of their former's unconventionality will fade; glimpses of this process in operation have been seen above in Schoen's (1992) results.

The neglect of research on cohabitation processes is also evident as regards this issue. How and why does living in a cohabiting relationship change people's ideas about the importance of marriage or about the nature of commitment in marriage? We do not yet know.

The End of Marriage?

The past generation has witnessed, in addition to cohabitation, a plethora of demographic changes that have occurred with enormous speed. Though the details may vary across different Western nations, these changes include (a) a rise in the incidence of premarital sexual intercourse, (b) a rise in age at first marriage, (c) a dramatic decline in marriage rates and total and age-specific childbearing (despite a rise in nonmarital childbearing), (d) a rise in the divorce rate, (e) a decline in the remarriage rate, and (f) a strong increase in the number of single-person households. In turn, the rise in premarital intercourse coupled with the steep decline in childbearing would not have been possible without the technological innovation of effective oral contraception from the early 1960s and secondarily the relaxation of legal prohibitions against abortion. In cohabitation the separation of sex from childbearing reduces the likelihood of nonmarital childbearing. As we have seen, despite frequent childbearing within cohabitation in continental Europe, North Americans and Australians generally postpone the arrival of children until after marriage.

Some observers have taken the rise in the age at first marriage and the decline in the rates of both first and later marriages as an indication that the institution of marriage is slowly disappearing. However, if cohabitation is regarded as a form of first union that is as valid as marriage, then much of the decline in first marriages is due to the rise in cohabitation. Indeed, by age 26 the first union for two thirds of a Dutch sample was cohabitation rather than marriage (Liefbroer, 1991); by age 23.5 the first union for one half of U.S. women and two thirds of men was cohabitation (Thornton, 1988); similar figures were found in Canada (Rao, 1990) and France (Leridon, 1990b). Young people are forming first unions at almost as early an age as they did before marriage rates declined (Bumpass et al., 1991). Cohabitation is by far the preferred type of second union in Sweden and Norway, largely contributing to the decline or delay in remarriage among the divorced; few women remarried without cohabiting first (Blanc, 1987).

In conclusion, it is evident that except for single-person households the demographic changes listed above are closely associated with cohabitation. By no means, however, is marriage going out of fashion; it is merely occupying less of the average adult's lifetime.

Concluding Observations

It appears, then, that the conclusions of earlier reviewers have substantially been supported by recent research. The most notable change over recent years has been the strong rise in large-sample demographic analyses rather than a continuation of the smaller but in-depth interview or questionnaire studies popular before 1985. As psychologists we were disappointed to discover so few recent writings on psychological or even social psychological processes in cohabitation. Beyond articles authored or coauthored by Lawrence Kurdek and a minor article by Tucker and O'Grady (1991), no articles on cohabitation have been published in journals that have *psychology* in their titles since Newcomb's (1987) review. This is despite Macklin's (1988) insightful psychosocial analysis of the complexities of dynamics and decision making within cohabiting couples. In contrast, as we have seen, recent methodological and statistical improvements have enabled demographers to untangle the relative rates of singlehood, cohabitation, marriage, and divorce in several Western countries and the effects of each on the others. We have learned much from them in the past decade.

We contend that the key psychological concept in the nexus between cohabitation and marriage is commitment, a woefully neglected concept in this context. Uneasiness about a lifetime commitment to the present partner or to the institution of marriage arises continually in surveys of cohabitors. Women's uneasiness about the institution of marriage now often stems from their awareness that it is still one of the major sites of gender inequality. Cohabiting women's feminist views (Cunningham & Antill, 1994) make them wary about the power of traditional marital roles to subvert their behavior, if not beliefs. The wish to protect their own and their children's interests while avoiding the often patriarchal assumptions of family law that sur-round marriage leads many to draw up cohabitation contracts that are legally enforceable (Hughston & Hughston, 1989; Kingdom, 1990).

Personal commitment is also a central social psychological concept, particularly in the attitude-change literature (Kiesler, 1971). To date, few theoretical frameworks have been devel-oped that explicitly incorporate commitment to a particular partner into the courtship → cohabitation → marriage sequence (for an exception, see Johnson, 1973). Drawing on Kelley's (1983) distinction between love and commitment, Lund (1985) made a promising beginning in this direction by demonstrating that investments in a relationship predicted commitment 4 months later, even when Time-1 love and commitment were par-tialed out. She interpreted this finding as support for a barrier model that regards commitment as "an attitude about continu-ing a relationship that is strengthened by a person's own acts of investing time, effort and resources in that relationship" (1985, p. 4). Evidence for this barrier model was much stronger than for a positive-pull model in which rewards and attitudes such as love predict relationship continuity. In this context Kurdek and Schmitt's (1986b) finding that cohabitors perceived fewer bar-riers to dissolution than married, gay, or lesbian relationships is intriguing. Though Lund's study involved a range of couples from daters to marrieds and did not separate cohabitors from others, it is tempting to speculate that cohabitors' lesser com-mitment to their partners, reviewed earlier, may stem from their lesser investments in the relationship.

Further theoretical and empirical development of the commit-ment concept in relation to cohabitation is necessary. For exam-ple, building on Lund's (1985) work, we need to find out whether cohabitors invest as many resources in their relation-ship as those who choose engagement or marriage. That is, do those couples who invest more in their relationships progress to greater commitment or do so more quickly than those who are reluctant to make such investments? Does cohabitation rep-resent a "holding pattern" for those who, for whatever reasons, are hesitant to make further investments or commitments to their relationship by, for example, marrying? Such hesitation may be more typical of some people than others. That is, due to the seminal work of Hazan and Shaver (1987), early child-parent attachment patterns have been implicated as relevant to intimate adult relationships. The three typical infant reactions to the "strange situation," namely, secure, avoidant, and anxious/ ambivalent attachment (Ainsworth, Blehar, Waters, & Wall, 1978), have also been identified as operating in adult relationships. In adults the avoidant attachment style is characterized by emotional extremes, jealousy, and fear of closeness and intimacy (Hazan & Shaver, 1987). Avoidant people tend to give priority to their own well-being and appear not to feel the same depth of love as either secure or anxious/ambivalent people (Shaver & Hazan, 1988). A straightforward prediction would argue that long-term cohabitors comprise disproportionately high numbers of avoidant individuals, as compared with those cohabitors who marry or those who marry without previous cohabitation. Indeed, as noted above, Cunningham and Antill (1994) found that the Rubin love scores of cohabitors were lower than those of daters or marrieds.

As another example of the relevance of commitment to cohabitation, it is clear that personal commitment to a partner must be separated from commitment to marriage as an institution; the two are likely to be independent of each other. Misunderstandings between cohabiting partners may easily arise through a confusion between these two meanings of commitment. That is, cohabitors may be reluctant to believe that their partner's hesitation about marriage is due to the partner's uneasiness about the institution of marriage rather than uneasiness about them as a potential spouse. After all, a rating of 50% in response to a question about the present likelihood of marriage may have vastly different meanings depending on the belief system of the rater. In general, the vast majority of cohabitors wish to marry someone, if not their partner, at some time in the future, but in certain groups, such as the previously married, this proportion is much lower.

Commitment to a particular partner is closely related to the concept of trust. Regardless of endless promises before the wedding about an egalitarian division of labor, it may be a rude surprise to many wives (and husbands)—both those who have and those who have not cohabited beforehand—to discover that their spouse's behavior has changed radically. Some believe that cohabitation before marriage can provide a simulacrum of marriage so that roles acceptable to both partners can be sorted out, and the assumptions of each partner can be put to the test. Thus cohabitors need not take predictions of future behavior so much on trust; they can see their partners in action in a marriage-like context and decide whether a potential marriage to that individual has promise.

Future psychological research on cohabitation must therefore pay close attention to the process of how cohabitors build trust in one another and grow in their commitment to one another. Whether a commitment to remain partnered to someone over the longer term and the trust that is closely implicated in that commitment is translated into marriage depends, of course, on the commitment of each partner to the institution of marriage. That too may change over time, possibly with each feeling so committed to each other on a personal level that each becomes more positive toward marriage as an institution. Newcomb's (1987) concepts of independence and relatedness are also essential; relatedness may be simply another way of construing commitment and trust. Each of these concepts—independence, relatedness, commitment to the institution of marriage, commitment to the particular partner, and trust—must be measured over time in order to predict the perceived likelihood of each cohabitor's marrying his or her partner, and with what consequences after the wedding. Such investigations may also provide us with an understanding of not only how people with certain predispositions approach the choice of different types of relationships, but also how the experience of having been in different types of relationships for varying lengths of time influences individuals' cognitive schemata about relationships (see Volume 1 of this series in this regard). As indicated earlier, we know that cohabitation makes people more positive towards cohabitation (Thornton, 1988), but we know little else about the changes that cohabitation creates in individuals or couples.

Good research on these issues—with or without samples of cohabiting couples—remains woefully lacking. In cohabitation, as elsewhere, process is the most important but also the most difficult phenomenon to study.

On the practice side, an important intervention would be the early identification and prevention of violence in cohabiting couples. We have seen how much aggression occurs in such couples, and ways must be found to intercede as early as possible in families so affected. In general, domestic violence has been ignored by the public at large for far too long. Due to the high levels of emotion involved and consequent violence, even police are apprehensive about intervening in "domestics." That is, police may be reluctant to make themselves the targets of possible violence, in part because of the lingering patriarchal belief that men have a right to "discipline" their partners; in this context see West (in press). Schoolteachers, social workers, and other helping professionals in frequent contact with the public should be especially alert to events occurring in cohabiting-couple families that may precipitate such violence (e.g., unemployment). Equally, it is clear that many stepchildren in cohabiting families are suffering from behavioral problems and low social competence (see Isaacs & Leon, 1988). Early identification of such children and appropriate intervention are essential for the sake of both the children and adults involved with them.

Cohabitation before marriage, and instead of marriage for those previously married, has become institutionalized throughout the Western industrialized world. It is impossible to imagine that this practice will dwindle away in the foreseeable future. It is therefore incumbent on those who profess a dedication to improving human welfare to discover ways in which to assist cohabiting couples in decision making about their future. Though the probability that any cohabiting relationship will lead to marriage is lower than the de facto title suggests, most cohabitors expect to marry someone eventually, so the most obvious avenue for such intervention is through marriage preparation courses. Issues surrounding commitment to one's partner and to the institution of marriage are obvious foci for such courses. It is essential to encourage couples to recognize that they can define a modus operandi within cohabitation or marriage that explicitly recognizes their respective but varying needs for commitment. They must be helped to understand that marriage need not carry an automatic set of patriarchal or other assumptions about the "proper" roles of husband and wife or father and mother, but rather that they can clarify for themselves what they want and need from their relationship, whether married or not, across the entire range of issues from the division of household tasks to sexual fidelity. The degree of desired independence and relatedness is central to these discussions (Newcomb, 1987). Once again, as elsewhere, communication is the key; the partners must have the courage to address these difficult and emotion-laden issues squarely, for the longer term benefit of both of them. Of course, this optimistic scenario is limited by the existence of powerful but subtle societal pressures toward conformity with gender stereotypes and cognitive schemata about heterosexual relationships and marriage that adults have internalized almost unconsciously during socialization.

Unfortunately, a large proportion of marriage preparation courses are conducted under the auspices of religious organizations and churches; as we saw earlier, cohabitors are notable in their rejection of religious observance. On the other hand, a study of 526 participants in Catholic marriage preparation courses in Minneapolis found that about half were currently cohabiting (Lally & Maddock, 1994), suggesting that religious proscriptions against cohabitation are not deterring many religious couples. However, given their ambivalence about or weak commitment to marriage to their present partner, many cohabitors would be reluctant to participate in marriage preparation courses if they were defined as such.

As we have seen, cohabitation is becoming the norm for young people in the Western world. This chronic trend away from "deviance" is likely to affect the nature and consequences of cohabitation in ways that currently we can only dimly foresee. It behooves social scientists and the helping professions, therefore, to continue to monitor this institution and those participating in it in order to improve our understanding and the long-term well-being of cohabitors and their dependents.

7

"Doesn't Anybody Stay in One Place Anymore?" An Exploration of the Under-Studied Phenomenon of Long-Distance Relationships

Mary E. Rohlfing

Studies on propinquity have long shown a positive relationship between geographic proximity and the development of friendly and romantic bonds (Bossard, 1932; Deutsch & Collins, 1958; Kennedy, 1943; Maisonneuve, Palmade, & Fourment, 1952). This research demonstrates that relationships are most often initiated by those who live geographically near one another because the more separated persons are, the more difficult it is for them to communicate with each other, thus the less likely they are to try. Less understood, though, is how relationships are carried on and maintained at a distance. Though it is obvious that persons cannot begin relationships until some force brings them into contact, we know little about the factors that serve to geographically separate those who were at one time proximal lovers and/or friends and who wish

173

to maintain their relationships, or how intimacy and closeness are maintained when partners are separated by time and space.

Although the U.S. Bureau of the Census (1992) claimed that geographic mobility is declining in the 1990s when compared to the 1980s, their figures show that nevertheless some 41.4 million Americans changed residences between March 1990 and March 1991. Though most stayed within the same municipality, county, or state, 14 million U.S. residents made an interstate move during that year. When the impact of geographic mobility is considered not only on the mover, but also on the network that he or she leaves behind, it is clear that relationship disruption due to geographic separation affects many more than just the 14 million Americans who move each year. Indeed, a study by Guldner and Swenson (1995) found that 70% of the college students they sampled had been in at least one long-distance romantic relationship (LDRR), and that at the time of the survey some 25% were currently so involved. My own studies (Rohlfing, 1990; Rohlfing & Healey, 1991) on long-distance friendship (LDF) indicate that these types of partnerships are even more common, with close to 90% of those sampled reporting that they had at least one "close" LDF.

Although the frequency of LDRRs and LDFs alone makes them a viable topic of study, even more important, such relationships should be studied for the challenges they pose to many of our taken-for-granted theoretical assumptions about the conditions under which interpersonal relationships are developed and maintained. Not only do these relationships force us to reconsider social exchange theories asserting that people terminate relationships that are difficult to maintain (Homans, 1961; Lloyd, Cate, & Henton, 1984; Thibaut & Kelley, 1959), they also suggest the importance of reexamining theories that focus solely on the behaviors or communicative strategies of relational partners. For these reasons and others, long-distance relationships have the potential to provide relationship researchers with a theoretically rich area of study.

This chapter explores long-distance romantic and friend relationships. Admittedly, to mix the two is unusual. After all, social scientists have long known that there are compelling theoretical and empirical reasons for keeping discussions of these relationships quite separate (Simmel, 1950). To date, though, no review of the long-distance relationship literature has been written; thus this rule is broken for what seem to be other good reasons. First, geographic separation is a relationship phenomenon that affects both romances and friendships, although not identically. Second, geographical relationship separation appears to be fairly common, and as such it is useful to gather what is known about these relationships to signal further directions for scholars interested in extending our knowledge of these relationships. Third, the impact of geographic separation on interpersonal relationships, regardless of whether they are romantic or platonic, has been sorely under-studied. This chapter, then, not only begins to rectify these concerns by reviewing the existing research on geographically separated relationships, but also may serve to map fruitful directions for future endeavors.

The chapter is divided into four sections. The first focuses on what defines geographically separated relationships. The second explores the impact of geographic separation on romantic relationships. The third section examines recent research on the processes at work in friendships of women who are geographically separated—an area of study that thus far has attracted little scholarly interest. The final section suggests possible directions for future research on both LDRRs and LDFs.

Defining Geographically Separated Relationships

Those who have studied geographically separated relationships have not always agreed on how best to operationally define them. For example, in recruiting premarried LDRRs, Guldner and Swenson's (1995) only criterion was that participants agreed with the statement "My partner lives far enough away from me that it would be difficult or impossible for me to see him or her every day."

In an analysis of the needs, coping strategies, and outcomes of those in LDRRs, however, Holt and Stone (1988) compared lovers residing at different distances from one another, and those who had face-to-face contact with different frequency. Participants were placed in particular geographical distance categories according to whether they lived (a) 0 to 1 miles apart, (b) 2 to 249 miles apart, or (c) more than 250 miles apart. The categories for visitation frequency consisted of those who (a) saw their lover more than once a week, (b) visited once a week to once a month, and (c) reunited less than once a month. Holt and Stone noted that these categories were arbitrarily selected and recommended that future researchers develop other typologies, such as Hillerbrand, Holt, and Cochran's (1986) tripartite classification of college student LDRRs.

Hillerbrand et al's (1986) categories of LDRRs include (a) those in which a student is newly separated from a high school romantic partner, (b) those in which one or both partners are graduating from college and are apart, and (c) those in which one or both partners are nontraditional students returning to college. As Holt and Stone (1988) pointed out, "These groups will tend to differ in both the age of the persons and the nature of the original relationship" (p. 141).

In two studies focusing on distal friendships, LDFs were defined as those in which friends have lived a minimum of 150 miles apart for 2 years or more, and who visit one another no more frequently than once a month (Rohlfing, 1990; Rohlfing & Healey, 1991).

To date, the variety of definitions for long-distance relationships has not been debilitating. In fact, the current dearth of studies on them makes almost any research on these relationships enlightening. Although complete agreement on how to define LDRRs and LDFs is probably neither necessary nor even wise, it may be useful to arrive at a consensus about the parameters of these relationships in the interests of deriving more meaningful research findings and creating theoretical statements regarding LDRRs and LDFs.

As we develop definitions of LDRRs, the criteria for operationalizing these relationships will necessarily differ from those defining LDFs; for just as romantic relationships differ from friendships, so, too, are these relationships distinct when they occur across geographic distances. For example, although friends may successfully sustain a distal relationship with visits occurring as infrequently as once every 3 to 5 years, with mediated communication (letters and telephoning) occurring as seldom as once annually (Rohlfing, 1990; Rohlfing & Healey, 1991), it is unlikely that such limited contact will sustain long-distance lovers. Indeed, romantic relationships are partially differentiated from platonic ones by virtue of the fact that they include behaviors necessitating physical proximity (fondling, caressing, kissing, and making love), whereas friendships do not. Further, it does not appear that the anticipation of living near one another again in the future is necessary for LDFs to endure, yet such expectations may be crucial to the maintenance of LDRRs. Whereas some lovers may be willing to separate only because they anticipate their separation to be temporary, those in LDFs rarely consider the potential for again living near one another to be a significant factor in their decisions to maintain LDFs (Rohlfing & Healey, 1991).

These expected differences, however, are at this time only speculative because no studies of LDRRs have yet explored possible relationships between the reasons lovers geographically separate and the anticipated length of such separations, and such factors as relationship satisfaction, commitment, coping strategies, and maintenance processes. It seems reasonable to expect, for example, that the coping strategies adopted by lovers separated for 2 months and the meanings attributed to those strategies would differ from those of a couple who anticipate a 2-year separation with only infrequent opportunities to visit during that time. Future studies should begin to ferret out some of these issues.

The establishment of some general operational parameters for what constitute LDRRs and LDFs, then, are necessary not only to provide insight into how LDFs and LDRRs differ but also to show how types of LDF and LDRR relationships vary.

Long-Distance Romantic Relationships

The Problems of Geographical Separation

In response to student demand, in the late 1970s Iowa State University's student YWCA and counseling service offered a series of workshops for those involved in LDRRs. Examining the outcomes of the program, Westefeld and Liddell (1982) posited that the workshops' popularity reflected the increase in premarried and married partners who believe it is possible and even desirable to separate in order to further individual education or career goals. One reason that the number of LDRRs is increasing may be the success of the feminist movement in decreasing the perception that women who pursue goals and aspirations independent of their male lovers and spouses are deviant. As the number of women attending college and attaining jobs requiring mobility increases, it is likely that so, too, will the prevalence of LDRRs.

In evaluating the workshops, Westefeld and Liddell found that LDRR partners face several difficulties and considerations that are particular to LDRRs. First, these relationships cost money to maintain. For those who are in college or living on a limited income, the cost of frequent telephoning and travel makes engaging in these activities as often as LDRR partners might like economically prohibitive. Another difficulty discussed by workshop participants is the problem of defining and negotiating their "in-town" relationships. Although those in LDRRs perceive their LDRRs to be intimate and close, many report that those in their proximal networks do not necessarily acknowledge or affirm this when their spouses or lovers are absent.

Third, LDRR couples report that they must be hyperconscious of how they spend time together when they reunite. As Gross

(1980) noted, those in LDRRs often have higher expectations about the quality of time spent with their partners than do those in close proximity relationships. When visits do not live up to expectations, partners in LDRRS often report feeling a degree of disappointment and stress about their relationships. A related problem discussed by those in LDRRs was the difficulty of assessing their relationships from a distance. Finally, Westefeld and Liddell found that those in LDRRs reported experiencing a more extreme range of emotions regarding their relationships than they did when they lived closer to their partners. Workshop participants noted that they commonly felt extreme happiness and anxiety about their relationships—sometimes within one 24-hour period.

Other researchers have identified additional factors particular to LDRRs. In a study of commuter marriages, Gross (1980) found that couples missed the luxury of daily discussions of "trivial" matters with their spouses. One husband, reflecting on what he found most difficult about being apart from his wife, said, "The lack of interpersonal communication—that sharing of little things that happened since you last talked to her, but after twenty-four hours, they're more trivial than they were to start with. There was a loss of that facet in our relationship" (p. 71). In a similar study, Gertsel and Gross (1984) reported that many in their sample noted that because so much of their discussion time took place on the telephone, they had no visual cues to gauge how their partners felt about particular topics.

Regarding the paradoxical blessings and curses of geographical separation, Gross (1980) reported that many of the married couples she interviewed felt that being apart allowed them time to concentrate on their jobs, school work, or other tasks; alternatively, when they did not get focused, they felt they were "wasting" time.

Gross's work is interesting, for it not only focuses on the problems associated with geographic separation, but also points to possible benefits of these relationships. Subsequent studies should examine other advantages that those in LDRRs derive from time spent living apart. Surely the success and prevalence of many LDRRs warrants a closer look at the perceived rewards of being apart to pursue independent goals, not just at the time of separation but also at the point when it is no longer necessary for lovers to live apart. Currently, we know little about how couples look back on and assess their separations in light of their present living situations. It would be useful to know whether lovers envision the time they spent apart as ultimately proving beneficial or detrimental to their individual and relational goals.

Satisfaction, Intimacy, and Commitment

Given the peculiar difficulties that those in LDRRs face, several researchers have sought to determine whether these relationships are less satisfying and intimate than proximal romances (Gertsel & Gross, 1982, 1984; Govaerts & Dixon, 1988; Guldner & Swenson, 1994; Holt & Stone, 1988; Shanor, 1987; Winfield, 1987) and whether relationship commitment is affected by geographic separation (Baxter & Bullis, 1986). In general, Guldner and Swenson (1995) stated that "these studies demonstrate the potential for maintaining . . . intimate, . . . satisfying [and committed] relationship[s] while separated" (p. 9).

Yet not all researchers concur. In a longitudinal study of geographically separated and proximal marriages, Rindfuss and Stephen (1990) found that spouses who were geographically separated at the beginning of the study were more likely than those who had been together to be divorced after 3 years. Critiquing this study, however, Guldner and Swenson (1994) noted that many of the geographically separated couples in the Rindfuss and Stephen sample were in the military, a group that has a higher divorce rate than the civilian population. They also pointed out that Rindfuss and Stephen's methodology did not allow for a precise analysis of the effects of distance, time spent separated, or preseparation factors. They speculated that if Rindfuss and Stephen's findings were compared to those failing "to find deficits in relationship outcomes or relationship qualities for geographically separated couples, . . . long-term detrimental effects of separation (if they exist) [might lie not] in the difficulties surrounding reunion [but] in the separation itself" (p. 21).

Thus although the limited numbers of studies that have investigated relationship satisfaction in LDRRs show that generally, at least, these relationships appear to be as satisfying and intimate as proximal ones, Gertsel and Gross (1982) and Holt and Stone's (1988) studies suggest that satisfaction and distance may interact in such a way that when geographical distance between partners and the infrequency of visits increases, relationship satisfaction decreases.

Although Govaerts and Dixon (1988) found no direct negative correlation between geographic separation and relationship satisfaction, they did find that those in commuter marriages derived less satisfaction from affectional communication than proximal married couples. Clearly, though, in enduring LDRRs, affectional needs must be at least partially met; thus future research should examine whether other relational processes, perhaps ones unique to these relationships, fulfill affectional needs for those in LDRRs. To date, most studies have relied almost solely on self-reports of the perceived effects of separation on relationship satisfaction, commitment, and affectional needs in LDRRs. If we are to have more precise analysis of the effects of distance, visitation frequency, and various other factors involved in LDRRs, it will be imperative to identify those processes that lead to particular psychological effects for partners in these relationships.

The Coping Strategies of Long-Distance Lovers

In a study that did explore some of the processes employed by those coping with geographical separation, Holt and Stone (1988) found partial support for the hypothesis that satisfaction is affected by one's "preference for visual or verbal response modes of cognitive processing" (p. 137) in LDRRs. Specifically, they noted that frequent visits had "a helpful effect on satisfaction for visualizers" (p. 139). They also discovered that those who lived between 2 to 249 miles apart and who visited less than once a month were the least satisfied group in their sample. They argued, then, that visiting at least once a month helps those in LDRRs cope with being apart, regardless of the amount of geographic distance between them, and regardless of one's tendency to prefer daydreaming about lovers or actually talking to them. As Holt and Stone noted, however, their study evaluated only two coping strategies: frequency of visits, and daydreaming (visualizing).

From their discussion with participants in workshops at Iowa State University, Westefeld and Liddell (1982) derived nine coping strategies that college students said they used in dealing with LDRRs. They are (a) recognizing that LDRRs are a widespread phenomenon; (b) developing additional and new support systems while separated; (c) developing creative ways to communicate (sending gifts, videotapes, and cassettes); (d) preparing for the separation by discussing relationship ground rules concerning going out with friends, telephoning, writing, and visiting; (e) using reunion time "wisely" by dealing with affectional and other needs, but also scheduling time for "fun"; (f) maintaining interpersonal "honesty"; (g) engaging in "open" communication; (h) developing and maintaining trust; and (i) focusing on the positive aspects of long-term separation.

Although these coping strategies have a certain intuitive appeal, it must be noted that Westefeld and Liddell's report is more anecdotal than empirical. Although the authors discussed the primary problems that participants in their workshop for college students in LDRRs reported, and the "solutions" they devised for dealing with them, the actual effects and success of these strategies for those coping with LDRRs have not been investigated. Further, Westefeld and Liddell did not specify either the frequency or the conditions under which these strategies are used. The inherent appeal of these strategies does, nonetheless, suggest directions for researchers who wish to learn more about how those in LDRRs deal with geographical separation.

In sum, research indicates that LDRRs are common and that there is little, if any, decrease in relationship satisfaction, intimacy, and commitment as long as lovers are able to reunite with some frequency (approximately once a month). In addition to visitation frequency, nine other strategies have been noted that may help some partners in LDRRs cope with their separation. Clearly, however, the most common processes that facilitate and militate against successful maintenance of LDRRs still need to be studied, for we know little about the individual psychological differences that may make geographical separation tolerable for some and intolerable for others. Finally, we also need to learn whether certain coping strategies are more effective than others and whether these strategies interact with geographical distance between lovers, the reasons lovers separate, and the length of time they spend apart. These considerations and others suggest that much work remains to be done on LDRRs.

Long-Distance Friendships

Although the available research on LDRRs is scant, even less attention has been paid to the phenomenon of LDFs. Perhaps due to the dearth of research on these relationships, Allan (1979) concluded that "in general, long-distance friendships are comparatively rare" (p. 65). Two studies indicate, however, that LDFs are far from uncommon; rather it is the investigation of them that is rare (Rohlfing, 1990; Rohlfing & Healey, 1991). Focusing on women's friendships exclusively, Rubin (1985), too, found that "many people maintain long-distance friendships, even best friendships, that are vital and alive—relationships that are kept . . . through regular contact by phone, letter, and intermittent visits" (p. 177). Although Allan's dismissal of LDFs is perhaps, then, overstated, it does appear that in some populations, at least, LDFs are more prevalent than in others. For example, Willmott (1987) found that geographic separation and the success of maintaining LDFs appear to be partially mitigated by the availability of economic resources to reinforce and sustain these bonds. Those with more money, he found, had more LDFs than people of a lower income status.

The Effects of Geographic
Separation on Friendships

Studying the factors that dissolve friendships during the transition from high school to college, Rose (1984) found geographic separation to be the factor most often associated with relationship disintegration. Similarly, a report of a reader survey (*N* = 40,000) published in *Psychology Today* (Parlee, 1979) indicated that regardless of their age, geographic separation was the most frequent reason readers cited for the dissolution of their friendship bonds.

Rose (1984) also discovered that in addition to being detrimental to friendships during the transition from high school to college, geographic separation was more devastating to men's friendships than women's. She concluded that "continuing friendships without . . . environmentally imposed contact . . . requires a cognitive shift to a concept of 'friend' in which . . . physical presence . . . is not necessary for the continuation of emotional bonds" (p. 276). She suggested that men's inability to maintain distal friends may be due a lack of awareness about and skills to utilize effective strategies that maintain "a stable level of emotional involvement without daily contact" (p. 276).

An explanation for the more debilitating impact of physical separation on men's friendships is found in the research findings suggesting that men's same-sex friendships are often based on activity sharing and situational-specific interests (Swain, 1989; Wood & Inman, 1993), rather than on the transituational intimate and emotional bonding that appears to be more prevalent among female friends (Aries & Johnson, 1983; Aukett, Richie, & Mill, 1988; Booth & Hess, 1974; Caldwell & Peplau, 1982; Eichenbaum & Orbach, 1988).

As Traynowicz (1986) pointed out, a mutual indication of the "availability of self as a subject to other beyond that called for by the context" (p. 197) is critical to the development and maintenance of intimate relationships. Thus, if the activities engaged in by friends are not unique or relationship specific, we can imagine that there is likely to be little perceived exigency to commit to the task of maintaining an LDF. LDFs may be more prevalent between women than men, then, because it more difficult to replace a friend who knows the intimate details of one's life and whom one has long depended on as a confidante than one who provides only companionship.

The Toll of Mobility on
Individuals and Friendships

Reisman (1970) wrote that the "transitory character of love of friends is a modern phenomenon" (p. 60) brought about by high mobility. "People who come and go," he said, "entertain the hope that their moves will increase" the number of their friendships (p. 83). However, studies investigating the consequences of mobility on interpersonal communication indicate that highly mobile individuals have fewer friendships and experience greater levels of anomie (Hunt & Butler, 1972; Parks, 1977).

The type of intimacy that is established only in dyadic relationships built on trust and time appears, then, to be lacking in many frequent movers' lives, despite the hope that increased access to people should also increase the number of friends that one has (Reisman, 1970). Indeed, it appears that when people are geographically separated from their friends, temporarily at least, they lack the sense of psychological well-being and emotional integration and stability (Duck, 1991) that is derived from being embedded in a well-established network of friendly relations (Parks, 1977).

What the Research Tells Us
About Long-Distance Friendships

Although research indicates that geographic separation is the most frequent cause of friendship dissolution, mobility seems to be more detrimental to some than to others. Specifically, the fewer economic resources friends have, the less likely it is that their distal bonds will endure. In addition, men's friendships appear to be potentially more negatively affected by geographic separation than women's. However, Rose's (1984) findings demonstrate that when bonds are based on activities requiring face-to-face contact, they are more likely to erode due to separation than are those predicated on emotional sharing, regardless of the sex of friends.

Although studies on anomie demonstrate a positive relationship between frequent mobility and the experience of estrangement and alienation, exactly why this is so has yet to be determined. Clearly, a variety of factors must be examined, such as the financial resources of frequent movers and the network of friends they leave behind, the type of communication that frequently mobile persons engage in with distal and proximal friends, and the strength of their friendship bonds prior to moving.

To date, few studies have attempted to discover how prevalent LDFs are. My own preliminary research indicates that out of nearly 250 people thus far surveyed, close to 200 claim they are presently maintaining at least one "close" LDF. An examination of the results from two other studies sheds light on processes by which women's LDFs are maintained and some of the reasons that these bonds are cultivated as well.

Women's Long-Distance Friendships

Because women's same-sex friendships tend to be based more on intimate and emotional discussions than men's same-sex friendships, Rose (1984) suggested that women may find it easier than men to make the transition from deriving relational pleasure from day-to-day contact to instead gleaning satisfaction from a history of emotional sharing. She also implied that the ability to make this shift may be an acquired skill. For these reasons, interviews were conducted with women over 25 years old. In all, four friendship pairs, or eight women, were interviewed.

In conducting these studies, I hoped to learn whether there are common communication patterns in women's LDFs and whether these patterns contribute to the vitality of their bonds. Further, I sought to determine if and how communication between such friends changes as a result of geographic and temporal separation. Finally, I wanted to know why women maintained these relationships despite the difficulties of doing so.

Patterns of Maintenance in Women's LDFs

The primary channel of communication used by these LDFs was the telephone. The frequency of calls between them ranged from once a month to once a year, but all reported that they wished they could call more frequently. The reasons they do not are the cost of calling and the lack of time available to spend on the phone.

Although all the women reported that they were generally satisfied with the quality of their telephone conversations, all expressed frustration regarding the level of intimacy that could be achieved through this medium. They also felt that the majority of their conversational time was spent "catching up" on changes concerning families, activities, and careers. These topics, it seems, were addressed at the expense of what one called "intimate self-disclosure about daily events." Another put it this way: "I know what she's doing, but I don't know how she feels about it."

Surprisingly, few of these friends exchanged letters and cards with any frequency. All of them said that when they did they enjoyed doing so, but almost all of them indicated that writing took too much time. Three women also expressed impatience with the amount of time it takes for letters and cards to be delivered. As one participant said, "When I want to talk to my friends, I want to talk to them now. I don't want to wait around for their written response."

Visits, like letter writing, were also infrequent among these friends; few of them saw each other more than once a year. Indeed, it was not uncommon for several years to lapse between visits. Although Jackie and Chris (friends for 33 years), had seen each other approximately five times during the 28 years they had lived apart, both remarked that it was now fortunate that Chris's daughters were attending college in the region of the country where Jackie lived, making it possible for the two of them to visit when Chris went to see them at school.

Interestingly, very few of the visits between these LDFs were planned solely for the sake of reuniting. Generally, these friends saw each other because there was some other reason to be in the area where their friend resided. When asked why this was so, none felt that she had enough money or time to travel only to visit her friend. All expressed dissatisfaction with the infrequency with which they were able to see one another.

When these friends did visit, they said that it was rare to spend time alone with one another, and that they missed doing so. Indeed, several mentioned that visits left them feeling "empty" because their time was divided between other commitments that had allowed them to reunite but did not allow them time to be alone to discuss issues of importance to them. One woman said, "We used to talk about our husbands and marriages, but now when we see each other our husbands are always around!" Another recalled a time when her family and her friend's family had gotten together for a skiing weekend. She spoke with relief that she and her friend were able to "send everyone to the mountain and ski while we stayed in the cabin all day drinking coffee and talking."

Impact on Conversational Topics

It was expected that because LDFs' conversations were now so dramatically truncated, topics discussed frequently when they lived near one another no longer would be. This assumption was accurate. For example, current events, movies, and books were no longer frequent topics of discussion, but when these friends lived closer to each other, these topics made up much of the daily "small talk" between them.

Although participants did not indicate a decline in the frequency with which they addressed personal issues per conversation (i.e., marriages, children, life plans, and goals), they did perceive a decline in the satisfaction derived from those discussions. Several reported that their conversations felt less "intimate" than they had once been. Interestingly, however, this was not reflected quantitatively in terms of the frequency with which they discussed seemingly intimate topics. It appears, then, that although the intimate details of each other's lives were still discussed, the infrequency of such conversations decreased the satisfaction derived from these discussions.

Gouldner and Strong (1987) noted that in contrast to lovers, friends report having greater difficulty explicitly discussing their relationships. They say that friends often feel uncomfortable telling each other how much they mean to them because the language for doing so seems better suited to describing romantic relationships than friendships. I was curious to learn whether geographic separation made it easier for these women to talk about their bonds, and wondered if doing so might actually be crucial to maintaining LDFs.

All of the participants said that they now frequently discuss the importance of their friendships and find doing so easier, whereas before being separated they did not. Several noted that although they do not often utter such explicit statements as "You mean a lot to me, I'm glad we're friends," they do tell each other that they are happy to still be "in touch" or that their bond is "still so strong." One woman said, "I never told her I loved her when I lived there, but I always do now." Thus it appears that discussions of the feelings each has for the other are one way that LDFs reaffirm the importance of their bond.

Change and Continuity:
Keeping the Tie That Binds

LDFs in these samples were ones predominantly based on mutual respect and a great deal of acceptance for the changes in each other's lives. Despite the miles that separate them, each seems to provide the other with a sense of history and relational continuity that is not endangered by the infrequency of day-to-day communication.

For example, when Jackie was asked to what she attributes her 33-year friendship with Chris, she replied, "We have a continuing respect for each other. I think she's done a lot of good things." When asked what her friend does, and if she works, Jackie said, "No, she has never worked, but she volunteers a lot, that's her work. She's had a busy and rewarding life." Chris's respect for Jackie is reciprocal. Chris noted that she is "proud" to have Jackie's friendship. "That's something that comes from age and time. I didn't know I was proud to have her as a friend in high school."

A respect for change also appears to be important to the longevity of LDFs. In each interview, participants spoke fondly of the growth they had seen their friends go through. For example, Sandy noted that when her relationships with Barbara began, she had viewed Barbara as a "role model" rather than as a "real friend." Eight years later, after talking each other through divorces, raising their children, and realizing individual life goals, Sandy reports that she now sees Barbara as a "peer." When Barbara spoke of Sandy, she seemed aware of the growth that Sandy had undergone, noting, "I used to intimidate the shit out of her, but not anymore. She can roll right over me if she wants to. Sandy's gotten tougher, and I respect that."

Liz and Rosanne spoke not so much about the changes in each other or their relationship, but instead about the continuity of their bond. Rosanne said that in her last visit with Liz she felt they had been able to "pick up" where they had "left off. . . . We are able to get right to the important stuff. We just don't cover as much of it now." When asked why she thought this was so, she replied, "It comes from openness and a sense of history."

Relationship history was also discussed by Tricia, not merely as the preservation of the past but as part of the foundation upon which her own sense of self is derived. Discussing who she had been when she and Miki met and lived near each other, Tricia said, "It's not who I am anymore, but it is who I was, and that's part of who I am."

In describing their friends, these women used such terms as *warm, nurturing, spontaneous, open, fun, solid, supportive,* and *admirable*. Barbara said of Sandy, "I love her like a sister. I feel the same way about her as I do my sisters, but I choose to feel this way about Sandy." Liz said of Rosanne, "We have a deep love and companionship. It's like a bonding of souls." About Jackie, Chris remarked, "The two words that I would use to describe our friendship are *enduring* and *promising*. We've come a long way and I expect it to flourish in the future."

Summary of the Research on
Women's Long-Distance Friendships

Women's LDFs do not demonstrate a consistent pattern of communication frequency. LDFs rarely exchange letters or cards, but rely on occasional telephone calls to keep in touch. These calls, though, may occur as frequently as once a month to only once a year, with no clear relationship between a sense of loss in relational intimacy and the frequency of those calls. All of these friends consider their LDFs to be significant relationships in their lives. All lament the lack of time they have to spend together and the constraining economic forces that do not permit them to visit and telephone and visit as frequently as they would like.

These women appear aware of one another's individual life changes and seem to value and honor them. They know they are not the same people they were when their friendships began, but seem comfortable with the changes they have endured in their relationships and as individuals. Although these women report satisfaction regarding these developments, they also note that it is the constancy and stability of their LDFs that makes these relationships gratifying.

The limited research on women's LDFs indicates that these are relationships built on an extensive history of shared emotions and intimate conversations. Although telephone conversations (the primary means of communicating in this sample) do not provide the level of intimacy that they would like, these women expressed a feeling of continued comfort in sharing the personal details of each other's lives. Interestingly, despite a sense of decreased satisfaction derived from doing so, it is the sharing of personal information that appears to be one of the most valued features of these bonds. Clearly, the phenomenon of LDFs is one ripe with research potential.

Future Directions in Studying Long-Distance Relationships

Currently, little is known about the effects of geographical separation on relationships generally, or how separation influences different subtypes of LDRRs and LDFs specifically. Although most of the research treats LDRRs as equal, it is reasonable to expect that geographical separation is experienced and managed differently by married and nonmarried partners and different subtypes within these more global relationship forms.

There are certain cultural expectations about how marriages are conducted. For example, although the number of geographically separated marriages may be increasing and thus becoming more acceptable, maintaining a marriage at a distance is still uncommon. We can expect that those in geographically separated marriages face different challenges than geographically separated nonmarried couples due to the cultural expectation that married partners should live together and perhaps sacrifice individual goals for the sake of the relationship.

Research also suggests (Hillerbrand et al., 1986; Holt & Stone, 1988) that there is wisdom in differentiating subtypes of LDRRs along other dimensions besides marriage. These studies note that relationship satisfaction and intimacy seem to be affected by the amount of time lovers spend apart and the distance between them. My own studies focused on enduring LDFs. It is not yet known whether satisfaction, intimacy, and other factors are experienced differently at different points in individual relational life cycles. Preliminary analysis of a longitudinal study on LDFs, however, indicates that some of those in LDFs experience a slight decrease in satisfaction and intimacy during the early stages of geographical separation, but that as these relationships endure, satisfaction and intimacy begin to increase or to stabilize at an acceptable level. Thus it may be useful to differentiate the psychological effects of separation and the accompanying processes of relationship maintenance at various phases within the temporal length of separation. But length of separation and geographical distance are only two ways to distinguish subtypes of long-distance relationships. The reasons that lovers and friends separate provide another way to categorize these bonds. No doubt the most useful way to differentiate such relationships will ultimately depend on the interests of particular investigators. Still, we need to better grasp some of the possible ways that these relationships can be classified so that effects of separation and the ways that distal partners manage their separation may be compared.

We need also to know more about the plans that persons in these relationships have to reunite, for it is feasible that distal lovers whose geographical separation lasts for a year or less will conduct and experience their relationships differently than those who anticipate separation for longer periods of time. Further research on these relationships, then, should begin to account for some of these factors in LDRRs and LDFs.

Another area of study on distal relations that should be investigated dovetails with the need to differentiate LDRR and LDF subtypes. Though studies indicate that satisfaction, intimacy, and commitment are generally not decreased in LDRRs, we know little about the levels of satisfaction, intimacy, or commitment of these partners *before* they were geographically separated; thus in many ways we are still merely guessing that geographical separation has no detrimental effects. In order to remedy this dilemma it will be useful for investigators to undertake longitudinal studies on these relationships to determine and dissect specific effects of distance on relationships across the relationship life cycle.

Further, we need to know more about *how* long-distance relationships are actually accomplished. Although point-in-time interviews and questionnaires give us some idea of the ways that people maintain relationships when they are geographically separated, such methods obscure important details of how social relationships are conducted. Studies that focus on how relational partners actually think, feel, and act about and with one another are needed to understand particular relationship stresses and various means by which couples handle these events processually.

Past research on the conditions of men's friendships seems to predict that men are less successful at maintaining LDFs, but we do not know how accurate this prediction is. Studies on the prevalence, factors, and processes of men's LDFs, then, would be useful. Such research would also contribute to understanding how gender is constructed in different relationships and allow us to see whether certain communication patterns are more prevalent in successful and failed LDFs and whether this varies with the sex of friends. Further, though the friendship literature expresses little confidence in males' abilities to maintain LDFs, clearly men in LDRRs are able to maintain those relationships. We need to know, then, whether the factors that contribute to some men's success in maintaining LDRRs can be extended to their LDFs.

At the current time, we know little about the variety of coping strategies that distal partners use and the effectiveness of those strategies. To date, only the frequency of visitations has been seriously studied. Clearly, distal lovers and friends use other strategies as well. Future research should focus more on those strategies and their effectiveness in the successful maintenance of LDFs and LDRRs. It would be helpful also to know if certain strategies are more effective at different points in the separation duration cycle.

Finally, we need to be more theoretically astute in our research on LDFs and LDRRs. If we are to better understand the variety of human bonds, including those carried out at a distance, we will need to consider ways that these relationships support and challenge existing social scientific theories. In doing so, we may need, too, to enter new research frontiers.

Changes in communication technologies are making it cheaper and easier for some to maintain relationships from afar. Videophones, for example, may help to alleviate some of what many in distal relations miss most, the opportunity to check verbal cues against visual ones during conversations. Further, as more people gain access to computer networks, the expense of staying in touch should decrease.

In addition, because individuals can send and respond to electronic "mail" when it is individually convenient, it is likely that this form of communication will be somewhat less constraining than the telephone.

These technologies, though, are by no means accessible to all. Further examination of the economic conditions that facilitate and prevent communication and their effect on the maintenance of certain bonds among particular groups of people would be useful.

An area of study undertaken by Couch (1986, 1987) and his associates (Couch & Hintz, 1975) may provide a rich theoretical framework for those interested in the study of both LDRRs and LDFs. Drawing from Simmel (1950) and Mead (1934), these scholars have concentrated extensively on how variations in shared pasts and expectations for the future shape the ongoing interactions that configure different relationship forms. Research on how dyadic negotiations are conducted by those who anticipate an extensive shared relational future as compared to those who expect to be mutually implicated in a relationship for only a short time, for example, may be useful for understanding how individuals construe and respond to relationship stresses and cope with disagreements and decisions when they are geographically separated. These are some of the questions that researchers might pursue in order to understand better how friends and lovers conduct and maintain relationships at a distance.

Conclusion

The current dearth of research on long-distance relationships presents investigators with a number of exciting challenges. This chapter has presented but a glimpse of what we know and what lies ahead for those who choose to study the effects of distance on relationships, and how those in distal relationships cope with and manage geographic separation. In understanding more about how relationships are affected by distance, we can learn more about the reciprocal influences between dyads and the environments in which they are embedded. Further, we can better appreciate the various phases and processes that dyadic relationships go through during their life cycles in a variety of conditions.

Often, people are forced to relocate through no choice of their own. Wars, economic instability, incarceration, family problems, marriages, births, deaths, and numerous other forces sometimes make it necessary for people to pack their belongings and move away from stable and supportive networks of family and friends. In studying relationships that are maintained despite geographical separation, we may learn more about the important generic principles of communication, psychology, and sociology in constructing social bonds and the importance of such bonds to the well-being of individuals and society.

8

Love at First Byte?
Building Personal Relationships
Over Computer Networks

Martin Lea

Russell Spears

Who are you my love? You are so numerous, so divided, all compartmented, even when you are there, entirely present and I speak to you. (Derrida, 1987, p. 193).

Joan . . . was a New York neuropsychologist in her late twenties, who had been severely disfigured in a car accident that was the fault of a drunken driver. The accident had killed her boyfriend. Joan herself spent a year in the hospital, being treated for brain damage, which affected both her speech and her ability to walk. Mute, confined to a wheelchair, and frequently suffering intense back and leg pain, [she] had at first been so embittered about her disabilities that she didn't want to live. [Then she was given] a

AUTHORS' NOTE: The authors are grateful to the editors and to Tom Postmes and Joe Walther for their insightful comments on a previous draft.

computer, modem and a subscription to CompuServe [a public computer network] to be used specifically to make friends on-line. . . . Joan could type—which is after all how one talks on a computer—and she had a sassy, bright, generous personality that blossomed in a medium where physicality doesn't count. Joan became enormously popular. . . . Over the next two years, she became a monumental on-line presence who served both as a support for other disabled women and as an inspiring stereotype-smasher to the able-bodied. Through her many intense friendships and (in some cases) her on-line romances, she changed the lives of dozens of women.

Thus it was a huge shock when, through a complicated series of events, Joan was revealed as being not disabled at all. More to the point, Joan, in fact, was not a woman. She was really a man we'll call Alex—a prominent New York psychiatrist in his early fifties engaged in a bizarre, all-consuming experiment to see what it felt like to be female, and to experience the intimacy of female friendship. (Van Gelder, 1985, pp. 94, 99)

Our discussion of personal relationships and computer networks focuses on three issues of central concern in this volume. The first issue concerns how relationship research currently privileges certain types of relationships while neglecting others. We describe relationships that have been observed in this new medium and identify a number of assumptions and biases underlying much social psychological theorizing that are common to both relationship research and media analyses. These proclivities foreshadow the conclusion that attraction and relationship development are primarily dependent upon face-to-face interaction. The second issue is about the need for theoretical extensions to cover these under-studied relationships. Here, however, we argue that the study of on-line relationships throws up various challenges that are not easily met by the addition of some simple contingencies to current social psychological models of relationship processes. We outline a model of situated social interaction that aims to recognize the constructionist dimensions of self, relationships, and technology, and give them a concrete social psychological grounding. By focusing on the social context for the development of "electronic relationships,"

rather than on interpersonal communication, we aim to under-
line the importance of viewing all personal relationships as socially situated. This approach has implications also for an issue
that underpins all of the volumes in the present series, namely
the central role of competence in relationships. Here we argue
that on-line communities provide a vivid illustration of how
competence in manipulating technical artifacts is also implicated in the essentially social process of constructing personal
relationships.

We begin, however, with a caveat. A comprehensive analysis
of personal relationships in computer-mediated communication (CMC) is presently limited by the paucity of available data.
Systematic studies of social interaction in CMC that focus on
personal relationships are few and far between. Experimental
studies of CMC that tend to concentrate on interaction within
groups have accumulated steadily and now form sufficient critical mass for meta-analysis (e.g., McLeod, 1992; Postmes &
Spears, 1993; Walther, Anderson, & Park, 1994). Although some
investigations conducted outside of the experimental laboratory report on uses of organizational CMC for social and recreational purposes (e.g., Finholt & Sproull, 1990; Ord, 1989), most
have focused on interactions and role relations within work-
related communication contexts (e.g., Fulk & Steinfield, 1990;
Zuboff, 1988). A more promising source of data is studies of the
voluntary use of bulletin boards by discussion groups that provide information about the group context of CMC as well as
occasional descriptions of individual relationship experiences
(e.g., Ogan, 1993; Smith & Balka, 1988; Wilkins, 1991). In addition, a small but significant corpus of anecdotal reports of
personal experiences of individual network participants has accumulated in the popular and specialist computer press. These
are interesting for the parallels and contrasts with normal social
relations that they highlight (e.g., Lewis, 1994; Van Gelder,
1985). Further data are found in a number of commentaries that
combine technical descriptions of computer-based communication networks and systems with (often speculative) conclusions
about their effects, but nevertheless contain some interesting

accounts of their social uses (e.g., Chesebro & Bonsall, 1989; Hiltz & Turoff, 1978; Rheingold, 1993). Last and most important, a handful of articles provide small ethnographies of particular network communities that have formed in bulletin boards or in multiuser software environments (e.g., Myers, 1987; Reid, 1994; Rosenberg, 1992). These provide the most systematic accounts of relating in CMC, and illustrate interesting issues concerning identity and gender relations in the absence of physical contact, although some of the observations may be specific to a particular computing subculture. In the absence of more directly related research, these data provide the descriptive base for our analysis of personal relationships mediated by communication technology.

Entering the
Computer-Mediated Social Environment

Computer-mediated communication has become an increasingly common form of human interaction. Unknown 25 years ago, today new communication networks span the world, connecting millions of computers in dozens of countries. In 1992 around 12 million people in the United States were regularly using electronic mail, and according to the Internet Society, its use is growing exponentially (Perry & Adam, 1992). A similar picture is emerging in other Western industrialized nations such as France, where 40% of the hours of domestic traffic on the national videotex service, Télétel, is devoted to message exchange among its 6 million users (Feenberg, 1992). To judge from present trends, we are fast approaching a time when the computer will be as ubiquitous a communication medium as the telephone is today.

Worldwide discussion groups abound in the computer medium, and sending a message to several thousand people is no more difficult than sending it to one person. This is made possible by software systems that allow users either to log in and exchange messages in real time in a shared file space (computer conferences) or to read messages previously left by other users and then leave their own messages to be read in turn by others (bulletin boards). UseNet alone carries around 1,500 different discussion groups, and a message sent to the most popular ones may be read by up to half a million people worldwide ("Top Ten Newsgroups," 1994). The computer medium therefore provides the means to communicate with vast audiences of strangers, a power hitherto primarily restricted to those members of a small elite with access to mass media.

As well as blurring the boundary between interpersonal and mass media, CMC also overcomes many of the barriers that we normally associate with communication at a distance. Communication is nearly instantaneous, and difficulties, delays, and costs do not increase in relation to the geographical distance between communicators (Rice & Bair, 1984). As a consequence of these factors, it is about as easy to communicate by computer with someone on the other side of the world as it is with someone in the next room. Many discussion groups are very active and provide sociable experiences despite the geographical separation of their members. For example, "social.culture.china" (a Chinese student network in the United States) exchanges an average of 40 messages per day among its estimated 20,000 members (Li, 1990). The sociability of these computer interactions is illustrated by a user of another bulletin board established to discuss the Gulf war, who offered the Turkish coffee house as a suitable comparison:

> People come and go, say a few witty things, argue politics, ask about help or information, share some news or an article they have recently read, or make announcements about something they are involved in. Friendships develop, people send each other private mail, eventually even get to talk to each other by telephone. *C. Bruce.* (Ogan, 1993, p. 187)

A strong sense of community is also felt by participants:

> We're a form of community: We offer each other support. . . . That's how I view chatting on the feminist computer network: checking in, exchanging ideas, telling a few stories, asking for

help on a project, creating community. *Judy Smith.* (Smith & Balka, 1988, p. 91)

This is an aspect of on-line relating that is frequently remarked upon by participants and recounted in press reports (e.g., Chesebro & Bonsall, 1989; Rheingold, 1993). In addition to the many available support networks that are dedicated to cancer patients, AIDS patients, victims of sexual abuse and so on, spontaneous demonstrations of social support also occur within on-line communities by members who have never met face to face (Lewis, 1994). Just as in "real life," these "virtual" social groups not only are concerned with exchanging information or debating the latest hot topic, but also provide a shared context for social interaction. The situation is superficially similar to a local community, interest group, or club, but differs crucially in that these groups exist independently of the normal physical and spatial reference points.

More important still, the absence of physical contact means that first impressions of individuals may be very different from those made salient by initial physical contact between communicators in face-to-face situations, where gender, age, physical attractiveness, and so on are immediately revealed. This is made clear in the Joan/Alex example described above and is frequently (if sometimes rather idealistically) celebrated by participants themselves (e.g., Herring, 1993; Van Gelder, 1985). However, the lack of face-to-face involvement in CMC offers more radical opportunities in relationship development than merely altering the timing and content of self-disclosures, as we hope to make clear. The visual anonymity of the communicators and the lack of co-presence—indeed the physical isolation—of the communicators add to the interaction possibilities, and for some this is the "magic" of on-line relationships (see, e.g., Myers, 1987).

Some of the effects of the absence of physicality in on-line interactions are most obvious in networks that are specifically dedicated to meeting other individuals and initiating on-line sexual relationships. For example, among the services provided on the French government-sponsored Télétel system, there are the "Messagerie-roses," made infamous by numerous press reports. These are conference systems in which people identify themselves by pseudonyms and "meet" to swap sexual banter or else collaborate in creating fantasy situations and roles and perhaps go on to simulate having sex together—"netsex" consists of typing fantasy descriptions at the keyboard, perhaps while masturbating (De Lacy, 1987; Marchand, 1988). Singles bulletin boards in the United States such as the San Francisco-based "The Back Door" ("dedicated to sex, smut and sleaze"; circa 2,000 subscribers) similarly function to support social-sexual interaction either exclusively on line or as a preliminary to "the real thing" ("Hi-Tech Sex," 1993; Poster, 1990). For some, these networks serve as a convenient shortcut to getting to know someone, avoiding the time and effort involved in face-to-face interaction. For others, the lack of physicality offers freedom to experiment with sexual fantasies devoid of the risks and complications normally attached to meeting others in the flesh:

> Typing back and forth is as far as I want to go for now. I'm a lot bolder than I would be in person; I'd never do that kind of talking face-to-face, or get into any of the fantasy roles. What I enjoy is that they'll never know who I am, yet we can talk about the most personal and specific things. *Julie.* ("Hi-Tech Sex," 1993, p. 26)

Whether CMC provides the technology for uninhibited sex liberated from the power relations and interpersonal complications that stem from involvement is a moot point that we take up later in the chapter. In addition, other, more enduring personal relationships emerge in CMC, and the fact that the interactants have not met face to face does not necessarily seem to mean that the relationships are any less "real" or significant for those involved. For example, two participants on Presbynet (an open conference for the Presbyterian church) declared after 2 months of exchanging messages with strangers they had never "met" that "I know some of these people better than some of my oldest and best friends" and that "I'm still constantly amazed at the 'companionship' and warmth one can find at the computer terminal" (Wilkins, 1991, pp. 56, 71). Similarly, on another system, a participant commented, "I have talked to some people for years without knowing where they live or their real names. Yet they are as much a presence in my life as if they were right in the room. They are my friends" (Kerr, 1982, p. C7).

Indeed, the fact that these friends populate a virtual world distinct from their real world would seem to be one of their attractions. As another contributor commented, "It can be very useful to have someone completely outside of one's normal life, to whom you can tell what's bothering you, because the people who are in your life are often the cause of what's bothering you" (Rosenberg, 1992, p. 8).

Some of the most interesting examples of electronic relationships occur in the MUDs, MOOs, and MUSHs: varieties of computer programs that provide "virtual" social environments that are accessible over the networks and whose structure relies on a strong architectural metaphor. Participants who log into a system such as WolfMOO assign themselves a "character" (a name plus a brief text description) and are then presented with a description of a room, a house, or a neighborhood, for example (rather than a computer file structure), and are able to navigate themselves around the building by issuing simple commands (Rheingold, 1993; Rosenberg, 1992). In their wanderings, players encounter other participants with whom they can converse and get to know, or they can enter rooms already full of people and join in the ongoing discussions. Participants who are proficient in computer programming can add to the software structure by building new features for themselves and others. Although many of these systems are designed as role-playing games, they should not be confused with adventure games (with which they share some features) because their primary function is conversation and social interaction.

Electronic mail, computer conferences, bulletin boards, and MUDs provide evidence that significant, strong, and often enduring personal relationships can emerge over the computer medium. Reid (1994) cited several accounts, in her study of cul-

tural formations over computer networks, given to her by female participants who had developed relationships through the
medium over the course of several months before finally meeting their on-line partners face to face and continuing their relationships—and in some cases getting married—in the physical
world.

> I met Mark, who I'm now married to, on a MUD. When I first met
> him I was living on the West Coast [of the United States] and he
> was on the East Coast. . . . We spent a lot of time chatting and we
> got closer and closer. It was really good—I could tell him anything
> and he was really supportive. . . . I could tell that he was interested
> in me, and at first I was reluctant to get involved but he was so
> nice and he said that he really loved me. . . . After a few months I
> had the chance to visit the East Coast, and we met while I was
> there. He was different from what I'd expected, mostly in the way
> he looked, but we really got along well, and I decided that I really
> did love him. He ended up getting a transfer to near where I lived
> and we got married last year. *Anonymous.* (Reid, 1994, p. 32)

To judge from these and other reports of social interaction in
CMC, it appears that personal relationships often develop in the
computer medium, some of which are exclusively maintained
on line, and others of which become integrated with normal,
face-to-face, social lives. Yet relationships that develop through
communication media do not fit easily into existing models of
attraction and intimacy. We argue that this shortcoming is due
to a number of assumptions and biases in the existing literature,
and these are now considered.

Assumptions and Biases
in Personal Relationship Research

1. We begin by considering a point made elsewhere, namely
that research on attraction and personal relationships has a restricted focus that is primarily on the development of intimacy
in the context of long-term relationships such as friendship and

marriage. It tends to ignore relationships that cross boundaries, such as "friendly lovers" (Gergen, 1991), and to treat as failures those that do not grow in intimacy or end in marriage (Delia, 1980). Similarly, the field virtually ignores negative relationships (such as enemies) or even the negative aspects of what are generally seen as positive relationships (Duck, 1994a). Although perhaps merely conforming to more widely held norms in this culture about what is desirable about relationships, these biases may be more difficult to sustain for relationships conducted over computer networks. This is not because transitory relationships, or "low-level romances" (Gergen, 1991), are more likely to occur in this medium (specifically, we argue that they are not), but because the vast public arenas in which much online relating is performed and the visibility and permanence of text are features that give these relationships and many of the hitherto private and ephemeral (oral) aspects of all relationships a renewed visibility (Zuboff, 1988). This visibility in turn invites a reappraisal of the neglected forms and aspects of relationships that are normally kept more hidden.

2. Numerous sociological studies have shown that we have a greater tendency to initiate relationships with those with whom we interact most frequently: our neighbors, workmates, fellow students, and the like (Athanasiou & Yoshioka, 1973; Gullahorn, 1952; Newcomb, 1963). Physical constraints on interaction have also meant that we are more likely to initiate relationships with people who are similar in race, religion, socioeconomic class, educational level, economic value, and so on (e.g., Kerckhoff, 1974; Woll & Cozby, 1987). One of the effects of the connectivity afforded by computer networks is that it vastly increases the "field of availables" for forming relationships far beyond the limits set by physical proximity—or even the extended horizons offered by other communication media. Whether the relaxation of constraints on the size and proximity of one's communication audience in the computer medium increases the diversity of people that we meet is an empirical question, but it nevertheless suggests that the process of identifying and communicating differentially with people is changed by the elec-

tronic medium (cf. Gandy, 1993). The criteria by which the preselection of our acquaintances is made for us are therefore rewritten around a variety of new issues, including technical issues, such as the compatibility of computer technology and network interconnections, in addition to more traditional economic and social issues (Lea, O'Shea, & Fung, 1994).

Of course, the use of communication media to overcome the physical and spatial limits on relationships is not a new phenomenon. People throughout the ages have been developing relationships at a distance by exchanging letters, or more recently by communicating via the telegraph and the telephone (Marvin, 1988). Furthermore, the proliferation of new media this century has given rise to new ways of meeting people: through newspaper lonely hearts columns, computer dating, telephone chat lines, video dating, and so on (e.g., Woll & Cozby, 1987). However, such instances are usually viewed as exceptional, antinormative ways of getting acquainted—as the last resort of the lonely or socially inadequate and at best as impoverished substitutes for face-to-face interactions. In short, mediated communication is neglected in personal relationship research, which focuses on direct face-to-face interaction as the primary vehicle for relationship formation.

3. In face-to-face interaction, aspects of our physical appearance normally act as powerful selection criteria for beginning relationships (e.g., Curran, 1973). In initial encounters, physical attractiveness is used to infer such qualities as personality, intelligence, similarity, and social desirability before these attributes have themselves been revealed (e.g., Dion, Berscheid, & Walster, 1972). Unsurprisingly then, physical attractiveness has featured as an important factor in several models of relationship development. For example, it acts as an early predictive filter cue to personality attributes and contributes to perceptions of equity in the relationship, both of which factors predict the likelihood of relationship continuation (Duck, 1977a; Walster, Walster, & Berscheid, 1978).

However, the relevance of physical attraction to relationship development is undermined in the computer medium. Where physical cues are unavailable, "love at first sight" would seem to be impossible. Instead of being at the forefront of face-to-face interactions, one's physical appearance recedes into the background in CMC, and its disclosure to others is under the control of the subject, who can choose when and how to reveal it. As a consequence, stage models of relationship development, or indeed our cultural expectations about how relationships develop that assume first and foremost an attraction between physical bodies, no longer work for us in this medium.

4. This focus on physicality and physical cues as a grounding for personal attraction points to a perhaps even more fundamental bias in personal relationships research. This concerns the emphasis on precisely the (inter)personal dimension of attraction and relationship formation and development. This view of relationships is no accident, but flows logically from the relatively individualistic conceptualization of both the self and social relations in much mainstream social psychology. Once the social dimension of attraction becomes acknowledged, this focus on the physical co-presence of individuals arguably becomes less critical. This social dimension refers to the importance of the wider social context in which relationships are embedded and in which they are constructed by those involved. In this sense, attraction and relationships are always more than a contract between two isolated individuals because they implicate resources and referents well beyond the interpersonal bond. The point is not just that the physical basis of attraction is at least partly culturally relative, but that notions such as lasting romantic love for another person are themselves inherently individualistic social constructions of Western culture. More specifically, to the extent that people are defined and can define themselves in terms of meaningful social identities (as a woman, as a feminist, etc.), these social self-categories can form the basis not only for a social self-worth, but also for a distinctively social attraction to others (Hogg, 1992; Turner, Hogg, Oakes, Reicher, & Wetherell, 1987). We return to this point in due course. Suffice it to say that the emphasis on individuals qua individuals, and the focus on relations of individual inter-

dependence and attraction that this implies, tends a priori to exclude attraction in contexts in which the individual is not physically present.

In line with this bias, the conclusion that enduring personal relationships in CMC are unlikely would seem to receive indirect support from much social psychological research. In addition to physical appearance, nonverbal cues such as voice, posture, and eye gaze are also concealed by the computer medium. These behaviors have long been regarded as the essential lubricants and regulators of social interaction, as well as further contributing to impression formation and the likelihood of developing acquaintanceship (e.g., Argyle & Dean, 1965; Patterson, 1973), Their lack of influence in the computer medium would therefore seem at the very least to make the formation of personal relationships difficult. Even more crucially, however, physical and nonverbal cues form an important channel for communicating emotional intimacy in relationships (Altman & Taylor, 1973; Reis & Shaver, 1988), so their absence in the computer context raises fundamental questions about whether and how intimacy can be achieved in this purely text medium. Furthermore, a number of perspectives suggest that these factors, together with spatial proximity, are means by which we judge relationships to be personal, close, and well adjusted (Clark & Reis, 1988; Huston & Levinger, 1978; Noller, 1987; Perlman & Fehr, 1987). In short, much research tends not only to presume face-to-face contact as the norm for personal relationships, but also to define personal relationships in terms of factors that are unique to this form of interaction.

5. More generally, physical and spatial metaphors are pervasive in discourses about relationships in this culture. As Surra and Huston (1987) pointed out, the idea that dating relationships are going from somewhere to somewhere is widespread. Lack of movement is an accepted reason for ending a relationship ("it wasn't going anywhere") as well as a reason for avoiding one ("I don't want to be tied down"). The process of relationship development has also been described in this way, acquaintanceship being a matter of moving from awareness of

the "outer" or "surface" aspects of another to penetrating his or her "inner" or "deeper" self (e.g., Altman & Taylor, 1973; Duck, 1977b). Duck (1994d; Duck & Pond, 1989) also noted the tendency for relationship researchers to construct relationships as if they had trajectories and to chart their "turning points along the pathways to success." Finally, the concept of a "close" relationship, readily understood by all and a central concept in personal relationship research, makes explicit reference to a spatial metaphor as a way of distinguishing rhetorically between relationships in terms of the strength and frequency of the interdependence between people's behaviors, emotions, and thoughts (Clark & Reis, 1988; Hendrick, 1989; Kelley et al., 1983). This general emphasis on the physical and spatial as means to elucidating relationship processes further encourages the assumption that mediated interactions that occur independently of such considerations are incapable of supporting intimacy and relationship development.

6. A related bias is seen in regard to the role of verbal communication in relationships, which is almost always equated with oral communication. Thus, for example, studies of intimacy focus mainly on the content of self-disclosures and on paralinguistic features such as conversational style in face-to-face interactions (Clark & Reis, 1988; Hornstein, 1985; Montgomery, 1984). More recent perspectives that recognize the important rhetorical role played by talk in constructing relationships do not necessarily escape this bias, even though they represent a considerable theoretical advance on viewing verbal communication merely as another channel through which social psychological processes are conveyed or expressed (e.g., Duck, 1994c, 1994d; Duck & Pond, 1989). By choosing to emphasize talk above other forms of discourse—written as well as oral—as the essential means by which relationships are constituted, relationships that are mainly or exclusively conducted at a distance and through a text-based communication medium such as CMC are implicitly (if unintentionally) excluded from this analysis.

Although this may seem a reasonable bias on balance, it partly reflects the contemporary elevation of the oral form over text in modern society; letters and postcards occupied a much stronger role in the development and maintenance of friendships and romantic relationships in the 19th century than they do today (Derrida, 1987; Van Gelder, 1985). However, as written discourse, CMC also shares many of the same characteristics as talk compared to traditional text. For example, it can be spontaneous and casual, and it shows intensive involvement with one's audience, features traditionally associated with spoken language and direct face-to-face interaction (Ferrara, Brunner, & Whittemore, 1991; Lea, 1991; Wilkins, 1991). On the other hand, as an asynchronous textual medium, CMC can emerge more as planned discourse than spontaneous talk, and its storage in the computer and presentation on the screen gives "online talk" a tangible, permanent presence that it is normally denied in the oral mode. This combination of features coupled with the disembodied presence of the subject makes CMC arguably a presentational medium par excellence, a point that not only resonates with Duck's (1994b) thesis about the (re)presentational functions of relationship talk, but also suggests how relationships can be built over computer networks in the absence of embodied presence.

7. Finally, we draw attention to the general neglect and restricted formulation of power in this field, even though feminist research has recently made welcome progress here (e.g., Wood, 1993c). In the mainstream of relationship research, power is usually conceptualized as the property of an individual that is allotted by an authority role and exerted upon a subordinate. Thus power tends to be discussed mainly in the context of children's relationships in which a parent or dominant sibling exerts power over a child (Adler & Furman, 1988; Mills & Grusec, 1988). In a similar vein, *power motivation* refers to an individual's desire to have strong impacts on others, and its level affects the choice of friends and marriage partners (McAdams, 1978). Once again, we see that the physical and spatial are implicated in the process. If power is conceptualized as an external force that is applied against the will of a reluctant other, its impact is presumably greatest when the interactants are in the physical

presence of one another, and by implication is reduced by their geographical separation in CMC (Spears & Lea, 1994).

To summarize our observations and conclusions so far, we argue that the prevailing conceptualizations of relationships and relationship processes predetermine the conclusion that personal relationships will be difficult to obtain and maintain via telecommunications media. These conceptualizations include emphasis on physical proximity, face-to-face interaction, and nonverbal communication and talk as the essential processes of relating, and a general tendency to use physical and spatial metaphors in describing and accounting for relationships. These biases and assumptions may arguably possess much ecological validity—after all, most human interaction is conducted face to face. However, it is important to draw the distinction between properties and processes that are simply the observed norm in relationships and those that are considered to be necessary prerequisites for relationships. The emergence of CMC as a pervasive communication medium that overcomes distance but denies physicality and nonverbal communication brings many of these underlying assumptions about relationship processes and definitions into focus, inviting their reappraisal. Having made these points in regard to research on personal relationships, we now consider how many of the same assumptions emerge once again in various theoretical perspectives on communication media, particularly in those that share the same metatheoretical basis in social psychology.

Perspectives on Communication Media

A number of macro-level perspectives on communication media also raise doubts about the possibility of establishing genuinely personal relationships through CMC. For example, Beninger (1987) argued that computer-based technologies provide the infrastructure for replacing a tradition of organic community based on interpersonal relationships with the superficial relationships of pseudocommunity. This development arises from the convergence between interpersonal and mass

media forms of communication that these new technologies allow, in which communications (such as computer mailings) that
bear all the characteristics of personalized messages can be
transmitted impersonally to a mass audience. Subjective judgments about the sincerity of the communication rest at least
partly on the inferred size of its intended audience. Thus face-
to-face communication above all else is assumed to be sincere
precisely because it seems intended only for us, whereas the
assumption becomes progressively more difficult to maintain
for the recipient of telecommunications. Similarly, Gergen
(1991) presented an image of the socially saturated self for
whom the slow, steady pace of traditional relationship development with a few significant others has given way to a barrage of
instant, transitory "microwave" relationships made possible and
at the same time constrained by the ever-increasing number of
strangers with whom we are brought into contact.

These media perspectives identify the removal of the require-
ment of embodied presence as the crucial factor in telecommunications underlying both the increased opportunities for
relating and the simultaneous reduction in the possibility of
establishing genuinely personal relationships. However, if
physical presence is entailed in the construct of close personal
relationships, as would appear from the above discussion, it is
difficult to see how it would be possible to conclude otherwise
than that the reduction of full co-presence in communication
media undermines opportunities for genuine, intimate personal
relationships. This position is most clearly seen in the "reduced
social cues" perspective on media within social psychology, and
we consider this next by way of introducing our own theoretical
position.

Within this general perspective are several related approaches, each of which argues in a different way that the styles
and outcomes of mediated interpersonal and group interaction
are determined primarily by the availability of social cues
within any given medium. The social presence model, for example, argues that the degree of social presence associated with
different media determines their social psychological effects
(Short, Williams, & Christie, 1976). Social presence is a subjec-

tive quality of the medium that is conceptually close to notions of intimacy (Argyle & Dean, 1965) and immediacy (Wiener & Mehrebian, 1968), so that media that are low in presence are judged to be impersonal, unsociable, cold, and insensitive. These judgments are in turn based on the objective capability of different media to communicate interpersonal cues via visual and/or auditory channels. Thus although all media share reduced social presence relative to the ideal of face-to-face interaction, CMC, as an asynchronous, text-based medium, should be much lower in social presence than most other media, such as the telephone or the videophone, and too impersonal, presumably, to sustain an intimate relationship.

Deterministic formulations about the effects of reduced cues in CMC appear in their most theoretically sophisticated form as the reduced social cues model (e.g., Kiesler, Siegel, & McGuire, 1984; Siegel, Dubrovsky, Kiesler, & McGuire, 1986). This approach argues that the reduction of social cues in CMC has a number of psychological and behavioral effects on individuals and groups. For example, it undermines leadership, power, and status, leading to greater equality of participation in CMC groups relative to face-to-face groups. It also encourages psychological states (such as deindividuation and reduced self-awareness), causing disinhibition and leading to deregulated, extreme, antinormative behavior. Like the earlier social presence research, much of this work was concerned with investigating a number of putative effects particular to groups, but it also has a number of implications for dyadic communication in this medium (e.g., Kiesler, Zubrow, Moses, & Geller, 1985; Sproull & Kiesler, 1986). Specifically, relative to face-to-face situations, communication in CMC should be more impersonal, negative, uninhibited, and equal. These are effects that, if true, would have the most profound implications for relating in this medium.

Interestingly, elements of these social psychological models and their predicted effects on human relationships resonate with earlier views about older communication technologies such as the telegraph and telephone. Notions of "presence," anxieties about the muddying of "social distance," and concerns about the social consequences of reduced communication bandwidth accompanying the widespread diffusion of these older media were voiced in the popular science journals of the 1890s. These articles often portrayed anecdotal accounts of dire consequences (such as betrayal, fraud, and abuse) that befell those who naively treated full and attenuated bandwidth as if they were socially equivalent. The reports in turn fueled debate among professional engineers and the general public as to how to defend social distances, customarily enforced and maintained by face-to-face cues, in a medium where strangers, criminals, and members of the lower classes could present themselves in an improperly intimate manner. They invited speculation and legal deliberation about the social circumstances in which a medium constituted "sufficient presence" to be judged as equivalent to face-to-face communication (Marvin, 1988, pp. 86-96). It is in these earlier electric media, rather than their modern computer counterparts, that we see the first examples of telecommunications placing friendship, courtship, and all manner of social interaction (including telegraphic marriage ceremonies) "on the line."

Strikingly similar processes have been traced in the discourses on the new computer-based communication medium nearly 100 years later (Lea & Giordano, in press; Lea, O'Shea, Fung, & Spears, 1992). Heim (1992) for example, suggested that without the direct experience of the human face in "cyberspace," warmth, trust, responsibility, and loyalty are replaced by an amoral indifference to human relationships. Similarly, articles in the popular press about uninhibited, asocial behavior, and the sinister personal and social implications of visual anonymity in computer-mediated communication (such as the Joan/Alex episode related above) have fed directly into social science models of the medium that in turn have helped shape popular ideas about the type of medium provided by computers.

Notions of presence, bandwidth, and reduced cues have had enormous influence in shaping subsequent views of mediated communication and its social effects (e.g., DeSanctis & Gallupe,

1987; Rice, 1984, 1993; Rutter, 1987), even though empirical research has failed to find much support for the type of deterministic effects that these concepts predict, and has even found directly contrary effects on occasion (e.g., Rice, 1984; Walther, 1994a, in press). The reduced cues perspective in general has been criticized for its failure to predict the considerable variability that can be observed in mediated interactions, or to recognize the influence of social context cues that are communicated largely independently of the richness of a medium (e.g., Lea et al., 1992; Lea & Spears, 1991 , 1992). Furthermore, as with personal relationship research, there is an overdependence on the physical and spatial, and on the exchange of nonverbal communication in situ, to communicate social norms and cues associated with interpersonal interaction (for reviews, see Spears & Lea, 1992; Walther et al., 1994). Rather than reproduce the substance of these critiques here, we focus instead on a number of conditions that arise in spite of, and in some cases because of, the lack of embodied presence and face-to-face interaction in CMC, and that in our view provide the basis for sociability and the emergence of relationships in the medium.

Conditions for Social Interaction in CMC

To begin with, the absence of physical and nonverbal cues should not be taken to mean that the computer medium is impersonal or devoid of social cues, or that the cues it transmits lack the subtlety of those communicated face to face. A high degree of socioemotional communication is observed in the medium even in task-oriented settings (e.g., Ord, 1989; Rice & Love, 1987; Walther, in press; Weedman, 1991), and recent studies of everyday CMC have identified many ways in which emotions and impressions are conveyed in this textual medium (e,g., Ferrara et al., 1991; Selfe & Meyer, 1991; Wilkins, 1991). Linguistic cues, for example, mark out men's contributions from women's. In one bulletin board study, men's messages were longer and used more "male language" (assertions, challenges, authoritative tone) than women's, which tended to use less confrontational and authoritative styles. The salience of these cues to gender is also revealed by their effects on participants' communication behavior, which are dependent in turn on the social context for communication. In work group discussions, women's messages tend to receive fewer responses (from men and women), and topics initiated by women were less likely to be taken up by the group (Herring, 1993), whereas in recreational situations, women's messages tend to receive more attention from men (Reid, 1994; Rosenberg, 1992).

Seasoned communicators in the computer medium become adept at using and interpreting textual signs and paralinguistic codes (various keyboard tricks, or "emotes," used to convey the intended emotional tone of a message), and even first-time users form impressions of other interactants' dispositions based on communication style (for recent reviews, see Lea & Spears, 1992; Walther & Tidwell, 1994). Noting the availability of these various cues, Walther (1992, 1993) argued that the putative depersonalizing effects observed in some studies of the computer medium arose simply because of experimentally imposed time constraints, which meant that less social information was passed in the slower, text-based medium compared to face to face. Given more time, sufficient social information can be conveyed for interactants to form impressions of each other and develop relational communication. A recent meta-analysis of experimental studies of CMC interactions, with time as the moderating variable, supports this reinterpretation of the social presence findings (Walther et al., 1994).

In contrast to the impersonal effects predicted by the reduced cues perspective, this account predicts that personal relationships can develop in CMC, albeit more slowly because the essential interpersonal processes—self-disclosure, development of trust, communication of intimacy, and so on—take longer than in the face-to-face situation (e.g., Walther, 1994b). But even if we dispense with the conclusion that CMC is an inherently impersonal medium, a problem that we saw in the earlier reduced cues models also pertains here. Common to all these approaches is the tendency to underestimate the effects of communicative behaviors that are trivial in purely informational terms but that nevertheless convey significant social meaning (Spears & Lea, 1992). Hanging up the phone unexpectedly is a familiar exemplar that has its equivalent in synchronous computer conferences, and the effects of response latency can be significant even in an asynchronous medium such as electronic mail. Indeed, a recent experimental study by Walther and Tidwell (1994) found that time sent and response latency interacted in CMC to affect perceptions of relational involvement by receivers. The "devastating" emotional impact of an unexpectedly long response latency in a critical phase during the development of a close personal relationship is also attested to by a respondent in Reid's computer ethnography (Reid, 1994, Appendix 2).

Furthermore, studies on impression formation and stereotyping have identified some of the processes by which we make significant inferences and attributions about people's personality, emotional state, and behavioral intentions on the basis of minimal cues (Fiske & Taylor, 1984). These are processes that are generally acknowledged to occur in interpersonal attraction and relationships (Huston & Levinger, 1978), but that have only just begun to be identified in CMC (e.g., Lea & Spears, 1992). Information conspicuous by its absence can also have informational significance and influence. Less can mean more, as observations about telephone sex lines and their equivalent in CMC would appear to testify. It is precisely the gaps in information as much as the information itself that give mediated sex its allure. Here a complex scenario of coordinated action, complete with sensory perceptions of tactility and odor, is constructed by the participants by drawing on a limited repertoire of cultural codes communicated in text (Stone, 1992). Furthermore, the success of crisis help lines is in large part due to the conditions of visual anonymity and physical isolation associated with telephone communication, which limit the amount of personal information revealed about the caller. These are precisely the conditions that encourage intimate self-disclosure and the development of trust in their counselors by persons seeking help in this way (Rutter, 1987). In group situations, these same conditions in CMC can promote more normative behavior, a greater sense of identification with the group, and more positive impressions of group members than face-to-face conditions in which the full range of channels for communicating interpersonal information is available (e.g., Lea & Spears, 1991, 1992). These conditions help to explain why self-help and counseling groups (e.g., for victims of sexual abuse) as well as netsex have become popular in the computer medium (e.g., Reid, 1994; Rheingold, 1993). It also suggests that acquaintanceship and relationship development are not dependent in any simple linear way upon the quantity of personal information that is exchanged in a given medium, as much as on the types of meanings that the interactants construct from the communication and the situations in which it occurs.

Social categorical cues are another important case in point, for although the communication of interpersonal cues that regulate communication or that identify the unique characteristics of people might be quite sensitive to the richness of a communication medium, information about the communicators that locates them in terms of particular social groups or wider categorizations within society would seem to be less dependent on communication bandwidth. Gender, for example, can be communicated as a single binary unit of information, but (as we have already noted) can be enormously influential in shaping the forms and conduct of relations. Similarly, power and status can be easily communicated as part of the meta-language of communication if they are not already apparent (Spears & Lea, 1992, 1994).

These and other observations suggest that relationships should not necessarily take longer to form in CMC (because of reduced bandwidth) than in face-to-face interaction, but that CMC has certain features that makes it more difficult to exchange some, and easier to exchange other types of relational communication. The effects on relationship development should therefore go beyond slowing the rate at which progress occurs, to alter the points in relationship development at which various processes can be observed. For this reason we might expect the process of forming relationships to be qualitatively different in the medium, and for some types of intimacy to develop more quickly and other types more slowly.

In sum, from our analysis so far, it would seem that the reduced cues approach to mediated communication and traditional approaches to interpersonal attraction and relationship development are similarly ill prepared to account for the development of personal relationships in the computer medium. Despite their independent development, these approaches share the same problematic, namely an overreliance on the physical and spatial aspects of interaction and on the communication of information in situ as the basis of genuine social relations.

In the remainder of this chapter we develop this argument further by introducing an alternative model to explain social interaction in CMC. In doing this we also discuss further problems shared by the approaches we have discussed so far, particularly their metatheoretical assumption of individualism and their conceptualization of a monolithic self corresponding to the physically embodied individual. Our aim is to explore the constructional aspects of relationships in this medium. In CMC the presentation of self is tilted away from the physical axis, over which we have little or no control, and this dissociation of the physical body from others' perceptions of ourselves paves the way for the manipulated presentation of alternative, ephemeral, and disposable selves through our relationships with others. This is a feature, moreover, that we consider highlights the constructional basis of all personal relationships, including those that arise from face-to-face interaction.

The SIDE Model of Mediated Communication

The social identification/deindividuation (SIDE) model was originally developed to explain various inconsistencies and contradictions in the reported behavior of groups and individuals communicating via computers. It was offered as a corrective to the dominant deterministic models of group CMC that were unable to explain, for example, the observation that groups communicating via computer sometimes exhibit more polarization than equivalent groups communicating face to face, but less polarization on other occasions (Lea & Spears, 1991; Spears, Lea, & Lee, 1990). The model explains these and other findings by reference to the contextual conditions, such an anonymity and physical isolation, associated with CMC, in combination with psychological states, such as deindividuation and self-awareness, that mediate the observed effects.

This approach is based on self-categorization theory (Turner et al., 1987), which in turn builds upon the insights of the earlier social identity tradition (Tajfel & Turner, 1986). Underlying the approach is the conceptualization of the self not as a fixed unitary entity associated with the individual, but as comprising a range of self-categories including personal identities (the characteristics that define the individual as a unique person) and social identities that define the individual in terms of membership of social groups (such as membership of an interest group) and social categorizations in society (such as gender). These different identities, which are made more or less salient depending on the social context, influence the communication and behavior of the individual to act in terms of the norms and standards associated with the salient identities. Consequently, the SIDE model does not rely necessarily on the on-line communication of informational cues for the operation of social norms, or even attraction. Although open to negotiation and development, both norms and the bases of attraction are nominally encoded within the social identities of the participants at the outset.

The SIDE model extends self-categorization theory and attempts to specify the situational conditions under which behavior normative to a particular self-category will be made appropriate and possible (Lea & Spears, 1992; Reicher, Spears, & Postmes, in press; Spears & Lea, 1992, 1994). It comprises two central elements: a cognitive element and a strategic element. The cognitive element refers to the level of identity or self-category made salient in a particular context (e.g., individual versus group identity), whereas the strategic element refers to the possibility or appropriateness of expression of behavior in line with the content of that self-category. Two important contextual features that we have identified as influencing the cognitive and strategic effects of CMC are isolation and anonymity. Isolation from others leads to an increase in self-attention (a cognitive effect) that enhances normative behavior and conformity to the salient self-category. With regard to anonymity, we distinguish between the anonymity of others to the person, and the degree of anonymity of the person to others, which to avoid confusion we refer to as *identifiability*. Anonymity of others to the self can increase perceptions of group homogeneity associated with the salient self-categorization (a cognitive effect), leading once more to normative behavior in line with the salient self-category. Identifiability of the self to others, on the other hand, influences self-presentation and accountability (a strategic effect), leading to the expression of normative behavior sanctioned or facilitated by the situation. Co-presence can also provide greater opportunities for the evaluation of social support from others (a strategic effect), which can encourage normative behavior that might otherwise be sanctioned under the surveillance of a powerful outgroup or authority.

Elsewhere we have presented the SIDE model in more detail and presented the theoretical and empirical evidence in support of the predicted contextually bound effects of CMC (Spears & Lea, 1992, 1994). Here, however, we confine discussion to some preliminary observations about the application of the model to account for the development of personal relationships in the medium. At the same time, these observations extend the constructional basis for contextualized effects. In much of our previous work, we have been mainly concerned to accumulate observations based on experimental studies in line with most other research in the social identity/self-categorization tradition (but for exceptions, see Lea et al., 1992; Postmes, Spears, & Lea, 1994). One unintended consequence of relying on a paradigm in which the contextual boundaries are largely predetermined by the experimenter is that it has tended to obscure the active efforts of participants themselves to construct appropriate contexts for their own interaction and behavior, suggesting perhaps that the model views CMC participants as passive recipients of externally imposed contextual factors (Walther, 1994b). We correct this omission by discussing some preliminary observations of participants' attempts to construct social contexts appropriate for the expression of certain identities in CMC, and by drawing on a recent analysis of the means by which power relations are constituted in CMC (Spears & Lea, 1994). At the same time we forge a link with other work within the self-categorization framework that is concerned with the construction of salient social self-categorizations by participants themselves through their discourses and other means available to them in situ (e.g., Reicher, 1994).

Identity and Power in CMC

The full significance of the importance assigned to the physical body in face-to-face interaction is perhaps most keenly felt by people with physical disabilities or disfigurements, whose encounters with others are more likely to be superficial, spurious, and ending in withdrawal by others (e.g., Bull & Rumsey, 1988; Goffman, 1963). Consequently the ability of the medium to distance communicators from the physical manifestations of the self is considered to be empowering for these and other groups who find themselves disadvantaged in face-to-face interaction (e.g., Hiltz & Turoff, 1978). The facility to optimize self-presentation in CMC through selective and strategic disclosures of the self (see Goffman, 1959) has been described by Walther (1994b) as a "hyperpersonal" quality of the medium. Decisions about whether and when to reveal the physical characteristics that have been traditionally considered to act as powerful initial selection criteria for decisions about forming relationships—gender, physical attractiveness, and so on, as well as stigma such as physical disability—are argued to be more under the control of the person to whom they belong in CMC. However, the SIDE perspective, in common with other broadly constructionist perspectives (Gergen & Davis, 1985), rejects the Cartesian concept of an essential self commensurate with the physical self and detached from the social situation. Self-presentation in these terms does not just reflect the presentation of selective aspects to form some socially acceptable face, as implied by classical self-presentation theory (e.g., Leary & Kowalski, 1990), nor is the medium seen as an opportunity to escape from the constraints of ordinary identity and interaction to create alternative selves and social relations, as implied by some of the liberatory rhetoric about "cyberspace" (for a review, see Fiqueroa-Sarriera, 1993). Instead, the presentation of the self is directly tied to the particular identity that is made salient in the social context, to the norms of its audience and its power of sanction (Reicher & Levine, 1994; Spears & Lea, 1994).

This is illustrated by brief consideration of power relations operating inside CMC. Although anonymity may provide optimal conditions for less powerful individuals and groups (e.g., women) to resist or challenge powerful others, it also makes it easier for the more powerful to manipulate others and facilitates the "darker side of relationships" (Duck, 1994a) by distancing the individual from the consequences of his or her actions. The example of Joan/Alex (described in the opening of this chapter) is a case in point. Here the cover of the alternative identity Joan created by Alex not only constitutes freedom to explore his male identity intrapersonally but also the opportunity to exploit the identity and trust in identity by others (see also Reid, 1994, Appendix 3; Rheingold, 1993, p. 164). Of course, not all relationships so formed are as unilaterally manipulative, or end as disastrously when the real gender is revealed, as in these encounters. Reid (1994, Appendix 2) presented a fascinating account (too detailed to be reproduced here) of a double-bluff between a woman (in real life) who presented herself as a male on line, and who became emotionally attached to a female on line who in reality was a man. At the critical moment at which their real genders were revealed to each other, their relationship floundered and only recovered (they eventually married) after they began their acquaintanceship over again, this time over the telephone as well as on line.

Nevertheless, the opportunities in CMC for exploiting power relations in personal relationships would seem undeniable if the relative absence of interpersonal cues in the medium serves to make social-categorical cues such as gender more salient and usable in the social situation, and thereby reinforces behaviors and forms of relating that are normative to the gender category. Within MUDs, there is evidence that women disguise their gender in order to avoid unwanted attention from males and in order to exploit the power associated with neutral or male identities. On the other hand, men's posing as women seems to be instigated with the predominantly male users (Balka, 1993; Marchand, 1988) and subculture in mind, precisely in order to attract the type of behavior often shown to women (i.e., chivalry and harassment) in a male-dominated society (Curtis, 1992). Occasionally too, there are examples of individuals who switch their gender regularly during participation in order to better manipulate the social situation in which they find themselves by exploiting prototypically gendered behavior from others (Reid, 1994; Rosenberg, 1992).

Manipulations of gender are not the only examples in CMC of attempts to construct on-line identities that break the connection between representation and reality that is forced upon us by interactions in the physical world (cf. Baudrillard, 1983). In certain MUDs, cultures are formed in which identities take the form of fantasy-style animals or characters drawn from myth and science fiction (Curtis, 1992; Reid, 1994). The names assigned to these fantasy selves can be extended by textual descriptions of the "embodied" identities. Though appearing to extend the possibilities for the presentation of the self beyond its usual human boundaries, the adoption of these kinds of identities does not liberate the participants from ordinary human relations. Rather, the adopted identities can be understood within the SIDE approach as providing anthropomorphic referents to human categorizations or characteristics (such as beauty and friendliness) for which the nominated identity is prototypical, and their behavior and the responses they invite are normative in terms of that self-category.

Far from providing liberation from existing power relations associated with personal relationships, CMC arguably provides a number of opportunities to further accentuate and reinforce them by increasing the salience of social self-categorizations in the relative absence of interpersonal information, CMC can also increase the sense of isolation and surveillance associated with "panoptic power" (Foucault, 1977; Spears & Lea, 1994). It should be clear from the above, then, that the communication conditions provided by CMC provide more complex implications for the formation of personal relationships than are suggested by merely altering the timing of disclosures, but that the absence of physicality does not in itself provide a freedom from some of the strictures that are associated with the embodied self.

Attraction in CMC

Given the increased salience of social categorical cues in CMC and the enhanced opportunities for presenting alternative selves drawn from these social self-categories, it follows that impressions formed (initially, at least) between participants in CMC are more likely to be in terms of these social categories than in terms of those aspects of the self that define participants as unique individuals. As already noted, interpersonal cues are more likely to be sensitive to the communication bandwidth of the medium of interaction and may therefore take longer and be more difficult to communicate than social cues, relative to face-to-face interaction. Under the social identity approach, the distinction between *social* attraction (i.e., attraction to those aspects of the self that are conferred by membership of or affiliation with certain social groups or categorizations) and *personal* attraction (i.e., attraction to the idiosyncratic aspects of an individual) is made explicit at the level of generative process. Social attraction is based on group processes (e.g., conformity,

stereotyping, intergroup differentiation), whereas personal attraction is based on interpersonal processes such as the development of intimacy (Hogg, 1992). Following this approach, social self-categorizations generate intragroup attraction because
they render self and other stereotypically identical (the other is
liked because the self is liked) and because they contribute to
self-esteem (the positively evaluated characteristics of the in-
group stereotype represented by the other are conferred on the
self). According to the SIDE model, the conditions of high group
salience and deindividuation (physical isolation and visual anonymity) that are engendered in bulletin board groups in CMC
increase the salience of the group. This promotes individuals'
attraction responses to others at the level of identity that is made
salient by their membership of that group, or by the factions or
subgroups that are formed during interaction with whom they
identify. If identity with the group is valued, then liking and
feelings of interdependence toward a particular other individual
are increased to the extent that the other is seen to be prototypical of the group (Lea & Spears, 1992).

In CMC, identification with a particular in-group can be sig-
naled merely by being a member of a discussion group, or computer network, or through debates that lead to the formation of
subgroups and factions. However, identifications are also made
salient and communicated by the adoption of pseudonyms and
character descriptions that increase the range of identifications
that can be made salient to self-presentation during interaction.
Communication style can also be interpreted by participants as
indicative of membership of particular groups and categorizations within society and responded to in terms of social rather
than personal attraction (Lea & Spears, 1992). It is interesting
to note that in the case of Joan/Alex and other examples of failed
electronic relationships that have received attention, the failure
is apparently due to the violation of assumed social self-categorizations discovered during interaction, whereas the personal
qualities of the individual (such as exceptional generosity, affection, intimacy, and concern for others in the case of Joan) remain the same (Van Gelder, 1985).

228 UNDER-STUDIED RELATIONSHIPS

The presentation of social self-categorizations and their interpretation by others provide a foundation for constructing personal relationships that is conceptually prior to any qualities
that are peculiar to the physical self or exclusively communicated through face-to-face interaction. In CMC, in which these
qualities are more open to strategic manipulation than in normal interpersonal interactions, their fundamental role in the
construction of relationships is highlighted. In face-to-face interaction, the influence of physical appearance on attraction,
rather than acting as an interpersonal cue to hidden personal
qualities, can be more readily understood in terms of attraction
to those fundamental social self-categorizations made salient by
the body.

At the same time, when couples are geographically separated
(i.e., physically isolated from one another as they are in CMC),
the salience of social category cues and the relative absence of
individuating information may be precisely the conditions that
fan the flames of passion and romance. A recent study by
Stafford and Reske (1990) found that written communication
between engaged partners who lived at a distance from each
other was highly correlated with adjustment, communication,
idealization, and love, whereas face-to-face communication was
negatively associated with these relationship variables. This suggests that the reduced salience of individuating cues in written
communication can encourage more romanticized constructions of the relationship in which one's perceptions of the individuating aspects of the other may be blurred by fantasy projec-
tions of an idealized other. Gergen (1991, pp. 66-67) made a
similar point, but seemed to invoke a rather different explanation. He argued that face-to-face relationships over time tend toward normalization and a leveling of emotional intensity, and
are accompanied by a high degree of surveillance by others,
whereas in the physical absence of the partner in electronic
communications there is greater opportunity for fantasies to
roam free, unhindered by the presence of the embodied other
or by the normalizing effects of surveillance typical of face-to-
face interaction. Gergen (1991) presented an image of technol-

ogy generally as capable of distancing the individual from the norms and constraints of community, family, and society, creating relationships that are no longer geographically located but can be taken up temporarily and independently of any enduring social context.

From the standpoint of the SIDE model, however, technology does not weaken the social conditions of communication so much as afford more efficient opportunities for constituting them. The constructions given to the self and to relationships are not freed by the absence of a physical setting so much as bound to the constraints of communication and behavior made normative and appropriate by the salience of specific social groups in particular contexts. Conditions of visual anonymity and isolation in CMC facilitate this process; furthermore, as we have argued above and elsewhere, many additional conditions associated with the communication technology, such as a large public forum, text-based communication, and efficient computer-based storage and retrieval capabilities, provide increased opportunities for surveillance and monitoring of personal relationships (Spears & Lea, 1994).

Shaping Technology/Building Relationships

In this final section, we explore some further ways in which identities and relationships may be constructed in CMC. Although we recognize the central role of discourse in this process, one of the most interesting aspects of the computer medium is the opportunity it affords to view the ways in which technology is also implicated in this process. Thus far, we have assumed the various features of the communication medium without considering their historical origins or the processes by which CMC systems such as electronic mail, computer conferencing, or the more complex multiuser interactive systems are designed. This is not to say, however, that the forms that these systems take are somehow inevitably produced (e.g., in response to users' "needs") or that their functions are necessarily determined by design. An approach that regards communication technologies as the stable products of a rational technical design process would be asymmetrical with the social constructionist perspective that we argue for with respect to the self and relationships. Instead, just as the latter can be viewed as tentative, exploratory, and ephemeral attempts to construct meanings from social situations, so can the process of technology development be seen as grounded in and constituted by these same social forces (e.g., Bijker, Hughes, & Pinch, 1987; Bijker & Law, 1992). In this respect, the process of building a communication medium should be regarded as "unfinished business" just as much as the relationships that are conducted through it (see Duck, 1990; Shotter, 1992).

Furthermore, there is a dynamic reciprocal influence between technology design and the contexts of use in which both technology and context mutually elaborate each other. This process is achieved rhetorically, through talk, social practices, and technical configurations (see Woolgar, 1991) and possibly appears in its most intimate form in computer-based communication technology, given the malleability of computer technology and the conduct of social life through the medium itself (Feenberg, 1992; Lea et al., 1992, 1994; Lea & Giordano, in press). This close interdependence can also be seen at work in the development of personal relationships over computer networks, in which determinations of what the technology is are dependent upon the forms of social interaction and human relationships that are conducted through it and in which at the same time the constructions of these relations are dependent upon the technology content that is negotiated during use.

For example, Myers (1987) described some of the processes by which new participants of a bulletin board mobilized the variety of possible technical configurations to create a suitable social context to construct their on-line identities and relationships with others. This involved direct appeals to the bulletin board operator to reconfigure the technical characteristics of the system in order to create an environment for interaction that suited their constructed identities, followed by the adoption of aliases (e.g., "Andromeda") that served to individuate the participants by drawing on referents to other social contexts. These new selves then gain meaning and social influence through the on-line relationships with others. Those who are most skilled at manipulating the interaction context, either technically, by reconfiguring the system architecture, or so-cially—for example, by helping others to create meaningful on-line identities—gain the most power and control over the communication behavior of others.

The process of constructing a technical context with the potential to control others is perhaps most clearly seen in systems such as WolfMOO that provide a programming language by which participants can build and manipulate new objects in the system (Rosenberg, 1992). Thus the WolfMOO environment is littered with artifacts that can act on the environment and on other people. For example, participants can build a "home" for their character that they design and furnish with "possessions." They "own" their home and can control access by others. Often, the programmed objects become a focus for conversation and achieve a social permanence: Participants can leave comments attached to objects for others to discuss subsequently. Thus the technical artifacts become yet further examples of social performance.

Individuals who show themselves to be the most competent, either socially or technically, become the leaders and accord themselves extra social and technical privileges by which they can reinforce their powerful position. In this culture, technical competence is highly valued and competes with social competence as a means of manipulating the context of the social interaction and as the route to greater power and influence. "Wizards" and "gods" promulgate the norms and values associated with the culture, police the system, and exact autocratic revenge on the perpetrators of wrongdoings by technical means (Reid, 1994). Technical competence also becomes a valuable currency in the formation of intimacy, as revealed by the respondent in Reid's (1994) study (cited earlier) who eventually married (in real life) her on-line partner:

I was really new to MUDs, really clueless, and he gave me a lot of help. He was teaching me how to build stuff, and he let me start building off of this castle he'd built. . . . We ended up building this castle together and everyone on the MUD treated us like a couple. . . . I was reluctant to get involved but he was so nice and he said that he really loved me and . . . we had this MUD marriage. It was so beautiful—I burst into tears in real life half way through it! *Anonymous.* (Reid, 1994, p. 32)

It has long been recognized that technical artifacts constitute social and political relations (Foucault, 1977; Winner, 1980). In personal relationships research, the importance of ownership and control over technical artifacts for the construction of intimate relationships is frequently underestimated, even though few with a knowledge of Western industrialized cultures would deny the influence of the automobile in shaping adolescent dating relationships. In CMC, however, these important influences are brought to the fore in a variety of guises. As a text medium, some of the most delicate and perhaps questionable bases of people's relationships that are reenacted daily through talk are freshly exposed to the actors themselves, to their partners, and to third parties (see Zuboff, 1988). Coupled with this, the immensely powerful information storage and search capabilities of computer technology mean that every word of every conversation ever conducted between two people via computer can be accurately retained and perfectly recalled at will by either party. Conversations are no longer tied to the time and place in which they were originated, but can be transported anywhere and reenacted at any time in the future. The permanence of text gives the process of constructing and reconstructing relationships through talk a new twist in the computer context. As well as recording the entire history of a relationship, the computer provides the technical means to carry out complex, detailed searches of a perfect memory to reveal details from the past, perhaps for evidence of lies and hypocrisy or to review a partner's unacceptable attitudes and behavior. In addition, the record is capable of being manipulated, edited, and restructured to order by the computer user to expose the underlying assumptions and complex associations of ideas used in the construction of relationships and to provide fresh angles from which to view the relationship. Examples of public broadcasts of private conversations, usually sexual in content, have already been noted in CMC (Reid, 1994; Rheingold, 1993). In short, CMC provides the technical as well as the social means to configure relationships in particular ways.

Summary

We have argued that a number of assumptions and biases in the prevailing conceptualizations about relationships and relationship processes prefigure the assumption that personal relationships will be difficult to obtain and maintain via telecommunications media. These include emphasis on physical proximity, face-to-face interaction, and nonverbal communication and talk as the essential processes of relating, and a general tendency to use physical and spatial metaphors in describing and accounting for relationships. Similar problems have been identified in models of communication media effects. Underlying both is an individualistic conception of self and social relations in social psychology and a tendency to ignore the social context of human interaction, so that the self is equated with the physical body and the foundations for attraction and relationship formation become dependent on the exchange of interpersonal information in situ. The SIDE model of situated social interaction is an attempt to ground a general social constructionist approach to conceptualizing self, relationships, and technology within concrete social psychological processes. We have tried to indicate how, by incorporating the social dimension of the self and attraction within relationship theory, this dependency on the physical co-presence of individuals can be overcome. In this way, the processes by which relationships are formed through communication media become explicable in the same terms as face-to-face relationships.

References

Aborampah, O. (1989). Black male-female relationships: Some observations. *Journal of Black Studies, 19,* 320-342.

Acitelli, L. K. (1988). When spouses talk to each other about their relationship. *Journal of Social and Personal Relationships, 5,* 185-199.

Ade-Ridder, L., & Brubaker, T. H. (1983). The quality of long-term marriages. In T. H. Brubaker (Ed.), *Family relationships in later life* (pp. 21-30). Beverly Hills, CA: Sage.

Adler, T. F., & Furman, W. (1988). A model for children's relationships and relationship dysfunctions. In S. W. Duck (Ed.), *Handbook of personal relationships* (pp. 211-229). Chichester, UK: John Wiley.

Aguirre, B. E., & Parr, W. C. (1982). Husbands' marriage order and the stability of first and second marriages for white and black women. *Journal of Marriage and the Family, 44,* 605-620.

Ainsworth, M. D., Blehar, M. C., Waters, E., & Wall, S. (1978). *Patterns of attachment: A psychological study of the strange situation.* Hillsdale, NJ: Lawrence Erlbaum.

Aldridge, D. P. (1991). *Focusing: Black male-female relationships.* Chicago: Third World Press.

Allan, G. (1979). *A sociology of friendship and kinship.* London: Allen & Unwin.

Allan, G. (1993). Social structure and relationships. In S. W. Duck (Ed.), *Social contexts of relationships* (pp. 1-25). Newbury Park, CA: Sage.

Allport, G. W. (1954). *The nature of prejudice.* New York: Addison-Wesley.

Althusser, L. (1976). *Essays in self-criticism.* London: Lowe & Brydone.

Altman, I., & T aylor, D. A. (1973). *Social penetration: The development of interpersonal relationships.* New York: Holt, Rinehart & Winston.

Amato, P. R. (1988). Parental divorce and attitudes toward marriage and family life. *Journal of Marriage and the Family, 50,* 453-461.

Anderson, S., Russell, C., & Schumm, A. (1983). Perceived marital quality and family life-cycle categories: A further analysis. *Journal of Marriage and the Family, 95,* 127-139.

Andrews, C. (1990). *Closeness and satisfaction in lesbian relationships.* Unpublished master's thesis, University of Washington.

Applegate, J. A. (1990). Constructs and communication: A pragmatic integration. In G. Neimeyer (Ed.), *Advances in personal construct psychology* (Vol. 1, pp. 203-230). Greenwich, CT: JAI.

Argyle, M., & Dean, J. (1965). Eye-contact, distance and affiliation. *Sociometry, 28,* 289-304.

Aries, E., & Johnson, F. (1983). Close friendship in adulthood: Conversational content between same-sex friends. *Sex Roles, 9,* 1183-1196.

Aronoff, J. (1967). *Psychological needs and cultural systems: A case study.* Princeton, NJ: Van Nostrand.

Aronoff, J., & Wilson, J. P. (1985). *Personality in the social process.* Hillsdale, NJ: Lawrence Erlbaum.

Asante, M. K. (1981). Black male and female relationship: An Afrocentric context. In L. Gary (Ed.), *Black men* (pp. 75-82). Beverly Hills, CA: Sage.

Athanasiou, R., & Yoshioka, G. (1973). The spatial character of friendship formation. *Environment and Behavior, 5,* 43-64.

Aukett, R., Richie, J., & Mill, K. (1988). Gender differences in friendship patterns. *Sex Roles, 19,* 57-66.

Axinn, W. G., & Thornton, A. (1992). The relationship between cohabitation and divorce: Selectivity or causal influence? *Demography, 29,* 357-374.

Bachrach, C. A. (1987). Cohabitation and reproductive behavior in the U.S. *Demography, 24,* 623-637.

Balakrishnan, T. R., & Chen, J. (1990). Religiosity, nuptiality and reproduction in Canada. *Canadian Journal of Sociology and Anthropology, 27,* 316-340.

Balakrishnan, T. R., Rao, K. V., Lapierre-Adamcyk, E., & Krotki, K. J. (1989). A hazard model analysis of the covariates of marriage dissolution in Canada. *Demography, 24,* 395-406.

Balka, E. (1993). Women's access to on-line discussions about feminism. *Electronic Journal of Communication, 3*(1). [Machine-readable file available through comserve@vm.its.rpi.edu].

Barker, J. R., Melville, C. W., & Pacanowsky, M. E. (1993). Self-directed teams at XEL: Changes in communication practices during a program of cultural transformation. *Journal of Applied Communication Research, 21,* 297-312.

Bateson, G. (1975). *Steps toward an ecology of mind.* New York: Ballantine.

Baudrillard, J. (1983). *Simulations* (P. Foss et al., Trans.). New York: Semiotext(e). (Original work published 1975)

Baxter, L. A. (1987). Symbols of relationship identity in relationship cultures. *Journal of Social and Personal Relationships, 4,* 261-279.

Baxter, L. A. (1988). A dialectical perspective on communication strategies in relationship development. In S. W. Duck, D. F. Hay, S. E. Hobfoll, W. Ickes, & B. Montgomery (Eds.), *Handbook of personal relationships* (pp. 257-273). London: John Wiley.

Baxter, L. A. (1990). Dialectical contradictions in relationship development. *Journal of Social and Personal Relationships, 7,* 69-88.

Baxter, L. A. (1993). The social and the personal of close relationships: A dialectical perspective. In S. W. Duck (Ed.), *Social contexts of relationships* (pp. 139-165). Newbury Park, CA: Sage.

Baxter, L. A., & Bullis, C. (1986). Turning points in developing romantic relationships. *Human Communication Research, 12,* 469-493.

Baxter, L. A., & Simon, E. P. (1993). Relationship maintenance strategies and dialectical contradictions in personal relationships. *Journal of Social and Personal Relationships, 10,* 225-242.

Bean, F. D., Curtis, R. L., Jr., & Marcum, J. P. (1977). Familism and marital satisfaction among Mexican Americans: The effects of family size, wife's labor force participation, and conjugal power. *Journal of Marriage and the Family, 39,* 759-767.

Beaujot, R. (1990). The family and demographic change in Canada: Economic and cultural interpretations and solutions. *Journal of Comparative Family Studies, 21,* 25-38.

Becerra, R. M. (1988). The Mexican American family. In C. H. Mindel, R. W. Habenstein, & R. Wright, Jr. (Eds.), *Ethnic families in America* (3rd ed., pp. 141-159). New York: Elsevier.

Becker, C. S. (1988). *Unbroken ties: lesbian ex-lovers.* Boston: Alyson.

Bell, Y. R., Bouie, C. L., & Baldwin, J. A. (1990). Afrocentric cultural consciousness and African-American male-female relationships. *Journal of Black Studies, 21,* 162-189.

Bellah, R. N., Madsen, R., Sullivan, W. M., Swidler, A., & Tipton, S. M. (1985). *Habits of the heart: Individualism and commitment in American life.* Berkeley: University of California Press.

Belsky, J., & Volling, B. (1987). Mothering, fathering, and marital interaction in the family triad during infancy. In P. Berman & F. Pedersen (Eds.), *Men's transitions to parenthood* (pp. 37-63). Hillsdale, NJ: Lawrence Erlbaum.

Bem, S. L. (1974). The measurement of psychological androgyny. *Journal of Consulting and Clinical Psychology, 45,* 196-205.

Beninger, J. R. (1987). Personalization of mass media and the growth of pseudo-community. *Communication Research, 14,* 352-371.

Bennett, N. G., Blanc, N. K., & Bloom, D. E. (1988). Commitment and the modern union. *American Sociological Review, 53,* 127-138.

Berger, C. R., & Bell, R. A. (1988). Plans and the initiation of social relationships. *Human Communication Research, 15,* 217-235.

Berger, P., & Kellner, H. (1975). Marriage and the construction of reality. In D. Brissett & C. Edgely (Eds.), *Life as theatre* (pp. 219-233). Chicago: Aldine.

Bernhardt, E., & Hoem, B. (1985). Cohabitation and social background: Trends observed for Swedish women born between 1936 and 1960. *European Journal of Population, 1,* 375-395.

Bernstein, B. (1974). *Class, codes, and control: Theoretical studies toward a sociology of language* (Rev. ed.). New York: Schocken.

Berry, J. W., Poortinga, Y. H., Segall, M. H., & Dasen, P. R. (1992). *Cross-cultural psychology: Research and applications.* Cambridge, UK: Cambridge University Press.

Berscheid, E. (1986). Mea culpas and lamentations: Sir Francis, Sir Isaac, and "the slow progress of soft psychology." In R. Gilmour & S. W. Duck (Eds.), *The emerging field of personal relationships* (pp. 267-310). Hillsdale, NJ: Lawrence Erlbaum.

Berzon, B. (1988). *Permanent partners: Building gay and lesbian relationships that last.* New York: E. P. Dutton.

Bijker, W. E., Hughes, T. P., & Pinch, T. J. (1987). *The social construction of technological systems: New directions in the sociology and history of technology.* Cambridge, MA: MIT Press.

Bijker, W. E., & Law, J. (1992). *Shaping technology/building society: Studies in sociotechnical change.* Cambridge, MA: MIT Press.

Billig, M. (1987). *Arguing and thinking: A rhetorical approach to social psychology.* New York: Cambridge University Press.

Billig, M., Condor, S., Edwards, D., Gane, M., Middleton, D., & Radley, A. (1988). *A social psychology of everyday thinking.* London: Sage.

Billingham, R. E., & Sack, A. R. (1987). Conflict tactics and the level of emotional commitment among unmarrieds. *Human Relations, 40,* 59-74.

Billingsley, A. (1968). *Black families in white America.* New York: Touchstone.

Black, L. E., & Sprenkle, D. H. (1991). Gender differences in college students' attitudes toward divorce and their willingness to marry. *Journal of Divorce and Remarriage, 14,* 47-60.

Blanc, A. K. (1987). Nonmarital cohabitation and fertility in the United States and western Europe. *Population Research and Policy Review, 3,* 181-193.

Bledsoe, C. (1990). Transformations in sub-Saharan African marriage and fertility. *Annals of the American Academy of Political and Social Science, 510,* 115-125.

Bloom, A. D. (1987). *The closing of the American mind.* New York: Simon & Schuster.

Blumer, H. (1969). *Symbolic interactionism: Perspective and method.* Englewood Cliffs, NJ: Prentice Hall.

Blumstein, P., & Schwartz, P. (1983). *American couples.* New York: William Morrow.

Bochner, A. (1984). The functions of human communication in interpersonal bonding. In C. Arnold & J. Bowers (Eds.), *Handbook of rhetorical and communication theory* (pp. 544-621). Boston: Allyn & Bacon.

Booth, A., & Hess, E. (1974). Cross-sex friendship. *Journal of Marriage and the Family, 36,* 38-47.

Booth, A., & Johnson, D. (1988). Premarital cohabitation and marital success. *Journal of Family Issues, 9,* 255-272.

Bossard, J. H. (1932). Residential propinquity as a factor in marriage selection. *American Journal of Sociology, 38,* 219-224.

Bracher, M., & Santow, G. (1990). The family histories of Australian women. *European Journal of Population, 6,* 227-256.

Bradley, D. (1990). Unmarried cohabitation in Sweden: A renewed social institution? *Journal of Legal History, 11,* 300-308.

Braithwaite, V. A., & Scott, W. A. (1991). Values. In J. P. Robinson, P. R. Shaver, & L. S. Wrightsman (Eds.), *Measures of personality and social psychological attitudes* (pp. 661-753). New York: Academic Press.

238 UNDER-STUDIED RELATIONSHIPS

Brehm, S. S. (1992). *Intimate relationships* (2nd ed.). New York: Random House.

Brooks, D. M., & Kennedy, G. E. (1989). British and American attitudes toward family relationships. *Psychological Reports, 64,* 815-818.

Brown, P., & Levinson, S. C. (1987). *Politeness: Some universals in language usage.* Cambridge, UK: Cambridge University Press.

Brown, P., Perry, L., & Harburg, E. (1977). Sex role attitudes and psychological outcomes for black and white women experiencing marital dissolution. *Journal of Marriage and the Family, 39,* 549-561.

Brown, R. (1965). *Social psychology.* New York: Free Press.

Brown, R. (1986). *Social psychology* (2nd ed.). New York: Free Press.

Brubaker, T. H. (1985). *Later life families.* Beverly Hills, CA: Sage.

Bull, R., & Rumsey, N. (1988). *The social psychology of facial appearance.* New York: Springer-Verlag.

Bumpass, L. L., Castro Martin, T., & Sweet, J. A. (1991). The impact of family background and early marital factors on marital disruption. *Journal of Family Issues, 12,* 22-42.

Bumpass, L. L., & Sweet, J. A. (1989). National estimates of cohabitation. *Demography, 26,* 615-625.

Bumpass, L. L., Sweet, J. A., & Cherlin, A. (1991). The role of cohabitation in declining rates of marriage. *Journal of Marriage and the Family, 53,* 913-927.

Burke, K. (1935). *Permanence and change.* New York: New Republic.

Burleson, B. R. (1987). Cognitive complexity. In J. C. McCroskey & J. A. Daly (Eds.), *Personality and interpersonal communication* (pp. 305-349). Newbury Park, CA: Sage.

Burr, W. R. (1970). Satisfaction with various aspects of marriage over the life cycle: A random middle class sample. *Journal of the Marriage and the Family, 32,* 29-37.

Burrell, G., & Morgan, G. (1979). *Sociological paradigms and organizational analysis.* London: Heinemann.

Buunk, B. P., & van Driel, B. (1989). *Variant lifestyles and relationships.* Newbury Park, CA: Sage.

Byrne, D. (1971). *The attraction paradigm.* New York: Academic Press.

Byron, R. F. (1976). Economic functions of kinship values in family businesses: Fishing crews in North Atlantic communities. *Sociology and Social Research, 60,* 147-160.

Caldwell, M., & Peplau, L. A. (1982). Sex differences in same-sex friendship. *Sex Roles, 8,* 721-732.

Cancian, F. (1987). *Love in America.* Cambridge, MA: Cambridge University Press.

Carlson, E., & Klinger, A. (1987). Partners in life: Unmarried couples in Hungary. *European Journal of Population, 3,* 85-99.

Carmichael, G. A. (1984). Living together in New Zealand: Data on coresidence at marriage and on de facto unions. *New Zealand Population Review, 10,* 41-53.

Carmichael, G. A. (1990). A cohort analysis of marriage and informal cohabitation among Australian men. *Australian and New Zealand Journal of Sociology, 27,* 53-72.

Castles, I. (1993). *Australia's families: Selected findings from the survey of families in Australia March 1992 to May 1992.* Canberra: Australian Government Printing Office.

Cavanaugh, J. C., & Parks, D. C. (1993). Vitality for life: Psychological research for productive aging. *APS Observer,* Vol. 2; Special Issue, Report 2, pp. 1-2. Published by the American Psychological Society

Chesebro, J. W., & Bonsall, D. G. (1989). *Computer-mediated communication: Human relationships in a computerized world.* Tuscaloosa: University of Alabama Press.

Chiari, J. (1975). *Twentieth-century French thought: From Bergson to Levi-Strauss.* New York: Gordian.

Clark, M. S., & Mills, J. (1979). Interpersonal attraction in exchange and communal relationships. *Journal of Personality and Social Psychology, 37,* 12-24.

Clark, M. S., Quellette, R., Powell, M. C., & Milberg, S. (1987). Recipient's mood, relationship type, and helping. *Journal of Personality and Social Psychology, 53,* 93-103.

Clark, M. S., & Reis, H. T. (1988). Interpersonal processes in close relationships. *Annual Review of Psychology, 39,* 609- 672.

Clark-Nicolas, P., & Gray-Little, B. (1991). Effects of economic resources on marital quality in black married couples. *Journal of Marriage and the Family, 53,* 645-655.

Clunis, D. M., & Green, G. D. (1988). *Lesbian couples.* Seattle, WA: Seal.

Cole, C. L. (1984). Marital quality in later life. In W. H. Quinn & G. H. Hughston (Eds.), *Independent aging: Family and social support perspectives* (pp. 72-90). Gaithersburg, MD: Aspen.

Collins, E. G. C. (1983, September/October). Managers and lovers. *Harvard Business Review,* pp. 142-153.

Collins, P. H. (1986). Learning from the outsider within. *Social Problems, 23,* 514-532.

Commission on Minority Participation in Education and American Life. (1988). *One-third of a nation.* Washington, DC: American Council on Education.

Conville, R. L. (1988). Relational transitions: An inquiry into their structure and function. *Journal of Social and Personal Relationships, 5,* 423-437.

Cook, N. D., & Kono, S. (1977). Black psychology: The third great tradition. *Journal of Black Psychology, 3,* 18-28.

Couch, C. J. (1986). Elementary forms of social activity. In C. J. Couch, S. L. Saxton, & M. A. Katovich (Eds.), *Studies in symbolic interaction: The Iowa school* (pp. 113-129). Greenwich, CT: JAI.

Couch, C. J. (1987). *Researching social processes in the laboratory.* Greenwich, CT: JAI.

Couch, C. J., & Hintz, R. A. (1975). *Constructing social life.* Champaign, IL: Stipes.

Crohan, S. E., & Veroff, J. (1989). Dimensions of marital well-being among white and black newlyweds. *Journal of Marriage and the Family, 51,* 373-383.

Cromwell, R. E., & Ruiz, R. A. (1979). The myth of macho dominance in decision making within Mexican and Chicano families. *Hispanic Journal of Behavioral Sciences, 1,* 355-373.

Cunningham, J. D., & Antill, J. K. (1994). Cohabitation and marriage: Retrospective and predictive comparisons. *Journal of Social and Personal Relationships, 11,* 77-93.

Curran, J. P. (1973). Examination of various interpersonal attraction principles in the dating dyad. *Journal of Experimental Research in Personality, 6,* 347-356.

Curtis, P. (1992). Mudding: Social phenomena in text-based virtual realities. In D. Schuler (Ed.), *DIAC-92: Directions and implications of advanced computing* (pp. 44-68). Palo Alto, CA: Computer Professionals for Social Responsibility.

Dansereau, F., & Markham, S. E. (1987). Superior-subordinate communication: Multiple levels of analysis. In F. M. Jablin, L. L. Putnam, K. H. Roberts, & L. W. Porter (Eds.), *Handbook of organizational communication: An interdisciplinary perspective* (pp. 343-388). Newbury Park, CA: Sage.

Davidson, A. G. (1991). Looking for love in the age of AIDS: The language of gay personals, 1978-1988. *Journal of Sex Research, 28,* 125-137.

Davis, S. K., & Chavez, V. (1985). Hispanic househusbands. *Hispanic Journal of Behavioral Sciences, 7,* 317-332.

Davis, V. T., & Singh, R. N. (1989). Attitudes of university students from India toward marriage and family life. *International Journal of Sociology of the Family, 19,* 43-57.

DeCotiis, T., & Petit, A. (1978). The performance appraisal process: A model and some testable propositions. *Academy of Management Review, 3,* 635-646.

De Lacy, J. (1987, July 31). The French are falling in love with their computers and through them. *New Yorker,* p. 92.

Delia, J. G. (1980). Some tentative thoughts concerning the study of interpersonal relationships and their development. *Western Journal of Speech Communication, 44,* 97-103.

Delia, J. G., O'Keefe, B. J., & O'Keefe, D. J. (1982). The constructivist approach to communication. In F. E. X. Dance (Ed.), *Human communication theory: Comparative essays* (pp. 147-191). New York: Harper & Row.

DeMaris, A. (1984). A comparison of remarriages with first marriages on satisfaction in marriage and its relationship to prior cohabitation. *Family Relations, 33,* 443-449.

DeMaris, A., & MacDonald, W. (1993). Premarital cohabitation and marital instability: A test of the unconventionality hypothesis. *Journal of Marriage and the Family, 55,* 399-407.

DeMaris, A., & Rao, K. V. (1992). Premarital cohabitation and subsequent marital stability in the United States: A reassessment. *Journal of Marriage and the Family, 54,* 178-190.

Derrida, J. (1987). *The postcard: From Socrates to Freud and beyond* (A. Bass, Trans.). Chicago: University of Chicago Press.

DeSanctis, G., & Gallupe, R. B. (1987). A foundation for the study of group decision support systems. *Management Science, 33,* 589-609.

Deutsch, M., & Collins, M. (1958). The effects of public policy in housing projects upon interracial attitudes. In E. Maccoby, T. M. Newcomb, & E. L. Hartley (Eds.), *Readings in social psychology* (pp. 612-623). New York: Holt, Rinehart & Winston.

Dickson, F. C. (1994). *Social interaction and health among older adults.* Manuscript submitted for publication.

References   241

Dietrich, K. T. (1975). A reexamination of the myth of the black matriarchy. *Journal of Marriage and the Family, 37,* 367-374.

Dillard, J. P., & Witteman, H. (1985). Romantic relationships at work: Organizational and personal influences. *Human Communication Research, 12,* 99-116.

Dindia, K. (1994). The intrapersonal-interpersonal dialectical process of self-disclosure. In S. W. Duck (Ed.), *Dynamics of relationships* (pp. 27-57). Newbury Park, CA: Sage.

Dindia, K., Fitzpatrick, M. A., & Kenny, D. A. (1989, November). *Self disclosure in spouse and stranger interaction: A social relations analysis.* Paper presented at the International Communication Association, New Orleans.

Dinnerstein, L., & Reimers, D. M. (1988). *Ethnic Americans: A history of immigration.* New York: Harper & Row.

Dinnerstein, L., Reimers, D. M., & Nichols, R. L. (1979). *Natives and strangers: Ethnic groups and the building of America.* New York: Oxford University Press.

Dion, K. K., Berscheid, E., & Walster, E. (1972). What is beautiful is good. *Journal of Personality and Social Psychology, 24,* 285-290.

Dorman, J. H. (1979). Ethnic groups and "ethnicity": Some theoretical considerations. *Journal of Ethnic Studies, 7,* 23-36.

D'Sousa, D. (1991). *Illiberal education: The politics of race and sex on campus.* New York: Free Press.

DuBois, W. E. B. (1986). *Writings.* New York: Harper & Row.

Dubos, R. (1974). *Of human diversity.* New York: Crown.

Duck, S. W. (1977a). Inquiry, hypothesis and the quest for validation: Personal construct systems in the development of acquaintance. In S. Duck (Ed.), *Theory and practice in interpersonal attraction* (pp. 379-404). London: Academic Press.

Duck, S. W. (1977b). *The study of acquaintance.* Farnborough, UK: Teakfield-Saxon House.

Duck, S. W. (1980). T aking the past to heart: One of the futures of social psychology. In R. Gilmour & S. W. Duck (Eds.), *The development of social psychology* (pp. 211-237). London: Academic Press.

Duck, S. W. (1988). *Relating to others.* Monterey, CA: Brooks/Cole.

Duck, S. W. (1990). Relationships as unfinished business: Out of the frying pan and into the 1990s [Editorial]. *Journal of Social and Personal Relationships, 7,* 3-28.

Duck, S. W. (1991). *Understanding relationships.* New York: Guilford.

Duck, S. W. (Ed.). (1994a). *Dynamics of relationships.* Newbury Park, CA: Sage.

Duck, S. W. (1994b). *Meaningful relationships: Talking, sense, and relating.* Newbury Park, CA: Sage.

Duck, S. W. (1994c). Steady as (s)he goes: Relationship maintenance as a shared meaning system. In D. J. Canary & L. Stafford (Eds.), *Communication and relationship maintenance* (pp. 45-60). New York: Academic Press.

Duck, S. W. (1994d). Stratagems, spoils and a serpent's tooth: On the delights and dilemmas of personal relationships. In W. R. Cupach & B. H. Spitzberg (Eds.), *The dark side of interpersonal communication* (pp. 3-24). Hillsdale, NJ: Lawrence Erlbaum.

242   UNDER-STUDIED RELATIONSHIPS

Duck, S. W., & Miell, D. E. (1984). Towards an understanding of relationship development and breakdown. In H. T ajfel, C. Fraser, & J. Jaspars (Eds.), *The social dimension: European perspectives on social psychology* (pp. 133-144). Cambridge, UK: Cambridge University Press.

Duck, S. W., & Pond, K. (1989). Friends, Romans, countrymen, lend me your retrospections: Rhetoric and reality in personal relationships. In C. Hendrick (Ed.), *Close relationships* (pp. 17-38). Newbury Park, CA: Sage.

Duck, S. W., Rutt, D. J., Hurst, M. H., & Strejc, H. (1991). Some evident truths about conversations in everyday relationships: All communications are not created equal. *Human Communication Research, 18,* 228-267.

Eckenrode, J., & Gore, S. (1989). *Stress between work and family.* New York: Plenum.

Eichenbaum, L., & Orbach, S. (1988). *Between women.* New York: Viking.

Eldridge, N. S., & Gilbert, L. A. (1990). Correlates of relationship satisfaction in lesbian couples. *Psychology of Women Quarterly, 14,* 43-62.

Ellis, D. (1989). Male abuse of a marriage or cohabiting female partner. *Violence and Victims, 4,* 235-255.

Ellis, D., & Dekeseredy, W. S. (1989). Marital status and woman abuse: The DAD model. *International Journal of the Sociology of the Family, 19,* 67-87.

England, P., & Farkas, G. (1986). *Households, employment, and gender: A social, economic and demographic view.* Hawthorne, NY: Walter de Gruyter.

Epstein, C. F. (1988). *Deceptive distinctions: Sex, gender, and the social order.* New Haven, CT: Yale University Press.

Faller, K. C. (1989). The role relationship between victim and perpetrator as a predictor of intrafamilial sexual abuse. *Child and Adolescent Social Work Journal, 6,* 217-229.

Feenberg, A. (1992). From information to communication: The French experience with videotex. In M. Lea (Ed.), *Contexts of computer-mediated communication* (pp. 168-187). London: Harvester-Wheatsheaf.

Feldman, H. (1974). Change in marriage and parenthood: A methodological design. In E. Peck & J. Senderowitz (Eds.), *Pronatalism: The myth of mom and apple pie* (pp. 206-226). New York: Thomas V. Crowell.

Feldman, S. P. (1985). Culture and conformity: An essay on individual adaptation in centralized bureaucracy. *Human Relations, 38,* 341-356.

Fennelly, K., Kandiah, V., & Ortiz, V. (1989). The cross-cultural study of fertility among Hispanic adolescents in the Americas. *Studies in Family Planning, 20,* 96-101.

Ferguson, D. M., Horwood, L. J., & Shannon, F. T. (1984). A proportional hazards model of family breakdown. *Journal of Marriage and the Family, 46,* 539-549.

Ferrara, K., Brunner, H., & Whittemore, G. (1991). Interactive written discourse as an emergent register. *Written Communication, 8,* 8-34.

Finholt, T., & Sproull, L. (1990). Electronic groups at work. *Organization Science, 1,* 41-64.

Fiqueroa-Sarriera, H. J. (1993, April). *Some body fantasies in cyberspace texts: A view from its exclusions.* Paper presented at the Conference of the International Society for Theoretical Psychology, Saclas, France.

Fishman, P. (1983). Interaction: The work women do. In K. Thorne & U. Henley (Eds.), *Language, gender, and society* (pp. 89-100). Rowley, MA: Newbury House.

Fiske, S. T., & Taylor, S. E. (1984). *Social cognition.* Reading, MA: Addison-Wesley.

Fitzpatrick, M. A. (1988). *Between husbands and wives: Communication in marriage.* Newbury Park, CA: Sage.

Fitzpatrick, M. A., & Best, P. (1979). Dyadic adjustment in relational types: Consensus, cohesion, affectional expression, and satisfaction in enduring relationships. *Communication Monographs, 46,* 167-178.

Foa, U. G. (1973). Interpersonal and economic resources. *Science, 171,* 345-351.

Foa, U. G., & Foa, E. B. (1974). *Societal structures of the mind.* Springfield, IL: Charles C Thomas.

Foucault, M. (1977). *Discipline and punish.* Harmondsworth, UK: Penguin.

Foucault, M. (1988). The political technology of individuals. In L. H. Martin, H. Gutman, & P. H. Hutton (Eds.), *Technologies of the self: A seminar with Michel Foucault* (pp. 145-162). Amherst: University of Massachusetts Press.

Frazier, E. F. (1939). *The Negro family in the United States.* Chicago: University of Chicago Press.

Frazier, P. A., & Cook, S. W. (1993). Correlates of distress following heterosexual relationship dissolution. *Journal of Social and Personal Relationships, 10,* 55-67.

French, M. (1985). *Beyond power: On women, men, and morals.* New York: Ballantine.

Frisbee, W. P., & Bean, F. D. (1978). Some issues in the demographic study of racial and ethnic populations. In F. D. Bean & W. P. Frisbee (Eds.), *The demography of racial and ethnic groups* (pp. 1-14). New York: Academic Press.

Frisbee, W. P., Bean, F. D., & Eberstein, I. W. (1978). Patterns of marital instability among Mexican Americans, blacks, and Anglos. In F. D. Bean & W. P. Frisbee (Eds.), *The demography of racial and ethnic groups* (pp. 143-163). New York: Academic Press.

Fulk, J., & Steinfield, C. (1990). *Organizations and communication technology.* Newbury Park, CA: Sage.

Gadamer, J.-G. (1989). *Truth and method* (2nd rev. ed., J. Weinsheimer & D. G. Marshall, Trans.). New York: Crossroad.

Gaines, S. O., Jr. (1993, March 4-7). *Familism and interpersonal resource exchange among Latinas and Latinos.* Paper presented at the 1993 Conference of the National Association for Ethnic Studies, University of Utah, Salt Lake City.

Gaines, S. O., Jr. (1994a). Exchange of respect-denying behavior among male-female friendships. *Journal of Social and Personal Relationships, 11,* 5-24.

Gaines, S. O., Jr. (1994b). Generic, stereotypic, and collectivistic models of interpersonal resource exchange among African American couples. *Journal of Black Psychology, 20,* 291-301.

Gaines, S. O., Jr., & Reed, E. S. (1994). Two social psychologies of prejudice: Gordon W. Allport, W. E. B. DuBois, and the legacy of Booker T. Washington. *Journal of Black Psychology, 20,* 8-28.

Gaines, S. O., Jr., & Reed, E. S. (1995). Prejudice: From Allport to DuBois. *American Psychologist, 50,* 96-103.

Gandy, O. (1993). *The panopticon sort: A political economy of personal information.* Boulder, CO: Westview.

Geertz, C. (1973). *The interpretation of cultures.* New York: Basic Books.

Gergen, K. J. (1969). *The psychology of behavior exchange.* Reading, MA: Addison-Wesley.

Gergen, K. J. (1991). *The saturated self: Dilemmas of identity in contemporary life.* New York: Basic Books.

Gergen, K. J., & Davis, K. E. (1985). *The social construction of the person.* New York: Springer-Verlag.

Gertsel, N., & Gross, H. E. (1982). Commuter marriages: A review. *Marriage and Family Review, 5,* 71-93.

Gertsel, N., & Gross, H. E. (1984). *Commuter relationships.* Beverly Hills: Sage.

Goffman, E. (1959). *The presentation of self in everyday life.* Garden City, NY: Doubleday.

Goffman, E. (1963). *Stigma: Notes on the management of spoiled identity.* Englewood Cliffs, NJ: Prentice Hall.

Goffman, E. (1967). *Interaction ritual: Essays in face to face behavior.* Garden City, NY: Doubleday.

Goffman, I. (1977). Arrangements between sexes. *Theory and Society, 4,* 301-331.

Goldner, V., Penn, P., Scheinberg, M., & Walker, G. (1990). Love and violence: Gender paradoxes in volatile attachments. *Family Process, 19,* 343-364.

Goldsmith, D. (1990). A dialectic perspective on the expression of autonomy and connection in romantic relationships. *Western Journal of Speech Communication, 54,* 537-556.

Gonzales, M. H., & Meyers, S. A. (1993). "Your mother would like me": Self-presentation in the personals ads of heterosexual and homosexual men and women. *Personality and Social Psychology Bulletin, 19,* 131-142.

Gordon, M. M. (1978). *Human nature, class, and ethnicity.* New York: Oxford University Press.

Gottman, J., Markman, H., & Notarius, C. (1977). The topography of marital conflict: A sequential analysis of verbal and nonverbal behavior. *Journal of Marriage and the Family, 39,* 461-477.

Gouldner, H., & Strong, M. S. (1987). *Speaking of friendship: Middle-class women and their friends.* New York: Greenwood.

Govaerts, K., & Dixon, D. (1988). ". . . Until careers do us part": Vocational and marital satisfaction in the dual-career commuter marriage. *International Journal for the Advancement of Counselling, 11,* 265-281.

Gross, H. E. (1980). Couples who live apart: Time/place disjunctions and their consequence. *Symbolic Interaction, 3,* 69-82.

Grunebaum, H. (1979). Middle age and marriage-affiliative men and assertive women. *American Journal of Family Therapy, 7*(3), 46-50.

Guldner, G. T., & Swenson, C. H. (1995). Time spent together and relationship quality: Long distance relationships as a test case. *Journal of Social and Personal Relationship, 12,* 313-320.

Gullahorn, J. T. (1952). Distance and friendship as factors in the gross interaction matrix. *Sociometry, 15,* 123-134.

Gutmann, D. L. (1977). The cross cultural perspective: Notes toward a comparative psychology of aging. In J. E. Birren & K. W. Schaie (Eds.), *Handbook for the psychology of aging* (pp. 167-1894). New York: Van Nostrand Reinhold.

Gwartney-Gibbs, P. A. (1986). The institutionalization of premarital cohabitation: Estimates from marriage license applications, 1970 and 1980. *Journal of Marriage and the Family, 48,* 423-434.

Haaken, J., & Korschgen, J. (1988). Adolescents and conceptions of social relations in the workplace. *Adolescence, 89,* 1-14.

Hall, C. S., & Lindzey, G. (1978). *Theories of personality* (3rd ed.). New York: John Wiley.

Hall, J. (1974). Interpersonal style and the communication dilemma: Managerial implications of the Johari Awareness model. *Human Relations, 27,* 381-399.

Halli, S. S., & Zimmer, Z. (1991). Common law union as a differentiating factor in the failure of marriage in Canada, 1984. *Social Indicators Research, 24,* 329-345.

Harding, S. (1991). *Whose science? Whose knowledge? Thinking from women's lives.* Ithaca, NY: Cornell University Press.

Harris, S. M., & Majors, R. (1993). Cultural value differences: Implications for the experiences of African-American men. *Journal of Men's Studies, 1,* 227-238.

Harry, J. (1982). Decision making and age differences among gay couples. *Journal of Homosexuality, 8,* 9-21.

Harry, J., & DeVall, W. B. (1978). *The social organization of gay males.* New York: Praeger.

Hasleton, S. (1975). Permissiveness in Australian society. *Australian Journal of Psychology, 27,* 257-267.

Hawkes, G. R., & Taylor, M. (1975). Power structure in Mexican and Mexican-American farm labor families. *Journal of Marriage and the Family, 37,* 807-811.

Hazan, C., & Shaver, P. (1987). Romantic love conceptualized as an attachment process. *Journal of Personality and Social Psychology, 52,* 511-524.

Hegel, G. W. F. (1910). *Phenomenology of mind* (J. B. Baillie, Trans.). Germany: Wurzburg & Bamburg. (Original work published 1807)

Heim, M. (1992). The erotic ontology of cyberspace. In M. Benedikt (Ed.), *Cyberspace: First steps* (pp. 59-80). Cambridge, MA: MIT Press.

Helmreich, R. L., Spence, J. T., Beane, W. E., Lucker, G. W., & Matthews, K. A. (1980). Making it in academic psychology: Demographic and personality correlates of attainment. *Journal of Personality and Social Psychology, 39,* 896-908.

Henderson, M., & Argyle, M. (1985). Social support by four categories of work colleagues: Relationships between activities, stress, and satisfaction. *Journal of Occupational Behaviour, 6,* 229-239.

Hendrick, C. (1989). *Review of social psychology and personality: Vol. 10. Close relationships.* Newbury Park, CA: Sage.

Hendrick, C., & Hendrick, S. (1988). Lovers wear rose colored glasses. *Journal of Social and Personal Relationships, 5,* 161-184.

Herring, S. C. (1993). Gender and democracy in computer-mediated communication. *Electronic Journal of Communication, 3*(2). [Machine-readable file available through comserve@vm.its.rpi.edu].

246   UNDER-STUDIED RELATIONSHIPS

Hess, R. D., & Handel, G. (1959). *Family worlds: A psychosocial approach to family life.* Chicago: University of Chicago Press.

Hillerbrand, E., Holt, P., & Cochran, S. (1986, April). *Long-distance relationships: An opportunity for growth.* Paper presented at the American College Personnel Association Convention, New Orleans.

Hiltz, S. R., & Turoff, M. (1978). *The network nation: Human communication via computer.* Reading, MA: Addison-Wesley.

Hi-tech sex. (1993, May). *Marie-Claire* (London ed.), pp. 22-25.

Hobart, C. (1993). Interest in marriage among Canadian students at the end of the eighties. *Journal of Comparative Family Studies, 24,* 45-61.

Hobart, C., & Grigel, F. (1992). Cohabitation among Canadian students at the end of the eighties. *Journal of Comparative Family Studies, 23,* 311-337.

Hochschild, A., with Manchung, A. (1989). *The double shift: Working parents and the revolution at home.* New York: Viking Penguin.

Hoffman, M. (1968). *The gay world.* New York: Basic Books.

Hogg, M. A. (1992). *The social psychology of group cohesiveness: From attraction to social identity.* London: Harvester-Wheatsheaf.

Holt, P. A., & Stone, G. L. (1988). Needs, coping strategies, and coping outcomes associated with long-distance relationships. *Journal of College Student Development, 29,* 136-141.

Homans, G. C. (1961). *Social behavior.* New York: Harcourt, Brace & World.

Honigmann, J. J. (1954). *Culture and personality.* New York: Harper & Brothers.

Hornstein, G. A. (1985). Intimacy in conversational style as a function of the degree of closeness between members of a dyad. *Journal of Personality and Social Psychology, 49,* 671-681.

Howard, J., Blumstein, P., & Schwartz, P. (1992). *Homogamy in intimate relationships.* Unpublished manuscript.

Hughston, D. S., & Hughston, G. A. (1989). Legal ramifications of elderly cohabitation. *Journal of Psychotherapy and the Family, 5,* 163-172.

Humphries, L. (1970). *Tearoom trade: Impersonal sex in public places.* Chicago: Aldine.

Hunt, G. J., & Butler, E. W. (1972). Migration, participation, and alienation. *Sociology and Social Research, 56,* 440-452.

Hunter, N. D., Michaelson, S. E., & Stoddard, T. B. (1992). *The rights of lesbian and gay men.* Carbondale: Southern Illinois University Press.

Huston, T. L., & Levinger, G. (1978). Interpersonal attraction and relationships. *Annual Review of Psychology, 29,* 115-156.

Huych, M. H., & Hoyer, W. J. (1982). *Adult development and aging.* Belmont, CA: Wadsworth.

Ickes, W. (1985). Sex-role influences on compatibility in relationships. In W. Ickes (Ed.), *Compatible and incompatible relationships* (pp. 187-208). New York: Springer-Verlag.

Ickes, W. (1993). Traditional gender roles: Do they make, and then break, our relationships? *Journal of Social Issues, 49,* 71-86.

Isaacs, M. B., & Leon, G. H. (1988). Remarriage and its alternatives following divorce. *Journal of Marriage and Family Therapy, 14,* 163-173.

Jablin, F. M. (1979). Superior-subordinate communication: The state of the art. *Psychological Bulletin, 86,* 1201-1222.

Jablin, F. M. (1982). Formal structural characteristics of organizations and superior-subordinate communication. *Human Commmunication Research, 8,* 338-347.

Jablin, F. M. (1985). Task/work relationships: A life span perspective. In G. M. Miller & M. L. Knapp (Eds.), *Handbook of interpersonal communication* (pp. 615-654). Beverly Hills, CA: Sage.

Jacobson, M. S., & Margolin, G. (1979). *Marital therapy: Strategies based on social learning and behavior exchange principles.* New York: Brunner-Mazel.

Johnson, M. P. (1973). Commitment: A conceptual structure and empirical application. *Sociological Quarterly, 14,* 395-406.

Johnson, M. P. (1991a). Commitment to personal relationships. In W. H. Jones & D. Perlman (Eds.), *Advances in personal relationships* (Vol. 3, pp. 117-143). London: Kingsley.

Johnson, M. P. (1991b). Reply to Levinger and Rusbult. In W. H. Jones & D. Perlman (Eds.), *Advances in personal relationships* (Vol. 3, pp. 171-176). London: Kingsley.

Jones, E. E. (1985). Major developments in social psychology during the past five decades. In G. Lindzey & E. Aronson (Eds.), *Handbook of social psychology* (3rd ed., Vol. 1, pp. 47-107). New York: Random House.

Jones, R. W., & Bates, J. E. (1978). Satisfaction in male homosexual couples. *Journal of Homosexuality, 3,* 217-224.

Joreskog, K. G., & Sorbom, D. (1979). *Advances in factor analysis and structural equation models.* Cambridge, MA: ABT.

Jourard, S. (1971). *The transparent self.* New York: D. Van Nostrand.

Kami, C. K., & Radin, N. L. (1967). Class differences in the socialization practices of Negro mothers. *Journal of Marriage and the Family, 29,* 302-310.

Kantor, J. R. (1982). *Cultural psychology.* Chicago: Principia.

Keating, N., & Cole, P. (1980). What do I do with him 24 hours a day? *Gerontologist, 20,* 84-89.

Keith, P., Powers, E., & Goudy, W. (1981). Older men in employment and retired families: Well-being and involvement in household activities. *Alternative Lifestyles, 4,* 228-241.

Keith, P. M., & Schafer, R. B. (1985). Equity, role strains, and depression among middle aged and older men and women. In W. A. Peterson & J. Quadagno (Eds.), *Social bonds in later life* (pp. 37-50). Beverly Hills, CA: Sage.

Keller, E. F. (1985). *Reflections on gender and science.* New Haven, CT: Yale University Press.

Keller, E. F. (1992). *Secrets of life, secrets of death: Essays on language, gender, and science.* New York: Routledge.

Kelley, H. H. (1983). Love and commitment. In H. H. Kelley, E. Berscheid, A. Christensen, J. H. Harvey, G. Levinger, E. McClintock, L. A. Peplau, & D. R. Peterson (Eds.), *Close relationships* (pp. 265-314). New York: W. H. Freeman.

Kelley, H. H., Berscheid, E., Christensen, A., Harvey, J. H., Huston, T. L., et al. (1983). *Close relationships.* New York: W. H. Freeman.

Kelly, G. A. (1955). *The psychology of personal constructs* (2 vols.). New York: Norton.

Kelly, J. A., St. Lawrence, J. S., Hood, H. V., & Brasfield, T. L. (1989). Behavioral intervention to reduce AIDS risk activities. *Journal of Consulting and Clinical Psychology, 57,* 60-67.

Kennedy, R. (1943). Premarital residential propinquity. *American Journal of Sociology, 48,* 580-584.

Kephart, W. M., & Jedlicka, D. (1988). *The family, society, and the individual* (6th ed.). New York: Harper & Row.

Kerckhoff, A. C. (1974). The social context of interpersonal attraction. In T. L. Huston (Ed.), *Foundations of interpersonal attraction* (pp. 61-78). New York: Academic Press.

Kerr, P. (1982, September 16). Now, computerized bulletin boards. *New York Times,* pp. C1, C7.

Kets de Vries, M. F. R., & Miller, D. (1984). *The neurotic organization.* San Francisco: Jossey-Bass.

Khoo, S.-E. (1987). Living together as married: A profile of de facto couples in Australia. *Journal of Marriage and the Family, 49,* 185-191.

Khoo, S.-E. (1988). Children in de facto relationships. *Australian Journal of Social Issues, 23,* 38-49.

Kiesler, C. A. (1971). *The psychology of commitment: Experiments linking behavior to belief.* New York: Academic Press.

Kiesler, S., Siegel, J., & McGuire, T. (1984). Social psychological aspects of computer-mediated communication. *American Psychologist, 39,* 1123-1134.

Kiesler, S., Zubrow, D., Moses, A. M., & Geller, V. (1985). Affect in computer-mediated communication: An experiment in synchronous terminal-to-terminal discussion. *Human-Computer Interaction, 1,* 77-104.

King, K. (1969). Adolescent perceptions of power structure in the Negro family. *Journal of Marriage and the Family, 31,* 751-755.

Kingdom, E. (1990). Cohabitation contracts and equality. *International Journal of the Sociology of Law, 18,* 287-298.

Kirpatrick, M. (1989). Middle age and the lesbian experience. *Women's Studies Quarterly, 17,* 87-96.

Kollock, P., Blumstein, P., & Schwartz, P. (1985). Sex and power in interaction: Conversational privileges and duties. *American Sociological Review, 50,* 34-46.

Kotkin, M. (1985). To marry or live together? *Lifestyles, 7,* 156-170.

Kurdek, L. A. (1991a). The dissolution of gay and lesbian couples. *Journal of Social and Personal Relationships, 8,* 265-278.

Kurdek, L. A. (1991b). Predictors of increases in marital distress in newlywed couples. *Developmental Psychology, 27,* 627-636.

Kurdek, L. A. (1993a). The allocation of household labor in gay, lesbian, and heterosexual married couples. *Journal of Social Issues, 49,* 127-139.

Kurdek, L. A. (1994). Conflict resolution styles in gay, lesbian, heterosexual nonparent, and heterosexual parent couples. *Journal of Marriage and the Family, 56,* 705-722.

Kurdek, L. A., & Schmitt, J. P. (1986a). Early development of relationship quality in heterosexual married, heterosexual cohabiting, gay, and lesbian couples. *Developmental Psychology, 22,* 305-309.

Kurdek, L. A., & Schmitt, J. P. (1986b). Relationship quality of partners in heterosexual married, heterosexual cohabiting, gay, and lesbian relationships. *Journal of Personality and Social Psychology, 51,* 711-720.

Kurdek, L. A., & Schmitt, J. P. (1987). Partner homogamy in married, heterosexual cohabiting, gay, and lesbian couples. *Journal of Sex Research, 23,* 212-232.

Lakoff, R. (1975). *Language and woman's place*. New York: Harper & Row.

Lally, C. F., & Maddock, J. W. (1994). Sexual meaning systems of engaged couples. *Family Relations, 43,* 53-60.

Lammermeier, P. J. (1973). The urban black family of the nineteenth century: A study of black family structure in the Ohio Valley, 1850-1880. *Journal of Marriage and the Family, 35,* 440-456.

Lamude, K. G., Daniels, T. D., & Graham, E. E. (1988). The paradoxical influence of sex on communication rules coorientation and communication satisfaction in superior-subordinate relationships. *Western Journal of Speech Communication, 52,* 122-134.

Landale, N. S., & Fennelly, K. (1992). Informal unions among mainland Puerto Ricans: Cohabitation or an alternative to legal marriage? *Journal of Marriage and the Family, 54,* 269-280.

Laner, M. R. (1978). Media Mating II: "Personals" advertisements of lesbian relationships. *Journal of Homosexuality, 4,* 41-61.

Lannamann, J. W. (1991). Interpersonal communication research as ideological practice. *Communication Theory, 1,* 179-203.

Larson, J. R. (1984). The performance feedback process: A preliminary model. *Organizational Behavior and Human Performance, 33,* 42-76.

Laudin, H. (1973). *Victims of culture*. Columbus, OH: Merrill.

Laurent, A. (1978). Managerial subordinacy: A neglected aspect of organizational hierarchies. *Academy of Management Review, 3,* 220-230.

Lea, M. (1991). Rationalist assumptions in cross-media comparisons of computer-mediated communication. *Behaviour and Information Technology, 10,* 153-172.

Lea, M., & Giordano, R. (in press). Representations of the group and group processes in CSCW research: A case of premature closure? In G. Bowker, L. Gasser, S. L. Star, & W. Turner (Eds.), *Bridging the great divide: Social science research, technical systems and cooperative work*. Cambridge, MA: MIT Press.

Lea, M., O'Shea, T., & Fung, P. (1994). *Constructing the networked organization: Changing organizational form and electronic communications*. Unpublished manuscript.

Lea, M., O'Shea, T., Fung, P., & Spears, R. (1992). "Flaming" in computer-mediated communication: Observations, explanations, implications. In M. Lea (Ed.), *Contexts of computer-mediated communication* (pp. 89-112). London: Harvester-Wheatsheaf.

Lea, M., & Spears, R. (1991). Computer-mediated communication, de-individuation and group decision-making. *International Journal of Man-Machine Studies, 39,* 283-301.

Lea, M., & Spears, R. (1992). Paralanguage and social perception in computer-mediated communication. *Journal of Organizational Computing, 2,* 321-342.

Leary, M. R., & Kowalski, R. M. (1990). Impression management: A literature review and two-component model. *Psychological Bulletin, 107,* 34-47.

Lee, G. R. (1988). Marital satisfaction in later life: The effects of nonmarital roles. *Journal of Marriage and the Family, 50,* 775-783.

Leo, J. (1993, May 24). Gay rights, gay marriages. *U.S. News & World Report,* p. 19.

Leridon, H. (1990a). Extra-marital cohabitation and fertility. *Population Studies,* 44, 469-487.

Leridon, H. (1990b). Cohabitation, marriage, separation: An analysis of life histories of French cohorts from 1968 to 1985. *Population Studies, 44,* 127-144.

Levinger, G. (1979). A social exchange view on the dissolution of pair relationships. In R. L. Burgess & T. L. Huston (Eds.), *Social exchange in developing relationships* (pp. 169-193). New York: Academic Press.

Levinger, G. (1991). Commitment vs. cohesiveness: Two complementary perspectives. In W. H. Jones & D. Perlman (Eds.), *Advances in personal relationships* (Vol. 3, pp. 145-150). London: Kingsley.

Levinger, G., & Huston, T. L. (1990). The social psychology of marriage. In F. D. Fincham & T. N. Bradbury (Eds.), *The psychology of marriage: Basic issues and applications* (pp. 19-58). New York: Guilford.

Levison, D. (1978). *The seasons of a man's life.* New York: Knopf.

Lewin, B. (1982). Unmarried cohabitation: A marriage form in a changing society. *Journal of Marriage and the Family, 44,* 763-773.

Lewis, G. K. (1963). *Puerto Rico: Freedom and power in the Caribbean.* New York: Harper.

Lewis, O. (1966). *La vida: A Puerto Rican family in the culture of poverty—San Juan and New York.* New York: Random House.

Lewis, P. H. (1994, March 8). Strangers, not their computers, build a network in time of grief. *New York Times,* pp. A1, D2.

Li, T. (1990). Computer-mediated communications and the Chinese students in the U.S. *The Information Society, 7,* 125-137.

Lieberman, S. (1956). The effects of changes in roles on the attitudes of role occupants. *Human Relations, 9,* 385-402.

Liefbroer, A. C. (1991). The choice between a married or unmarried first union by young adults: A competing risk analysis. *European Journal of Population, 7,* 273-298.

Lin, Y. H., & Rusbult, C. E. (in press). Extending the investment model of commitment processes: The effects of normative support, centrality of relationship, and traditional investment variables. *Journal of Social and Personal Relationships, 12.*

Lloyd, S. A., Cate, R. M., & Henton, J. M. (1984). Predicting pre-marital relationship stability: A methodological refinement. *Journal of Marriage and the Family, 46,* 71-76.

Locke, H., & Wallace, K. (1959). Short marital adjustment and prediction tests: Their reliability and validity. *Marriage and Family Living, 21,* 251-255.

Lowenthal, M. F., & Robinson, B. (1976). Social networks and isolation. In R. H. Binstock & E. Shanas (Eds.), *Handbook of aging and the social sciences* (pp. 432-456). New York: Van Nostrand Reinhold.

Lund, M. (1985). The development of investment and commitment scales for predicting continuity of personal relationships. *Journal of Social and Personal Relationships, 2,* 3-23.

Lynch, J. M., & Reilly, M. E. (1985/1986). Role relationships: Lesbian perspectives. *Journal of Homosexuality, 12,* 53-69.

Macklin, E. D. (1974, November). Going very steady. *Psychology Today, 6,* 53-59.

Macklin, E. D. (1987). Nontraditional family forms. In M. B. Sussman & S. K. Steinmetz (Eds.), *Handbook of marriage and the family* (pp. 320-323). New York: Plenum.

Macklin, E. D. (1988). Heterosexual couples who cohabit nonmaritally: Some common problems and issues. In C. S. Chilman, E. W. Nunnally, & F. M. Cox (Eds.), *Variant family forms* (pp. 56-72). Newbury Park, CA: Sage.

Maisonneuve, J., Palmade, G., & Fourment, C. (1952). Selective choices and propinquity. *Sociometry, 5,* 135-140.

Marchand, M. (1988). *A French success story: The Minitel saga* (M. Murphy, Trans.). Paris: Larousse.

Marin, G., & Marin, B. V. (1991). *Research with Hispanic populations.* Newbury Park, CA: Sage.

Markman, H. J. (1988). A longitudinal study of couples interactions: Implications for understanding and predicting the development of marital distress. In K. Hahlweg & N. Jacobson (Eds.), *Marital interaction: Analysis and modification* (pp. 253-281). New York: Guilford.

Marvin, C. (1988). *When old technologies were new: Thinking about electric communication in the late nineteenth century.* Oxford, UK: Oxford University Press.

Maslow, A. H. (1954). *Motivation and personality.* New York: Harper & Brothers.

Mathis, R., & T anner, Z. (1991). Cohesion, adaptability, and satisfaction of family systems in later life. *Family Therapy, 18,* 47-60.

McAdams, D. P. (1985). *Power, intimacy, and the life story: Personological inquiries into identity.* Homewood, IL: Dow Jones-Irwin.

McAdams, D. P. (1988). Personal needs and personal relationships. In S. W. Duck (Ed.), *Handbook of personal relationships* (pp. 7-22). Chichester, UK: John Wiley.

McAdoo, H. P. (1978). Factors related to stability of upwardly mobile black families. *Journal of Marriage and the Family, 40,* 761-776.

McCall, G. J., & Simmons, J. L. (1978). *Identities and interaction: An examination of human associations in everyday life* (Rev. ed.). New York: Free Press.

McCarthy, T. (1987). General introduction. In K. Baynes, J. Bohman, & T. McCarthy (Eds.), *After philosophy: End or transformation* (pp. iii-xii). Cambridge: MIT Press.

McClelland, D. C. (1987). *Human motivation.* New York: Cambridge University Press.

McDonald, G. (1981). Structural exchange and marital interaction. *Journal of Marriage and the Family, 43,* 825-839.

McLeod, P. L. (1992). An assessment of the experimental literature on electronic support of group work: Results of a meta-analysis. *Human Computer Interaction, 7,* 257-280.

McWhirter, D. P., & Mattison, A. M. (1984). *The male couple: How relationships develop.* Englewood Cliffs, NJ: Prentice Hall.

Mead, G. H. (1934). *Mind, self, and society.* Chicago: University of Chicago Press.

Mead, M. (1966, July). Marriage in two steps. *Redbook, 127,* 48-52.

Mellinger, G. D. (1956). Interpersonal trust as a factor in communication. *Journal of Abnormal Social Psychology, 52,* 304-309.

252   UNDER-STUDIED RELATIONSHIPS

Melton, W., & Thomas, D. L. (1976). Instrumental and expressive values in mate selection of black and white college students. *Journal of Marriage and the Family, 38*, 509-517.

Miao, G. (1974). Marital instability and unemployment among whites and non-whites, the Moynihan Report revisited—again. *Journal of Marriage and the Family, 36*, 77-86.

Mills, R. S. L., & Grusec, J. E. (1988). Socialization from the perspective of the parent-child relationship. In S. W. Duck (Ed.), *Handbook of personal relationships* (pp. 177-192). Chichester, UK: John Wiley.

Mindel, C. H. (1980). Extended familism among urban Mexican Americans, Anglos, and blacks. *Hispanic Journal of Behavioral Sciences, 2*, 21-34.

Mindel, C. H., Habenstein, R. W., & Wright, R., Jr. (1988). Family lifestyles of America's ethnic minorities: An introduction. In C. H. Mindel, R. W. Habenstein, & R. Wright, Jr. (Eds.), *Ethnic families in America* (3rd ed., pp. 1-14). New York: Elsevier.

Mirande, A. (1977). The Chicano family: A reanalysis of conflicting views. *Journal of Marriage and the Family, 39*, 747-756.

Mirande, A. (1985). *The Chicano experience: An alternative perspective*. South Bend, IN: University of Notre Dame Press.

Montgomery, B. M. (1984). Behavioral characteristics predicting self and peer perceptions of open communication. *Communication Quarterly, 32*, 233-240.

Mook, D. G. (1983). In defense of external invalidity. *American Psychologist, 38*, 379-387.

Moore, K. A., & Stief, T. M. (1991). Changes in marriage and fertility behavior: Behavior versus attitudes of young adults. *Youth and Society, 22*, 362-386.

Moore, M., Blumstein, P., & Schwartz, P. (1994). *The power of motherhood: A contextual evaluation of family resources*. Manuscript submitted for publication.

Moses, A. E., & Hawkins, Jr., R. O. (1982). *Counseling lesbian women and gay men*. St. Louis, MO: C. V. Mosby.

Myers, D. (1987). "Anonymity is part of the magic": Individual manipulation of computer-mediated communication contexts. *Qualitative Sociology, 10*, 251-266.

Myrdal, G. (1944). *An American dilemma: The Negro problem and Negro democracy*. New York: Harper.

Newcomb, M. D. (1981). Unmarried heterosexual cohabitation. In S. Duck & R. Gilmour (Eds.), *Personal relationships 1: Studying personal relationships* (pp. 131-164). London: Academic Press.

Newcomb, M. D. (1986a). Cohabitation, marriage and divorce among adolescents and young adults. *Journal of Social and Personal Relationships, 3*, 473-494.

Newcomb, M. D. (1986b). Sexual behavior of cohabitors: A comparison of three independent samples. *Journal of Sex Research, 22*, 492-513.

Newcomb, M. D. (1987). Cohabitation and marriage: A quest for independence and relatedness. *Applied Social Psychology Annual, 7*, 128-156.

Newcomb, T. M. (1963). Stabilities underlying changes in interpersonal attraction. *Journal of Abnormal and Social Psychology, 66*, 376-386.

Noller, P. (1987). Nonverbal communication in marriage. In D. Perlman & S. Duck (Eds.), *Intimate relationships: Development, dynamics and deterioration* (pp. 149-176). Newbury Park, CA: Sage.

Nussbaum, J. F., Thompson, T., & Robinson, J. D. (1989). *Communication and aging.* New York: Harper & Row.

O'Connell, L. (1984). An exploration of exchange in three social relationships: Kinship, friendship, and the market-place. *Journal of Social and Personal Relationships, 1,* 333-346.

Office of Population Census and Surveys. (1987). *General Household Survey.* London: HMSO Publications.

Ogan, C. (1993). Listserver communication during the Gulf War: What kind of medium is the electronic bulletin board? *Journal of Broadcasting and Electronic Media, 37,* 177-196.

O'Keefe, B. J., & Delia, J. G. (1982). Impression formation and message production. In M. E. Roloff & C. R. Berger (Eds.), *Social cognition and communication* (pp. 33-72). Beverly Hills, CA: Sage.

Okin, S. M. (1989). *Justice, gender and the family.* New York: Basic Books.

Olson, D., McCubbin, H., Barnes, H., Larsen, A., Muxen, M., & Wilson, M. (1983). *Families: What makes them work.* Beverly Hills: Sage.

Omi, M., & Winant, H. (1986). *Racial formation in the United States: From the 1960s to the 1980s.* New York: Routledge.

Ord, J. (1989). Who's joking? The information system at play. *Interacting With Computers, 1,* 118-128.

Orthner, D. (1975). Leisure activity patterns and marital satisfaction over the marital career. *Journal of Marriage and the Family, 37,* 91-102.

Pacanowsky, M. E., & O'Donnell-Trujillo, N. (1983). Organizational communication as cultural performance. *Communication Monographs, 50,* 126-147.

Padilla, A. M., & Lindholm, K. J. (1984). Hispanic behavioral science research: Recommendations for future research. *Hispanic Journal of Behavioral Sciences, 6,* 13-32.

Padilla, F. M. (1985). *Latino ethnic consciousness: The case of Mexican Americans and Puerto Ricans in Chicago.* South Bend, IN: University of Notre Dame Press.

Parker, S., & Kleiner, R. J. (1966). Characteristics of Negro mothers in single-headed households. *Journal of Marriage and the Family, 28,* 507-513.

Parks, M. R. (1977). Anomie and close friendship communication networks. *Human Communication Research, 4,* 48-57.

Parlee, M. B. (1979, October). The friendship bond. *Psychology Today,* pp. 43-54, 113.

Patterson, M. L. (1973). Compensation in nonverbal immediacy behaviors. *Sociometry, 36,* 237-252.

Pearson, J. (1992). *Lasting love: What keeps couples together.* Dubuque, IA: William C. Brown.

Peplau, L. A. (1991). Lesbian and gay relationships. In J. C. Gonsiorek & J. D. Weinrich (Eds.), *Homosexuality: Research implications for public policy* (pp. 177-196). Newbury Park, CA: Sage.

Peplau, L. A., Cochran, S., Rook, K., & Padesky, C. (1978). Loving women: Attachment and autonomy in lesbian relationships. *Journal of Social Issues, 34,* 7-27.

Peplau, L. A., Padesky, C., & Hamilton, M. (1982). Satisfaction in lesbian relationships. *Journal of Homosexuality, 8,* 23-35.

Perlman, D., & Fehr, B. (1987). The development of intimate relationships. In D. Perlman & S. Duck (Eds.), *Intimate relationships: Development, dynamics and deterioration* (pp. 13-42). Newbury Park, CA: Sage.

Perry, T. S., & Adam, J. A. (1992, October). Special report/electronic mail. *IEEE Spectrum,* pp. 22-33.

Phillips, G. M., & Wood, J. T. (1983). *Communication and human relationships: The study of interpersonal communication.* New York: Macmillan.

Phinney, J. S. (1991). Ethnic identity and self-esteem: A review and integration. *Hispanic Journal of Behavioral Sciences, 13,* 193-208.

Pope, H. (1969). Negro-white differences in decisions regarding illegitimate children. *Journal of Marriage and the Family, 31,* 756-764.

Porterfield, E. (1978). *Black and white mixed marriages.* Chicago: Nelson-Hall.

Poster, M. (1975). *Existential Marxism in postwar France: From Sartre to Althusser.* Princeton, NJ: Princeton University Press.

Poster, M. (1990). *The mode of information: Poststructuralism and social context.* Chicago: Polity.

Postmes, T., & Spears, R. (1993, September). *A meta-analysis of deindividuation research: How "anti" is antinormative behavior.* Paper presented at the 10th General Meeting of the European Association for Experimental Social Psychology, Lisbon, Portugal.

Postmes, T., Spears, R., & Lea, M.. (1994). *Difference and development of norms in computer-mediated communications.* Unpublished manuscript, University of Amsterdam.

Pryor, J. B., & Merluzzi, T. V. (1985). The role of expertise in processing social interaction scripts. *Journal of Experimental Social Psychology, 21,* 362-379.

Putnam, L. L. (1983). The interpretive perspective: An alternative to functionalism. In L. L. Putnam & M. E. Pacanowsky (Eds.), *Communication and organizations: An interpretive approach* (pp. 31-54). Beverly Hills, CA: Sage.

Quinn, R. E. (1977). Coping with Cupid: The formation, impact, and management of romantic relationships in organizations. *Administrative Science Quarterly, 22,* 30-45.

Ramirez, M., III. (1983). *Psychology of the Americas: Mestizo perspectives on personality and mental health.* New York: Pergamon.

Ramirez, M., III. (1984). Assessing and understanding biculturalism-multiculturalism in Mexican-American adults. In J. L. Martinez & R. H. Mendoza (Eds.), *Chicano psychology* (2nd ed., pp. 77-94). Orlando, FL: Academic Press.

Rao, K. V. (1990). Marriage risks, cohabitation and premarital births in Canada. *European Journal of Population, 6,* 27-49.

Rawlins, W. K. (1989). A dialectical analysis of the tensions, functions, and strategic challenges of communication in young adult friendships. In J. A. Andersen (Ed.), *Communication Yearbook 12* (pp. 157-189). Newbury Park, CA: Sage.

Reicher, S. D. (1994). Collective action and the (re)construction of the self. In A. Oosterwegel & R. Wicklund (Eds.), *The self in European and North American culture: Development and processes.* Amsterdam: Kluwer.

Reicher, S. D., & Levine, M. (1994). Deindividuation, power relations between groups and the expression of social identity: The effects of visibility to the outgroup. *British Journal of Social Psychology, 33,* 145-163.

Reicher, S. D., Spears, R., & Postmes, T. (in press). A social identity model of deindividuation phenomena. *European Review of Social Psychology, 6.* Chichester, UK: John Wiley.

Reid, E. (1994). *Cultural formations in text-based virtual realities.* Unpublished master's thesis, University of Melbourne.

Reis, H. T. (1982). An introduction to the use of structural equations: Prospects and problems. In L. Wheeler (Ed.), *Review of personality and social psychology* (Vol. 3, pp. 255-287). Beverly Hills, CA: Sage.

Reis, H. T., & Shaver, P. (1988). Intimacy as an interpersonal process. In S. W. Duck (Ed.), *Handbook of personal relationships* (pp. 367-389). Chichester, UK: John Wiley.

Reisman, J. M. (1970). *Anatomy of friendship.* New York: Irvington.

Renzetti, C. M. (1992). *Violent betrayal: Partner abuse in lesbian relationships.* Newbury Park, CA: Sage.

Rheingold, H. (1993). *The virtual community: Homesteading on the electronic frontier.* Reading, MA: Addison-Wesley.

Rice, R. E. (1984). Theories old and new: The study of new media. In R. E. Rice (Ed.), *The new media: Communication, research and technology* (pp. 55-80). Beverly Hills, CA: Sage.

Rice, R. E. (1993). Media appropriateness: Using social presence theory to compare traditional and new organizational media. *Human Communication Research, 19,* 451-484.

Rice, R. E., & Bair, J. H. (1984). New organizational media and productivity. In R. E. Rice (Ed.), *The new media: Communication, research and technology* (pp. 185-215). Beverly Hills, CA: Sage.

Rice, R. E., & Love, G. (1987). Electronic emotion: Socio-emotional content in a computer-mediated communication network. *Communication Research, 14,* 85-108.

Riessman, C. (1990). *Divorce talk: Women and men make sense of personal relationships.* New Brunswick, NJ: Rutgers University Press.

Rindfuss, R. R., & Stephen, E. H. (1990). Marital noncohabitation: Separation does not make the heart grow fonder. *Journal of Marriage and the Family, 52,* 259-270.

Rios, D. I. (1993). *Mexican American audiences: A qualitative and quantitative study of ethnic subgroup uses for mass media.* Unpublished doctoral dissertation, University of Texas at Austin.

Roberts, K. H., & O'Reilly, C. A. (1974). Failures in upward communication: Three possible culprits. *Academy of Management Journal, 17,* 205-215.

Rohlfing, M. E. (1990, November). *Communicating long-distance friendship.* Paper presented at the annual convention of the Speech Communication Association, Chicago.

Rohlfing, M. E., & Healey, A. C. (1991, May). *Keeping the tie that binds: The communicative patterns of geographically separated female friends.* Paper presented at the annual convention of the International Communication Association, Miami.

Rollins, B. C., & Cannon, K. (1974). Marital satisfaction over the family life cycle: A reevaluation. *Journal of Marriage and the Family, 36,* 271-282.

Rollins, B. C., & Feldman, H. (1970). Marital satisfaction over the family life cycle. *Journal of Marriage and the Family, 32,* 20-28.

Rose, S. M. (1984). How friendships end: Patterns among young adults. *Journal of Social and Personal Relationships, 1,* 267-277.

Rose, S. M., & Frieze, I. H. (1989). Young singles' scripts for a first date. *Gender and Society, 3,* 258-268.

Rosenberg, M. S. (1992). Virtual reality: Reflections of life, dreams and technology; An ethnography of a computer society. *Electronic Journal on Virtual Culture, 1.* [Machine readable file available through listserv@kentvm.kent.edu].

Ross, M. W. (1983). *The married homosexual man.* Boston: Routledge & Kegan Paul.

Roucek, J. S., & Eisenberg, B. (1982). Introduction: The new awareness. In J. S. Roucek & B. Eisenberg (Eds.), *America's ethnic politics* (pp. 1-27). Westport, CT: Greenwood.

Rubin, L. B. (1985). *Just friends.* New York: Harper & Row.

Rusbult, C. E. (1987). Responses to dissatisfaction in close relationships: The exit-voice-loyalty-neglect model. In D. Perlman & S. W. Duck (Eds.), *Intimate relationships: Development, dynamics, deterioration* (pp. 209-238). London: Sage.

Rusbult, C. E. (1991). Commentary on Johnson's "Commitment to personal relationships": What's interesting, and what's new? In W. H. Jones & D. Perlman (Eds.), *Advances in personal relationships* (Vol. 3, pp. 151-169). London: Kingsley.

Rusbult, C. E., & Buunk, B. P. (1993). Commitment processes in close relationships: An interdependence analysis. *Journal of Social and Personal Relationships, 10,* 175-204.

Rusbult, C. E., Insko, C. A., Lin, Y. W., & Smith, W. A. (1990). Social motives underlying rational versus selective exploitation: The impact of instrumental versus social-emotional allocator orientation on the distribution of rewards in groups. *Journal of Applied Social Psychology, 20,* 984-1025.

Rutter, D. R. (1987). *Communicating by telephone.* Oxford, UK: Pergamon.

Samson, J.-M., Levy, J. J., Dupras, A., & Tessier, D. (1991). Coitus frequency among married or cohabiting heterosexual adults: A survey in French-Canada. *Australian Journal of Marriage and Family, 12,* 103-109.

Sanchez-Ayendez, M. (1988). The Puerto Rican American family. In C. H. Mindel, R. W. Habenstein, & R. Wright, Jr. (Eds.), *Ethnic families in America* (3rd ed., pp. 173-195). New York: Elsevier.

Sarantakos, S. (1991). Cohabitation revisited: Paths of change among cohabiting and non-cohabiting couples. *Australian Journal of Marriage and Family, 12,* 144-155.

Scanzoni, J. (1975). Sex roles, economic factors, and marital solidarity in black and white marriages. *Journal of Marriage and the Family, 37,* 130-144.

Schaefer, R. T. (1988). *Racial and ethnic groups* (3rd ed.). Glenview, IL: Scott, Foresman.

Schellenberg, J. A. (1978). *Masters of social psychology: Freud, Mead, Lewin, and Skinner.* New York: Oxford University Press.

Schmidt, A., & Padilla, A. M. (1983). Grandparent-grandchild interaction in a Mexican-American group. *Hispanic Journal of Behavioral Sciences, 5,* 181-198.

Schoen, R. (1992). First unions and the stability of first marriages. *Journal of Marriage and the Family, 54,* 281-284.

Schumm, W. (1979). Marital satisfaction over the family life cycle: A critique and proposal. *Journal of Marriage and the Family, 41,* 7-12.

Schumm, W. R., McCollum, E. E., Bugaighis, M. A., Jurich, A. P., Bollman, S. R., & Reitz, J. (1988). Differences between Anglo and Mexican American family members on satisfaction with family life. *Hispanic Journal of Behavioral Sciences, 10,* 39-53.

Schutte, J. G., & Light, J. M. (1978). The relative importance of proximity and status for friendship choices in social hierarchies. *Social Psychology, 41,* 260-264.

Selfe, C. L., & Meyer, P. R. (1991). Testing claims for on-line conferences. *Written Communication, 8,* 163-192.

Shachar, R. (1991). His and her marital satisfaction: The double standard. *Sex Roles, 25,* 451-467.

Shanor, K. (1987). *How to stay together when you have to be apart.* New York: Warner.

Shaver, P. R., & Hazan, C. (1988). A biased overview of the study of love. *Journal of Social and Personal Relationships, 5,* 473-501.

Short, J., Williams, E., & Christie, B. (1976). *The social psychology of telecommunications.* Chichester, UK: John Wiley.

Shotter, J. (1992). What is a "personal relationship"? A rhetorical-responsive account of "unfinished business." In J. H. Harvey, T. L. Orbuch, & A. L. Weber (Eds.), *Attributions, accounts and close relationships* (pp. 19-39). New York: Springer-Verlag.

Shotter, J. (1993). *Conversational realities: The construction of life through language.* Newbury Park, CA: Sage.

Shweder, R. A. (1991). *Thinking through cultures: Expeditions in cultural psychology.* Cambridge, MA: Harvard University Press.

Siegel, J., Dubrovsky, V., Kiesler, S., & McGuire, T. (1986). Group processes in computer-mediated communication. *Organizational Behavior and Human Decision Processes, 37,* 157-187.

Sillars, A. L., Burggraf, C. S., Yost, S., & Zietlow, P. H. (1992). Conversational themes and marital relationship definition: Quantitative and qualitative investigations. *Human Communication Research, 19,* 124-154.

Silverstein, C. (1981). *Man to man: Gay couples in America.* New York: William Morrow.

Simmel, G. (1950). *The sociology of Georg Simmel.* New York: Free Press.

Skinner, B. F. (1972). *Beyond freedom and dignity.* New York: Knopf.

Smith, J., & Balka, E. (1988). Chatting on a feminist computer network. In C. Kramarae (Ed.), *Technology and women's voices. Keeping in touch* (pp. 82-97). New York: Routledge & Kegan Paul.

Smith, T. W. (1990). The polls—a report: The sexual revolution. *Public Opinion Quarterly, 54,* 415-435.

Sollors, W. (1986). *Beyond ethnicity: Consent and descent in American culture.* New York: Oxford University Press.

Spada, J. (1979). *The Spada Report.* New York: Signet.

Spanier, G. B. (1983). Married and unmarried cohabitation in the U.S.: 1980. *Journal of Marriage and the Family, 45,* 277-288.

Spanier, G. B., Lewis, R. A., & Cole, C. L. (1975). Marital adjustment over the family life cycle: The issue of curvilinearity. *Journal of Marriage and the Family, 37,* 263-268.

Spears, R., & Lea, M. (1992). Social influence and the influence of the "social" in computer-mediated communication. In M. Lea (Ed.), *Contexts of computer-mediated communication* (pp. 30-65). London: Harvester-Wheatsheaf.

Spears, R., & Lea, M. (1994). Panacea or panopticon? The hidden power in computer-mediated communication. *Communication Research, 21,* 427-459.

Spears, R., Lea, M., & Lee, S. (1990). De-individuation and group polarization in computer-mediated communication. *British Journal of Social Psychology, 29,* 121-134.

Spence, J. T. (1985). Gender identity and its implications for the concepts of masculinity and femininity. *Nebraska Symposium on Motivation, 32,* 59-95.

Spence, J. T., Deaux, K., & Helmreich, R. L. (1985). Sex roles in contemporary American society. In G. Lindzey & E. Aronson (Eds.), *The handbook of social psychology* (3rd ed., Vol. 2, pp. 149-178). New York: Random House.

Spence, J. T., Helmreich, R. L., & Stapp, J. (1974). The Personal Attributes Questionnaire: A measure of sex role stereotypes and masculinity-femininity. *JSAS Catalog of Selected Documents in Psychology, 4,* 43-44.

Spencer, T. (1994). Transforming relationships through ordinary talk. In S. W. Duck (Ed.), *Dynamics of relationships* (pp. 58-85). Newbury Park, CA: Sage.

Spickard, P. R. (1989). *Mixed blood: Intermarriage and ethnic identity in twentieth-century America.* Madison: University of Wisconsin Press.

Sproull, L., & Kiesler, S. (1986). Reducing social context cues: Electronic mail in organizational communication. *Management Science, 32,* 1492-1512.

Stafford, L., & Reske, J. R. (1990). Idealization and communication in long-distance premarital relationships. *Family Relations, 39,* 274-279.

Stamp, G. H. (1991, November). *The transition to parenthood through communication: A case study of the management of dialectic tension.* Paper presented at the annual meeting of the Speech Communication Association, Chicago.

Stamp, G. H., & Banski, M. A. (1992). The communicative management of constrained autonomy during the transition to parenthood. *Western Journal of Communication, 56,* 281-300.

Staples, R. (1972). The matricentric family system: A cross-cultural examination. *Journal of Marriage and the Family, 34,* 156-165.

Staples, R. (1985). Changes in black family structure: The conflict between family ideology and structural conditions. *Journal of Marriage and the Family, 47,* 1005-1013.

Staples, R. (1988). The black American family. In C. H. Mindel, R. W. Habenstein, & R. Wright, Jr. (Eds.), *Ethnic families in America* (3rd ed., pp. 303-324). New York: Elsevier.

Staples, R., & Mirande, A. (1980). Racial and cultural variations among American families: A decentennial review of the literature on minority families. *Journal of Marriage and the Family, 42,* 887-903.

Steere, G. H. (1981). The family and the elderly. In F. J. Berghorn & D. E. Schafter (Eds.), *The dynamics of aging* (pp. 289-309). Boulder, CO: Westview.

Stephan, W. G. (1985). Intergroup relations. In G. Lindzey & E. Aronson (Eds.), *The handbook of social psychology* (3rd ed., Vol. 2, pp. 599-658). New York: Random House.

Stets, J. E., & Straus, M. A. (1989). The marriage license as a hitting license: A comparison of assaults in dating, cohabiting, and married couples. *Journal of Family Violence, 4,* 161-183.

Stewart, J. (1991). A postmodern look at traditional communication postulates. *Western Journal of Speech Communication, 55,* 354-379.

Stinnett, N. J., Carter, L. M., & Montgomery, J. E. (1972). Older persons perceptions of their marriage. *Journal of Marriage and the Family, 34,* 665-670.

Stone, A. R. (1992). Will the real body please stand up? Boundary stories about virtual cultures. In M. Benedikt (Ed.), *Cyberspace: First steps* (pp. 81-119). Cambridge: MIT Press.

Streib, G., & Beck, R. (1980). Older families: A decade review. *Journal of Marriage and the Family, 42,* 937-956.

Stryker, S. (1991). Consequences of the gap between the "two social psychologies." In C. W. Stephan, W. G. Stephan, & T. F. Pettigrew (Eds.), *The future of social psychology* (pp. 83-97). New York: Springer-Verlag.

Stryker, S., & Stratham, A. (1985). Symbolic interactionism and role theory. In G. Lindzey & E. Aronson (Eds.), *Handbook of social psychology* (3rd ed., Vol. 2, pp. 311-378). New York: Random House.

Sullivan, H. S. (1953). *The interpersonal theory of psychiatry.* New York: Norton.

Surra, C. A. (1987). Reasons for changes in commitment: Variation by courtship type. *Journal of Social and Personal Relationships, 4,* 17-33.

Surra, C. A., & Huston, T. L. (1987). Mate selection as social transition. In D. Perlman & S. Duck (Eds.), *Intimate relationships: Development, dynamics and deterioration* (pp. 88-120). Newbury Park, CA: Sage.

Swain, S. (1989). Covert intimacy: Closeness in men's friendships. In B. Risman & P. Schwartz (Eds.), *Gender in intimate relationships* (pp. 71-86). Belmont, CA: Wadsworth.

Szapocznik, J., & Hernandez, R. (1988). The Cuban American family. In C. H. Mindel, R. W. Habenstein, & R. Wright, Jr. (Eds.), *Ethnic families in America* (3rd ed., pp. 303-324). New York: Elsevier.

Tajfel, H., & Turner, J. C. (1986). The social identity theory of intergroup behavior. In S. Worchel & W. G. Austin (Ed.), *Psychology of intergroup relations* (pp. 7-24). Chicago: Nelson-Hall.

Tamir, L., & Antonucci, T. (1981). Self-perception, motivation, and social support through the family life cycle. *Journal of Marriage and the Family, 43,* 151-160.

Tanfer, K. (1987). Patterns of premarital cohabitation among never-married women in the United States. *Journal of Marriage and the Family, 49,* 483-497.

Tannen, D. (1990). *You just don't understand: Women and men in communication.* New York: Ballantine.

Taylor, J., & Rogers, J. (1993). Relationship between cultural identity and exchange disposition. *Journal of Black Psychology, 19,* 248-265.

Teachman, J. D., & Polonko, K. A. (1990). Cohabitation and marriage stability in the United States. *Social Forces, 69,* 207-220.

Teachman, J. D., Thomas, J., & Paasch, K. (1991). Legal status and the stability of coresidential unions. *Demography, 28,* 571-586.

Thibaut, J. W., & Kelley, H. H. (1959). *The social psychology of groups.* New York: John Wiley.

Thompson, E. H., & Walker, A. J. (1989). Gender in families: Women and men in marriage, work, and parenthood. *Journal of Marriage and the Family, 51,* 845-871.

Thomson, E., & Colella, U. (1992). Cohabitation and marital stability: Quality or commitment? *Journal of Marriage and the Family, 54,* 259-267.

Thorne, B., & Henley, N. (Eds.). (1975). *Language and sex: Difference and dominance.* Rowley, MA: Newbury House.

Thornton, A. (1988). Cohabitation and marriage in the 1980s. *Demography, 25,* 497-508.

Thornton, A. (1989). Changing attitudes toward family issues in the United States. *Journal of Marriage and the Family, 51,* 873-893.

Thornton, A. (1991). Influence of the marital history of parents on the marital and cohabitational experiences of children. *American Journal of Sociology, 96,* 868-894.

Thornton, A., Axinn, W. G., & Hill, D. H. (1992). Reciprocal effects of religiosity, cohabitation, and marriage. *American Journal of Sociology, 98,* 628-651.

Ting-Toomey, S. (1991). Intimacy expressions in three cultures: France, Japan, and the United States. *International Journal of Intercultural Relations, 15,* 29-46.

Tompkins, P. K., & Cheney, G. (1985). Communication and unobtrusive control in contemporary organizations. In R. D. McPhee & P. K. Tompkins (Eds.), *Organizational communication: Traditional themes and new directions* (pp. 179-210). Beverly Hills, CA: Sage.

Top ten newsgroups. (1994, August). *Wired,* p. 36.

Traynowicz, L. (1986). Establishing intimacy. In C. J. Couch, S. L. Saxton, & M. A. Katovich (Eds.), *Studies in symbolic interaction: The Iowa school* (pp. 195-208). Greenwich, CT: JAI.

Treas, J. (1975). Aging and the family. In D. S. Woodruff & J. E. Birren (Eds.), *Aging* (pp. 92-108). New York: Van Nostrand.

Triandis, H. C. (1990). Cross-cultural studies of individualism and collectivism. *Nebraska Symposium on Motivation, 39,* 41-133.

Triandis, H. C., Hui, C. H., Albert, R. D., Leung, S., Lisansky, J., Diaz-Loving, R., Plascencia, L., Marin, G., Betancourt, H., & Loyola-Cintron, L. (1984). Individual models of social behavior. *Journal of Personality and Social Psychology, 46,* 1389-1404.

Triandis, H. C., Marin, G., Lisansky, J., & Betancourt, H. (1984). Simpatia as a cultural script of Hispanics. *Journal of Personality and Social Psychology, 47,* 1363-1375.

Triandis, H. C., Weldon, D., & Feldman, J. (1972). *Black and white hardcore and middle class subjective cultures: A cross-validation.* Champaign: University of Illinois.

Trinkoff, A. M., Ritter, C., & Anthony, J. C. (1990). Prevalence and self-reported consequences of cocaine use. *Drug and Alcohol Dependence, 26,* 217-225.

Troll, L. E. (1971). The family of later-life: A decade review. *Journal of Marriage and the Family, 33,* 263-290.

Troll, L. E. (1982). *Continuations: Adult development and aging.* Monterey, CA: Brooks/Cole.

Trost, J. (1979). *Unmarried cohabitation.* Vasteras, Sweden: International Library.

Trujillo, N. (1985). Organizational communication as cultural performance: Some managerial considerations. *Southern Speech Communication Journal, 50,* 201-224.

Trussell, J., & Rao, K. V. (1989). Premarital cohabitation and marital stability: A reassessment of the Canadian evidence. *Journal of Marriage and the Family, 51,* 535-540.

Tucker, B. M., & Taylor, R. J. (1989). Demographic correlates of relationship status among black Americans. *Journal of Marriage and the Family, 51,* 655-665.

Tucker, M. W., & O'Grady, K. E. (1991). Effects of physical attractiveness, intelligence, age at marriage, and cohabitation on the perception of marital satisfaction. *Journal of Social Psychology, 131,* 253-269.

Tuller, N. R. (1978). Couples: The hidden segment of the gay world. *Journal of Homosexuality, 3,* 331-343.

Turner, J. C., Hogg, M. A., Oakes, P. J., Reicher, S. D., & Wetherell, M. S. (1987). *Rediscovering the social group: A self-categorization theory.* Oxford, UK: Basil Blackwell.

U.S. Bureau of the Census. (1992). *Geographical Mobility, March 1990 to March 1991* (Current Population Reports, P20-463). Washington, DC: Government Printing Office.

Vance, C. S. (1984). *Pleasure and danger: Exploring female sexuality.* Boston: Routledge & Kegan Paul.

Van Gelder, L. (1985, October). The strange case of the electronic lover. *Ms.,* pp. 94, 99, 101-104, 117, 123-124.

VanYperen, N. W., & Buunk, B. P. (1991). Equity theory and exchange from a cross-national perspective. *Journal of Social Psychology, 131,* 5-20.

Vetere, V. A. (1982). The role of friendships in the development and maintenance of lesbian love relationships. *Journal of Homosexuality, 8,* 51-65.

Waite, L. J., Goldscheider, F. K., & Witsberger, C. (1986). Nonfamily living and the erosion of traditional family orientations among young adults. *American Sociological Review, 51,* 541-554.

Wallace, A. F. C. (1970). *Culture and personality* (2nd ed.). New York: Random House.

Walster, E., Walster, G. W., & Berscheid, E. (1978). *Equity: Theory and research.* Boston: Allyn & Bacon.

Walther, J. B. (1992). Interpersonal effects in computermediated interaction: A relational perspective. *Communication Research, 19,* 52-90.

Walther, J. B. (1993). Impression development in computer-mediated interaction. *Western Journal of Communication, 57,* 381-398.

Walther, J. B. (1994a). Anticipated ongoing interaction versus channel effects on relational communication in computer-mediated interaction. *Human Communication Research, 20,* 473-501.

Walther, J. B. (1994b). *Computer-mediated communication: Impersonal, interpersonal, and hyperpersonal interaction.* Unpublished manuscript, Department of Communication Studies, Northwestern University.

Walther, J. B. (in press). Relational aspects of computer-mediated communication: Experimental observations over time. *Organization Science.*

Walther, J., Anderson, J. F., & Park, D. W. (1994). Interpersonal effects in computer-mediated interaction: A meta-analysis of social and antisocial communication. *Communication Research, 21,* 460-487.

Walther, J. B., & Tidwell, L. C. (1994, August). *Nonverbal cues in computer-mediated communication, and the effects of chronemics on relational communication.* Paper presented at the annual meeting of the Speech Communication Association, New Orleans.

Warren, C. A. B. (1974). *Identity and community in the gay world.* New York: John Wiley.

Webber, R. A. (1970). Perceptions of interactions between superiors and subordinates. *Human Relations, 23,* 235-248.

Weedman, J. (1991). T ask and non-task functions of a computer conference used in professional education: A measure of flexibility. *International Journal of Man-Machine Studies, 34,* 303-318.

Welte, C. R. (1979). Interrelationships of individual, cultural, and pan-human values. In G. G. Haydu (Ed.), *Experience forms: Their cultural and individual place and function* (pp. 269-294). New York: Mouton.

Werner, H. (1957). The concept of development from a comparative and organismic point of view. In D. D. Harris (Ed.), *The concept of development* (pp. 125-146). Minneapolis: University of Minnesota Press.

West, J. T. (1995). Understanding how the dynamics of ideology influence violence between intimates. In S. W. Duck & J. T. Wood (Eds.), *Confronting Relationship Challenges* (pp. 129-149). Thousand Oaks, CA: Sage.

Westefeld, J. S., & Liddell, D. (1982). Coping with long- distance relationships. *Journal of College Student Personnel, 23,* 550-551.

Wexley, K. N., Alexander, R. A., Greenwalt, J. P., & Couch, M. A. (1980). Attitudinal congruence and similarity as related to interpersonal evaluations in superior subordinate dyads. *Academy of Management Journal, 23,* 320-330.

Wexley, K. N., & Pulakos, E. D. (1983). The effects of perceptual congruence and sex on subordinates' performance appraisal of their managers. *Academy of Management Journal, 26,* 666-676.

White, J. L. (1984). *The psychology of blacks: An Afro-American perspective.* Englewood Cliffs, NJ: Prentice Hall.

White, J. L., & Parham, T. A. (1990). *The psychology of blacks: An African-American perspective* (2nd ed.). Englewood Cliffs, NJ: Prentice Hall.

White, J. M. (1987). Premarital cohabitation and marital stability in Canada. *Journal of Marriage and the Family, 49,* 641-647.

White, J. M. (1989). Reply to comment by Trussell and Rao: A reanalysis of the data. *Journal of Marriage and the Family, 51,* 540-544.

Whitman, W. (1881). *Leaves of Grass* (7th ed.). Boston: Osgood & Company.

Whitney, C. (1990). *Uncommon lives: Gay men and straight women.* New York: New American Library.

Whyte, M. K. (1990). *Dating, mating, and marriage.* New York: Aldine.

Wiener, M., & Mehrebian, A. (1968). *Language within language: Immediacy, a channel in verbal communication.* New York: Appleton-Century-Crofts.

Wiersma, G. E. (1983). *Cohabitation, An alternative to marriage? A cross-national study*. Boston: Martinus Nijhoff.

Wiggins, J. S. (1979). A psychological taxonomy of trait-descriptive terms: The interpersonal domain. *Journal of Personality and Social Psychology, 37*, 395-412.

Wiggins, J. S. (1991). Agency and communion as conceptual coordinates for the understanding and measurement of interpersonal behavior. In W. Grove & D. Cicchetti (Eds.), *Thinking clearly about psychology* (Vol. 2, pp. 89-113). Minneapolis: University of Minnesota Press.

Wilkins, H. (1991). Computer talk: Long-distance conversations by computer. *Written Communication, 8*, 56-78.

Williams, N. (1990). *The Mexican American family: Tradition and change*. Dix Hills, NY: General Hall.

Willie, C. V. (1985). *Black and white families: A study in complementarity*. Bayside, NY: General Hall.

Willie, C. V., & Greenblatt, S. L. (1978). Four "classic" studies of power relationships in black families: A review and look to the future. *Journal of Marriage and the Family, 40*, 691-694.

Willmott, P. (1987). *Friendship networks and social support*. London: Policy Studies Institute.

Wills, T. A., Weiss, R. L., & Patterson, G. R. (1974). A behavioral analysis of the determinants of marital satisfaction. *Journal of Consulting and Clinical Psychology, 42*, 802-811.

Wilmot, W. W. (1994). Relationship rejuvenation. In D. J. Canary & L. Stafford (Eds.), *Communication and relational maintenance* (pp. 255-273). San Diego, CA: Academic Press.

Winfield, P. (1987). *Commuter marriage: Living together, apart*. New York: Columbia University Press.

Winner, L. (1980). Do artifacts have politics? *Daedalus, 109*, 121-136.

Wiseman, J. P. (1986). Friendship: Bonds and binds in a voluntary relationship. *Journal of Social and Personal Relationships, 3*, 191-212.

Wolf, D. G. (1979). *The lesbian community*. Berkeley: University of California Press.

Woll, S. B., & Cozby, P. C. (1987). Videodating and other alternatives to traditional methods of relationship initiation. In W. H. Jones and D. Perlman (Eds.), *Advances in personal relationships* (Vol. 1). Greenwich, CT: JAI.

Wood, J. T. (1982). Communication and relational culture: Bases for the study of human relationships. *Communication Quarterly, 30*, 75-83.

Wood, J. T. (1992a). *Spinning the symbolic web: Human communication as symbolic interaction*. Norwood, NJ: Ablex.

Wood, J. T. (1992b). Telling our stories: Narratives as a basis for theorizing sexual harassment. *Journal of Applied Communication Research, 20*, 349-363.

Wood, J. T. (1993a). Engendered relationships: Interaction, caring, power, and responsibility in intimacy. In S. W. Duck (Ed.), *Social contexts of relationships* (pp. 26-54). Newbury Park, CA: Sage.

Wood, J. T. (1993b). Enlarging conceptual boundaries: A feminist critique of research on interpersonal relationships. In S. Bowen & N. Wyatt (Eds.), *Transforming visions: Feminist critiques of speech communication* (pp. 19-49). Cresskill, NJ: Hampton.

Wood, J. T. (1993c). Gender, communication, and competence in close relationships. In S. W. Duck (Ed.), *Social contexts of relationships* (pp. 26-54). London: Sage.

Wood, J. T. (1994a). *Gendered lives: Communication, gender, and culture.* Belmont, CA: Wadsworth.

Wood, J. T. (1994b). Nonmajority members of academe. In G. M. Phillips, D. S. Gouran, S. Kuehn, & J. T. Wood, *Survival in the academy* (pp. 55-71). Cresskill, NJ: Hampton.

Wood, J. T. (1994c). Saying it makes it so: The discursive construction of sexual harassment. In S. Bingham (Ed.), *Conceptualizing sexual harassment as discursive practice.* Westport, CT: Praeger.

Wood, J. T. (1994d). *Who cares? Women, care, and culture.* Carbondale: Southern Illinois University Press.

Wood, J. T. (1995). *Relational communication: Change and continuity in personal relationships.* Belmont, CA: Wadsworth.

Wood, J. T. (in press). Feminist scholarship and research on personal relationships. *Journal of Social and Personal Relationships.*

Wood, J. T., & Cox, J. R. (1993). Rethinking critical voice: Materiality and situated knowledges. *Western Journal of Communication, 57,* 278-287.

Wood, J. T., Dendy, L. L., Dordek, E., Germany, M., & Varallo, S. (1994). The dialectic of difference: A thematic analysis of intimates' meanings for differences. In K. Carter & M. Presnell (Eds.), *Interpretive approaches to interpersonal communication* (pp. 115-136). New York: SUNY Press.

Wood, J. T., & Inman, C. C. (1993). In a different mode: Masculine styles of communicating closeness. *Journal of Applied Communication Research, 21,* 279-295.

Woolgar, S. (1991). Configuring the user: The case of usability trials. In J. Law (Ed.), *A sociology of monsters: Essays on power, technology and domination* (pp. 57-102). London: Routledge.

Wu, Z., & Balakrishnan, T. R. (1992). Attitudes towards cohabitation and marriage in Canada. *Journal of Comparative Family Studies, 23,* 1-12.

Yamaguchi, K., & Kandel, D. B. (1985). Dynamic relationships between premarital cohabitation and illicit drug use: An event-history analysis of role selection and role socialization. *American Sociological Review, 50,* 530-546.

Yamaguchi, K., & Kandel, D. B. (1987). Drug use and other determinants of premarital pregnancy and its outcome. *Journal of Marriage and the Family, 49,* 257-270.

Yelsma, P. (1986). Marriage versus cohabitation: Couples' communication practices and satisfaction. *Journal of Communication, 36,* 94-107.

Yerby, J., Buerkel-Rothfuss, N., & Bochner, A. P. (1990). *Understanding family communication.* Scottsdale, AZ: Gorsuch, Scarisbrick.

Zeff, S. B. (1982). A cross-cultural study of Mexican American, black American, and white American women at a large urban university. *Hispanic Journal of Behavioral Sciences, 4,* 245-261.

Zinn, M. B., & Eitzen, D. S. (1987). *Diversity in American families.* New York: Harper & Row.

Zuboff, S. (1988). *In the age of the smart machine: The future of work and power.* New York: Basic Books.

Author Index

Subject Index

About the Contributors

John K. Antill is Associate Professor of Psychology at Macquarie University, where he has taught since 1973. He was educated at Sydney University, where he majored in mathematical statistics, and at Oxford University, where, as a Rhodes Scholar, he studied philosophy and psychology. He completed his Ph.D. at the University of Michigan. Since then his major area of interest has been sex roles: their nature, measurement, antecedents, and consequences. The focus of his teaching has been on psychological measurement and assessment, survey research, and survey design. He is particularly interested in the application of psychological knowledge and has conducted several large-scale surveys concerning the behavior, knowledge, and attitudes of teenagers regarding road safety. He has written over 50 research papers, book chapters, and reports and is a Fellow of the Australian Psychological Society.

John D. Cunningham completed a B.A. in psychology in 1969 at Yale University and then studied social psychology at the University of California, Los Angeles, obtaining a Ph.D. in 1975. Since then he has taught at Macquarie University, Sydney, Australia, where he is currently Senior Lecturer in Psychology. He teaches social psychology, health psychology, and survey research methodology. He has conducted research on cohabitation for 20 years. His other research interests include gender-linked personality traits, the intersection of work and family roles, psychological aspects of childbirth, and environmental management. A member of the Australian Psychological Society and an affiliate of the American Psychological Association, he is the author of over 40 journal articles and book chapters.

Fran C. Dickson, Ph.D. (Bowling Green State University, 1982), is Assistant Professor in the Department of Human Communication Studies at the University of Denver, Colorado. She has been involved in studying communication and aging for a number of years. More recently, she has been focusing on later-life couples' communication using a narrative approach.

Steve Duck is Daniel and Amy Starch Research Professor at the University of Iowa, where he holds an appointment in the Department of Communication Studies and an adjunct appointment in the Department of Psychology. He founded and is editor of the *Journal of Social and Personal Relationships,* has edited two editions of the *Handbook of Personal Relationships,* and founded the International Network on Personal Relationships, the professional organization for scholars and practitioners with interests in this field, which now has over 1,200 members. He has written or edited over 30 books on relationships.

Stanley O. Gaines Jr., is Assistant Professor in the Department of Psychology at Pomona College and in the Intercollegiate Department of Black Studies at the Claremont Colleges. His primary research interests include cultural value orientations, ethnicity, personality characteristics, and gender as influences on interpersonal resource exchange, responses to partners' dissatisfaction, and other personal relationship processes. He has published conceptual and empirical articles in a number of journals, including *Journal of Black Psychology, Journal of Social* *and Personal Relationships, Basic and Applied Social Psychology,* and *American Psychologist.*

Michelle Huston is a graduate student in the Department of Sociology at the University of Washington. She holds a Bachelor's degree in sociology from the State University of New York at Plattsburgh (1992). Although the focus of her interests changes periodically, she always seems to come back to the exploration of sexuality and gender. She is currently working on a master's thesis and another book chapter about the construction and negotiation of gender in gay and lesbian relationships.

Martin Lea (Ph.D., Lancaster University, U.K.) holds a lectureship in psychology at the University of Manchester together with a fellowship from the U.K. Joint Research Council Initiative in Cognitive Science/Human Computer Interaction. His current research interests are predominantly in the sociology and social psychology of computers and communication technology. He recently edited the book *Contexts of Computer-Mediated Communication.*

Mary E. Rohlfing is Assistant Professor in the Department of Communication at Boise State University. Her research interests include the study of long-distance friendships, the relationship between accounts and negotiations, and the role of women in the production of popular culture. She received her Ph.D. in communication research from the University of Iowa in 1993.

Pepper Schwartz is Professor of Sociology at the University of Washington and Associate Chair of the department. Her most recent book is *Peer Marriage: How Love Between Equals Really Works* (1994). She is also coauthor (with Philip Blumstein) of *American Couples* (1983), a study of heterosexual and homosexual couples.

Russell Spears (Ph.D., Exeter University, U.K.) is a Senior Lecturer at the Department of Social Psychology, University of

Amsterdam. His research interests include social stereotyping, intergroup relations, social influence, and social psychological aspects of computer-mediated communication. He is currently editor of the *British Journal of Social Psychology*.

Julia T. Wood is Nelson R. Hairston Distinguished Professor of Communication Studies at the University of North Carolina at Chapel Hill, where she teaches and conducts research on personal relationships and gender, communication, and culture. Within those areas she has written or coauthored eight books, coedited four others, and published more than 60 articles and chapters in books. She also co-founded the National Conference on Research on Gender and Communication.

Theodore E. Zorn (Ph.D., 1987, University of Kentucky) is Associate Professor of Communication Studies at the University of North Carolina at Chapel Hill. His research focuses on interpersonal communication in organizations, particularly on how social cognitive and communicative processes mutually interact and the role of these processes in enabling people to attain personal and professional goals. His recent research has been published in *Communication Yearbook, Management Communication Quarterly, International Journal of Personal Construct Psychology, Communication Education,* and *Southern Communication Journal.*